Smith Wigglesworth

ON THE

POWER *of* Scripture

MORE BOOKS WRITTEN OR COMPILED
BY ROBERTS LIARDON

Breaking Controlling Powers
God's Generals: Why They Succeeded
and Why Some Failed
God's Generals: The Roaring Reformers
God's Generals: The Revivalists
John G. Lake: The Complete Collection of His Life Teachings
John G. Lake on Healing
Kathryn Kuhlman: A Spiritual Biography
of God's Miracle-Working Power
Sharpen Your Discernment
Smith Wigglesworth: The Complete Collection of His Life Teachings
Your Power in the Holy Spirit

Also Available
God's Generals Video Collection (12 DVDs)

Smith Wigglesworth

ON THE

POWER

of Scripture

ш

WHITAKER
HOUSE

All Scripture quotations are taken from the King James Version of the Holy Bible.

SMITH WIGGLESWORTH ON THE POWER OF SCRIPTURE

Compiled by Roberts Liardon
Roberts Liardon Ministries
P.O. Box 2989
Sarasota, Florida 34230
www.robertsliardon.com

ISBN: 978-1-60374-094-4
Printed in the United States of America
© 2009 by Roberts Liardon

Whitaker House
1030 Hunt Valley Circle
New Kensington, PA 15068
www.whitakerhouse.com

Library of Congress Cataloging-in-Publication Data

Wigglesworth, Smith, 1859–1947.
    [Smith Wigglesworth speaks to students of the Bible]
    Smith Wigglesworth on the power of Scripture / by Smith Wigglesworth;
compiled by Roberts Liardon.
        p. cm.
    Originally published: Smith Wigglesworth speaks to students of the Bible. Tulsa,
Okla. : Albury Pub., ©1998.
    Summary: "Bible courses taught by Smith Wigglesworth and transcribed exactly as
they were delivered to Bible students, including rarely recorded question and answer
sessions"—Provided by publisher.
    ISBN 978-1-60374-094-4 (trade pbk. : alk. paper) 1. Pentecostal churches—
Great Britain—Sermons. 2. Sermons, English. I. Liardon, Roberts. II. Title.
III. Title: On the power of Scripture.
    BX8762.Z6W58 2009
    252'.0994—dc22
                                    2008054166

3 4 5 6 7 8 9 10 11 12   **WH**   16 15 14 13 12 11 10

Contents

INTRODUCTION

Some people speak words that can change a situation; others speak words that change a destiny. Smith Wigglesworth was a nation- shaker, a destiny maker. He has always been one of my favorite generals of God because of his bold, uncompromising approach to faith in God and His Word.

For the last ten years, I have traveled extensively throughout Europe, Australia, New Zealand, South Africa, and America, searching for and collecting Wigglesworth material. I have gathered everything from shorthand stenography notes he made to the grand piano that belonged to him.

Wigglesworth did not have his own Bible school. Instead, he would be the guest speaker at many different Bible schools, much like many teachers and preachers are today. As I studied the way he conducted his Bible school sessions and interacted with the students, it made a great impression on my life. This book features questions posed by students that are thoughtful and real, and Wigglesworth's answers to these questions, although spoken many years ago, are still relevant today.

What you are about to read is very bold. Few have been able to convey strong spiritual truths in the simple yet effective way that Smith Wigglesworth did. I believe the present truth of his words will refresh you. That's why I have separated the lectures he delivered at Bible schools from my other collections of his teachings. This special edition is a historical sequel to the books God's Generals: *Why They Succeeded and Why Some Failed* and *Smith Wigglesworth: The Complete Collection of His Life Teachings*. True to my previous publications, I have also made certain that this interaction between Wigglesworth and his Bible students is an unedited documentation of what was actually spoken.

I hope my years of research and study will make a deep impression on you and help solidify your destiny with God. Enjoy it; then, go out and run in the strength from heaven!

—*Roberts Liardon*

Smith Wigglesworth

Supplementary Remarks on First Study

These are the days of the dispensation of the Holy Ghost. I find in Galatians 3:14 that there is an especially blessed way to receive the Holy Ghost:

That the blessing of Abraham might come on the Gentiles through Jesus Christ; that we might receive the promise of the Spirit through faith.

When you have the right attitude, your faith becomes remarkably active. Faith cannot be remarkably active in a dead life; it is active only when your sins have been forgiven, your body is clean, and your life is made right. When these things are true, the Holy Ghost comes, and faith is the evidence.

Why should we tarry for the Holy Ghost? Why should we wrestle and pray for living faith to be made ready? In John 16:7–8, we find the reason:

It is expedient for you that I go away: for if I go not away, the Comforter will not come unto you; but if I depart, I will send him unto you. And when he is come, he will reprove the world of sin, and of righteousness, and of judgment.

That is why the Holy Ghost is to come into your body. First of all, when your sin is gone, you can see clearly to speak to others. But Jesus does not want you to pick the mote out of someone else's eye while a beam remains in your own eye.

(See Matthew 7:1–5.) When your own sins are gone, then the Holy Ghost is to convince the world of sin, of righteousness, and of judgment.

Only when a person is filled with the Holy Ghost can he bind the power of Satan. Satan has a right, he thinks, and will have a short time to exhibit it as the prince of the world, but he can't be prince as long as there is one person filled with the Holy Ghost. That is the reason why the church will go before tribulation.

How could you resist coming into the place where you are filled with the life and power of the Holy Ghost? I command you first to halt and then to march.

Halt! Think! What is the attitude of your life? Are you thirsty? Are you longing? Are you willing to pay the price? Are you willing to forfeit in order to have? Are you willing to allow yourself to die that He may live? Are you willing for Him to have right-of-way of your heart, your conscience, and all that you are? Are you ready to have God's deluge of blessing pour into your soul?

Are you ready? You ask, "What for?" That you may be changed forever. Receive the Holy Ghost. Be filled with divine power forever.

RECEIVING THE HOLY GHOST

If you would believe half as much as you ask, you would receive. Many people do not receive the Holy Ghost because they are continually asking and never believing. In Matthew 7:7, Jesus said, *"Ask, and it shall be given you; seek, and ye shall find; knock, and it shall be opened unto you."*

Everyone who asks receives. He who is asking is receiving. He who is seeking is finding. The door has been opened right now; that is, God's present Word. The verse does not say, "Ask and ye shall not receive." Believe that asking is receiving, seeking is finding, and to him who is knocking, the door is being opened.

Faith has it. Faith claims it because it has got it. *"Faith is the substance of things hoped for, the evidence of things not seen"* (Hebrews 11:1). As sure as you have faith, God will give you grace overflowing, and when He comes in, you will speak as the Spirit giveth utterance.

QUESTIONS AND ANSWERS

Q: When we have a strong impression to do a thing, how do we know that it is the Holy Spirit speaking?

A: Hundreds of people are struggling to have the mind of God. The first thing to understand is that when you are living in the perfect will of God, you will only that which is purposed in His will. If you are not living in that perfect attitude toward God, you may have any number of thoughts originating in your own nature, which you will find brings you into difficulty. It is the easiest thing to get the mind of the Lord when your whole heart desires only what He wills. That mind-set will save you from a thousand troubles.

Are you so in touch with God that the desire of your mind is pure regarding that thing you want to be done? Does your desire have the sanction of purity? Would Christ desire that thing? If so, the moment you pray, you will have the witness of the Spirit, and your request will coincide with the will of God.

Difficulties come when people desire the Lord's revelation in a carnal manner, or when they lead carnal lives. Ask yourself questions similar to the following: *Why am I in this meeting? Why do I want to live? Why do I want to go to this convention?*

Why do I want to be a pastor? Why am I feeling anxious this morning? Act and you will be freed. If I can find out that I want to be in Angeles Temple for a reason other than bringing glory to God and extending His kingdom, then I am in sin. If I want to be heard, I am wrong. If I want to be seen, I am wrong. If I want to be honored, I am wrong.

But if I want Christ; if I want to preach because I want to advocate His glorious gospel; if I want to be seen only because I want to exhibit His Spirit; if I am here for the advancement of the glory of Christ—then things are as easy as possible.

Q: What shall I do when the devil bothers me in the night?

> *Are you up where light increases?*
> *Reach above all earthly good,*
> *Where the life of the sinning ceases,*
> *Where the Spirit comes in flood.*
> *Bring me higher up the mountain.*
> *Into fellowship with Thee.*
> *In Thy light I'll see the fountain*
> *And the blood that cleanseth me.*

> *The blood of Jesus cleanses me just as much when I am asleep as when I am awake.*

A: The blood of Jesus cleanses me just as much when I am asleep as when I am awake, and I believe the Word when it says that the devil shall have no power over me. (See Mark 6:7.) You have a right to go into your bedroom and say, "I rebuke every evil spirit," and you will sleep through the night in the safe shadow of God's protection.

If your mind continues to be troubled at night, you must not go to sleep without first putting yourself and your entire household under the blood of Jesus, where you can sleep safely, for the blood of Jesus blocks the devil's access.

Q: Is the baptism of the Holy Spirit essential to the rapture?

A: No. It is a good thing to be baptized with the Holy Ghost because it is a wonderful thing to know that when the church goes, the Holy Ghost will not be here anymore. So, it appears that the Holy Ghost goes with the church. The Word of God says that Jesus will bring with Him all who have fallen asleep in Him. (See 1 Thessalonians 4:14.) And there are thousands who are asleep in Jesus but were never baptized in the Holy Ghost; however, He is going to bring them, too, so it is evident that they are there.

Luke 22:16, 18 says, "For I say unto you, I will not any more eat thereof, until it be fulfilled in the kingdom of God....For I say unto you, I will drink of the fruit of the vine, until the kingdom of God shall come."

When Jesus said, "The kingdom of God is within you" (Luke 17:21), He was talking about the new creation. He was referring to the new deposit of life that He had given, for He was the life of the world; it would be impossible, He said, for Him to eat or drink again until the kingdom had come.

Every person who has the kingdom within him will be there. It doesn't say anything about the baptism; it says the kingdom will be present at the supper.

The baptism of the Holy Ghost is for revelation. The baptism of the Holy Ghost is to take the things of Jesus and reveal them to us. The baptism of the Holy Ghost is to be a focus.

Supposing you put a great magnifying glass onto the smallest thing. What would it do? The Holy Ghost is the greatest magnifier of the life, the gifts, and the ministry of the King. And the King, when the Holy Ghost comes, is coronated. In the process of coronation, the Holy Ghost comes into the body; Jesus becomes King and the Holy Ghost becomes the revealer of Kingship.

Q: Is the church going through the tribulation?

A: We have a clear teaching in Thessalonians about the rapture, which clearly says, "*He who now letteth will let, until he be taken out of the way*" (2 Thessalonians 2:7).

As sure as anything, the devil is having power given to him at this day, and he will have more power given to him until he is manifested. He will increase his liberties until he becomes the prince of the earth. At the same time, there is increasing velocity, divine power, quickening, and revelation of the saints. Today, we are living in a day of revelation of the Holy Ghost like none that has been before. This is the great open door of ministry, and as He is letting in that power, and before the devil is made prince, we will be off.

If you are ready for translation, you are ready for anything.

Q: Will the bride be taken out after we get the glory?

A: Yes, the bride is in the body. She will not be seen until just before the marriage. Till then, she will be veiled. Even now, God is quickening many people in a remarkable way and they are preparing to pay the price for holiness and separation. This is the intense desire of the bridal position, or the church.

Now, don't assume that you are in the bride. Rather, prove yourself to be worthy to be taken out of the body as the bride. Think about it often and do not be fooled, for many people are misled, thinking themselves to be manifestations of the bride. It is absolute folly and foolishness. The bride will be taken out right in the kingdom.

A sinner who is saved by grace and has the full assurance that Christ dwelleth within, and his only desire and highest thought is to do the will of God and lead sinners to Christ.

Q: Is it possible for Satan to bring things about so that he can deprive such a person of the privilege of receiving the Holy Ghost in all His fullness?

A: Two things you will have to put up before you. There might be some self-righteousness destroyed, but you will find that Satan will not be able to defeat you or anybody else from receiving the Holy Ghost.

Q: If a person says he has been born again but has not been baptized with the Holy Ghost, loves God but he realizes there is something within that wars against the Spirit, will he be saved?

A: They are not saved because of that. They are saved because they believe. A person is saved only on faith.

Q: Are we baptized into the church or are we born again into the church?

A: We are not made a member of the church nor of the body of Christ either by water baptism or by the baptism of the Holy Spirit. We are born into the family of God the moment that we believe, and we belong to the body. The Word of God is very clear on this. You belong to the First Begotten, you belong to the mystical body the moment you believe. Baptism in water is form unto death. There are no merits in it either one way or the other. There isn't a thing about it that would make you more heavenly in any way. But it is obedience, and it is good conscience that obeys. The baptism of the Spirit has nothing to do with this. It is "baptism by the same Spirit" into revelation of the knowledge and the mysteries of God.

Q: Explain "One Lord, one faith, one baptism" (Ephesians 4:5).

A: It is the baptism of the Spirit, because it is in the Epistles. The baptism in water is in the Acts of the Apostles, or the Gospels.

Q: Should everyone who speaks in an unknown tongue in prophecy pray that he may interpret?

A: Prophecy is clearly understood. Tongues are not prophecy. Tongues never prophesy. Prophecy is speaking right out by the power of the Spirit in languages you know.

Q: Once saved, are you always saved?

A: You were saved by believing. Keep on believing and you will land.

Q: Will there be anybody saved on earth after the body is taken?

A: The 144,000, which is perfectly Jewish. They will go through great tribulation because of the Word, and people, if they are saved at all, will be saved by the Word, but not by the Spirit. The Holy Ghost will have gone with the body. But the 144,000 will be Jewish. They know the Word and they will go through by the Word. They will even die for the Word.

Q: What is the backslider's position regarding the kingdom of heaven?

A: The backslider's position is exactly like the man who was away from home. When he returned, the father said, "This is my son, which was astray." A backslider has always a chance to return. The Lord loves the backslider, and He always makes it possible for him to return.

Praying for the Sick
July 6, 1927

We need to be very near God so that every day brings us nearer to the goal, which has so many things in it. The terrestrial body will be so beautiful in every way to take in all the glories and all the expression of heaven. I want to provoke you to this holy, inward interest so that you may have a share. I look forward to the Word of God where it says that He will bring many sons into glory. I long to make you hungry to be sons of God, hungry to be worthy of redemption; make you so you cannot rest...you feel you are reaching the prize of the mark of your high calling in Christ Jesus, that you must come into a place where you could earnestly contend for the faith delivered unto you, that there should be no lack in your life but you should be filled with the Spirit, filled with the grace of the Spirit, moved by almightiness.

BE READY

God has so many things for us in this day that we must be ready. That is the reason why I try to provoke you to holiness, intensity of desire, an inward cry after God.

O Lord, help me! Help me, that I may earnestly contend, leaving all things before me and pressing forward to the prize.

Are you ready today? Are you anxious today? Are you willing today? Oh, it was wonderful that they were willing in the day of their visitation. It is lovely to be in a place where we can say, "*Mine eyes have seen thy salvation*" (Luke 2:30).

Are you ready? What for? To be so moved this afternoon by the power of God that this day shall be eclipsed on every line because of God taking me on with Him.

Are you ready? What for? To so lose yourself in God today that you will not claim your earthly rights but claim the heavenly rights of God.

Are you ready? What for? That you may so cry aloud that the Lord Himself will be the only One that can satisfy the desire of your heart.

THE PLACE OF REIGNING

If you are going on with God, you cannot be fed with natural bread. The people who are going on with God have to have the bread that cometh down, and you know it is very fresh every day. It is very special bread because it just meets the need of every heart. The disciples knew it. They were listening to His voice as He was saying marvelous words, yet they knew that there was such a freshness about it that they said, "*Evermore give us this bread*" (John 6:34).

Now this is the bread that came down from heaven, even the Son of God, who gave His life for the world. Remember that He has so wonderfully overcome the power of Satan and all the powers of disease and all the powers of sin till there is a perfect place in Christ Jesus where we may be free from sin, sickness, disease, and death; it is one of the greatest positions that God has for us.

If I were to select a word this afternoon to meet your need, you would find it very clearly in Romans 8:

> *There is therefore now no condemnation to them which are*
> *in Christ Jesus, who walk not after the flesh, but after the*

Spirit. For the law of the Spirit of life in Christ Jesus hath made me free from the law of sin and death.

(Romans 8:1–2)

DIVINE PERSONAL PLAN

You see it is as clear, as definite, and as personal as it could be. As we enter into these divine, personal plans today, we will find that sin is dethroned, disease can't hold its seat, death has lost its sting, and victory is in Christ Jesus. How? Reigning in life by Christ Jesus. To reign in life means that you are over every human weakness on every line. To reign means to say that you are on the rock and everything else is under your feet.

Jesus has made for us, everyone, a place of victory that we may reign as kings over our bodies in every way and over all thoughts of evil. Remember: Thoughts of evil are of Satan. Evil thoughts come from within.

> *Jesus has made for us, everyone, a place of victory that we may reign as kings over our bodies in every way and over all thoughts of evil.*

Is any among you afflicted? let him pray.   (James 5:13)

Whenever I go to homes to pray for the sick, I turn to this Scripture because it is Scripture that is used. It belongs to the church. Are any of the church people sick? Then they call for the elders. The elders go and anoint the sick one with oil. I have had so many revelations on this that I see I must give it to you today in as simple a form as possible.

This is the key note: *"Is any among you afflicted? let him pray."* This is one of many marvelous words that God has been revealing to me on the line of sicknesses.

Healing through Anointed Handkerchiefs

Before I left home, we were having some meetings in Belfast, Ireland, and the Lord was very graciously blessing us. The crowds were gathering, many needy cases were helped, God was blessing souls. A great many people began inviting us to see them in their homes to pray for the sick.

This is a very difficult thing to do, but God has made a plan for us to take care of this emergency. Here is our Sister McPherson in Chicago; we know as well as anything that she cannot reach hundreds who are longing for her. She never will reach them; she cannot reach them. She has neither the strength nor the power to go and run from place to place.

Paul was in the same place at Ephesus. The cry was coming from all over, and Paul knew there could be something that could reach this kind of need, and so he had a revelation. Paul was great on revelation and then wrote revelation down. And so we have that word in the nineteenth chapter of the Acts, so beautifully put:

> *And God wrought special miracles by the hands of Paul: So that from his body were brought unto the sick handkerchiefs or aprons, and the diseases departed from them, and the evil spirits went out of them.* (Acts 19:11–12)

Paul would pray over the handkerchief or the apron, then send it to the suffering one and the disease would be healed.

I want to tell you a story about this to create in you a great blessing which shall come to those who know about it, those we cannot reach.

Poisoned Beer

I was in Liverpool when a woman came to me and said, "I would like you to pray for my husband. He comes home every night drunk."

"Why," I said, "my dear sister, God has made a way for that."

"What way is it?" she asked.

"If you have a handkerchief," I said. "I will pray over it."

She opened her bag, brought out a handkerchief, and in the name of Jesus I laid my hands upon the handkerchief, prayed, and gave it back to her.

"What shall I do with it?" she asked.

"Place it upon his pillow," I answered.

"But he will be drunk."

"It makes no difference; he will have his drunken head on the promise of God."

She took the handkerchief and placed it on the pillow. He came home drunk. He knew nothing about the handkerchief. He slept all night, awoke in the morning—for anything he knew, just as he was before.

Of course, it was his natural desire to call at the first saloon for some beer. He got the beer and began to take it when instantly he was convinced there was poison in the beer and said to the man, "What have you done with that beer?"

"I have done nothing with it," the man answered.

"I know you have; I wouldn't take it for the world."

Cautious about Poison

He went to another place, called for a glass of beer again, put it to his lips, more cautiously, was more convinced than ever that there was poison in it.

He said to the man, "Why?! Has all Liverpool agreed to poison me?"

He worked all the morning, then went at noon as usual to get his beer for his lunch. This time he was convinced that

Liverpool had agreed to poison him, and he talked so much about it that he was asked to leave the place.

At night he was not going to go home without the beer. This time he was so enraged at the people who served him the beer because he was convinced of poison that they had to throw him out of that place.

ASKED FOR PRAYER

He went home without a drink, and his wife said, "My dear, why are you home so early?"

"You ought to pray for me," he said.

"Oh, I am."

"But you don't know all Liverpool has agreed to poison me." As he told her the story, she said, "Can't you see how the grace of God has covered you today? Can't you see how you have been delivered?"

He was awakened to consciousness, and that night, he was blessedly saved. And I am a witness he became a wonderful worker for God.

A woman sent a handkerchief. She had a cancer, was just at the point of death. They placed the handkerchief on her instantly. God sent new life through her. She was healed that day.

I could go on like that, but there is no need. Look! It is the Book. It is not Wigglesworth. It is the Book. That was God's remedy for people like me and Mrs. McPherson and others of us who cannot teach the people.

In our meetings in Norway and Sweden, five hundred handkerchiefs were brought for prayer at one meeting. In Ceylon, one thousand were brought at one meeting.

Move Biblically

When God moves, you will move biblically. When you move biblically, you will move savingly, healingly, cleansingly, and heavenly.

Is Anyone Sick?

Is there anyone sick? Is there anyone sick in this place?

This is what I ask when I get into a sick room. Why? I will tell you a story, which will explain.

My daughter is a missionary from Africa. I am interested in helping to support missionaries all over, besides Africa, for I love missionary work.

We had a missionary out in China who, by some means or other, got rheumatism. I have no Word for rheumatism, only "devil possessed." Rheumatism, cancers, tumors, lumbago, neuralgia—all these things I give only one name: the power of the devil working in humanity. When I see consumption, I see demon-working power there. All these things can be removed.

When Jesus went into Peter's wife's mother's house, what did He really do? Did He cover her up with a blanket and put a hot water bottle to her feet? If He did not do that, why didn't He do it? Because He knew it was demons that had all the heat of hell in them. He did the right thing: He rebuked the fever and it left.

Outside the Plan

So we ought to do the right thing with these diseases.

This missionary came home to Belfast from China, enraged against the work of God, enraged against God, enraged against everything. She was absolutely outside the plan of God.

While this missionary was in Belfast, God allowed her to fall down the steps and some way dislocate her backbone till they had to lift her up and carry her to her bed. God allowed it.

You be careful about falling out with God because of something wrong with your body. Get right with God first before you fall out with Him.

There came the day of visiting. She asked for me to come. When I went to the room, I looked at her and said, "Is there anybody sick in this room?"

No response.

"Is there anyone sick in this room?"

No response.

"Well," I said, "we will wait while somebody moves."

By and by she says, "Yes, I am sick."

"All right, we have found you out then. You are in the room. Now, the Word of God says when you are sick, pray. When you pray" I said, "I will anoint you, I will pray for you, but not before."

It took her almost a quarter of an hour to yield, the devil had got such possession of her. But, thank God, she yielded. Then she cried and she cried, and her body, by the power of God, was shaken loose and she was made free—when she repented, not before.

> *We have a need to see that God wants us to be blessed, but first of all, He wants us to be ready for the blessing.*

Talk about Blessings

Oh, what would happen if everybody in this place would repent today! Talk about blessings! The glory would fall so they couldn't get out of the place. We have a need to see that God wants us to be blessed, but first of all, He wants us to be ready for the blessing.

God Has the Second Chance

I want to take you to another word about this:

Brethren, if any of you do err from the truth, and one con-
vert him; let him know, that he which converteth the sinner
from the error of his way shall save a soul from death, and
shall hide a multitude of sins.　　　(James 5:19–20)

One thing God is showing to me, which causes me to deal very faithfully with the sick, people is this: if the first remedy that you have taken from the doctor's bottle had healed you, you would not have been here; so you are only giving God the next chance.

If we would be as faithful to God as we have been faithful to doctors, we would all have been healed. But we have been unfaithful and there is need of repentance.

Some people, after they have been healed, go back to medicine This nineteenth verse I have read shows what the Bible says about that. People preach on this and turn it into a salvation message; it has nothing to do with salvation. It is a healing message. It is full of life. *"Brethren, if any of you do err from the truth"* (James 5:19). What is erring from the truth? After God has healed you once, then using your remedies. After you have tried all you can get of all kinds of things and it doesn't move you, then you are in a queer place and someone comes along and turns you *"from the error of* [your] *way"*—he saves you from your sin of turning from God to seek other means and saves you from death.

God is so merciful after all that. What I am doing today is turning you from the error of your ways, getting you back to God.

Look to God, only believe that His atoning blood is sufficient, and you may be healed from every weakness.

BELIEVE AND BE HEALED

The God who told Moses to make a pole and put a brazen serpent upon it, that whoever looked could be healed, now says, "The brazen serpent is not on the pole, Jesus is not on the cross, so now *believe*, and you shall be healed if you *believe*."

You cannot look to the cross, you cannot look to the serpent, but you can believe, and if you believe you can be healed, God means you to be helped today.

COMPLETE VERSUS PARTIAL HEALING

I want everybody to know that Wigglesworth does not believe in partial healings.

Then what does Wigglesworth believe?

I believe in complete healing. If it is not manifested, it is there all the same. It is indolent because of inactive faith, but it is there, God has given it.

How do I know?

"They shall lay hands on the sick, and they shall recover" (Mark 16:18).

Whose word is that? That is God's Word. So I have faith today, hallelujah! Even repeating the Word gives me more faith.

Interpretation of Tongues:

> *Why dost thou doubt when God, even the Lord, hath come to cast the devil out, that you may know that you are free from all things by the blood of Jesus?*

We are in a great place. The Lord is in the midst of us. You are to go away free today.

PRAYER HEALS A DISLOCATED HEART

I like the thought, *"Himself took our infirmities, and bare our sicknesses"* (Matthew 8:17).

I want to tell you a remarkable story. One day I was standing at the bottom of Shanklin Road, Belfast, Ireland, with a piece of paper in my hand, looking at the addresses of where I had to go to, when a man came over and said to me, "Are you visiting the sick?"

"Yes," I said.

"Go there," he said, and pointed to a house nearby.

I knocked at the door—no reply. Knocked again, and then a voice inside said, "Come in!" So I opened the door and walked in. Then a young man pointed to me to go up the stairway.

BEGAN TO PRAY

When I got up onto the landing there was a door wide open, so I walked right into the doorway and found a woman sitting up on the bed. As soon as I looked at her, I knew she couldn't speak to me, so I began to pray. She was moving backwards and forwards, gasping for breath, and I knew she was beyond answering me.

When I prayed, the Lord said to me distinctly, the Holy Spirit said, "Read Isaiah 53."

So I opened the Book and began to read, "*Who hath believed our report? and to whom is the aim of the LORD revealed? For he shall grow up before him as a tender plant, and as a root out of a dry ground*" (Isaiah 53:1–2), and so forth.

When I got to the fifth verse, "*He was wounded for our transgressions, he was bruised for our iniquities: the chastisement of our peace was upon him; and with his stripes we are healed*," the woman shouted, "I am healed!"

"Oh!" I said. "Woman, tell me."

She said, "Three weeks ago I was cleaning down the house. In moving some furniture, I strained my heart—it moved out of its place. The doctors have examined me and said that I should die with suffocation, and truly it has been often as though I should die with suffocation. But last night, in the middle of the night, I saw you come into the room. When you saw me you knew I could not speak, so you began to pray. Then you opened to Isaiah 53 and read until you came to the fifth verse, and when you read the fifth verse I was completely healed. That was vision; now it is a fact."

So I know the Word of God is still true.

Interpretation of Tongues:

> *Stretch out thy hand, for the Lord thy God is so nigh unto thee He shall take thee and so place thee in His pavilion of splendor that if thou wilt not go out any more but remain stationary in the will of God, He shall grant thee the desire of thy heart.*

Now, that is a word from the Lord. You will never get anything more distinctly from the Lord than that. People miss the greatest plan of healing because of moving from one thing to another. Become stationary. God wants you to take the Word. Claim the Word. Believe it. That is the perfect way of healing: turn not to the right hand nor to the left, but believe God.

God's Presence Heals

I believe we ought to have people in this meeting loosed from their infirmities without being touched. More and more, I see that the day of visitation of the Lord is upon us, that the presence of the Lord is here to heal. We should have people healed in these meetings while I am speaking, healed under the unction of the Spirit.

I have been preaching faith along lines so that you may definitely claim your healing. I believe if you listen to the Word, if you are moved to believe, and if you stand up while I pray, you will find that healing virtue will loose you.

Interpretation of Tongues:

> *In the depths God has come and moves, and moves in the very inner working of the heart till the Spirit of the Lord has perfect choice, brings forth that which shall resound to His glory forever. The Lord is in the midst of it. Those that are bound are made free from captivity.*

God wants you to have a living faith now, to get a vital touch, shaking the foundation of all weakness. When you were saved, you were saved the moment you believed, and you will be healed the moment you believe.

PRAYER

Father, into Thy gracious, glorious care we take these people and present them to Thee, that Thou shouldest keep them from falling, keep them from the error of the ways of the wicked, deliver them from all evil. Let Thy mercy be with them in their homes, in their bodies, in every way.

God Bless You!
Bible Study #4 – July 8, 1927

God bless you! When He blesses, no one can curse. When God is with you, it is impossible for anyone to be against you. When God has put His hand upon you, every way will open with benediction to others. The greatest thing that God has allowed us to come into is the plan of distrib-uting His blessing to others. *"I will bless thee...and thou shalt be a blessing"* (Genesis 12:2).

When we know the power of God Almighty, we need never be afraid of any weapon that is formed against us, believing that the Lord of Hosts will rise up and stand against the enemy.

God's power upon us, His wonderful benediction of us, His provident of promise written down for us is to make us ready—in every day, under all circumstances—to know that He who promised will surely fulfill.

What a wonderful Christ! God has chosen for us in the midst a blessing, the power of the Highest overshadoweth, the glory of the Lord is rearward and before us. Who is able to withstand that almightiness?

God, breathe upon us this morning so that we may receive the enduement, enriched with all the enrichment of heaven, crowned with blessing.

Lead Us through Victory

The Lord shall lead us forth, from victory unto victory, the Lord's people. Oh, what a blessing to know that we are the fruit of the Lord! His people are the precious fruit of the earth.

I am not afraid to say these things to you because I know God means to bless you. Why should you go away without blessing when God has promised you to have a measure that cannot be measured? Why should you fear when God would remove fear?

Are you ready? You say, "What for?" Oh! For His blessing that shall fill your life, overflow you, change you.

Are you ready? "What for?" To get a childlike simplicity and look into the face of the Father and believe that all His promises are yea and amen to you.

Are you ready? "What for?" To be awakened into that spirit of acquaintance that believes all things and dares to ask the Father.

First Corinthians 13: A Balancer

This morning I wish to take up the thirteenth chapter of 1 Corinthians. This chapter is between the twelfth and fourteenth; it is a dovetail, or union, of those three chapters together, bringing us into a place where we see. The twelfth chapter deals with the gifts, the fourteenth chapter deals with ministry of gifts, and the thirteenth chapter deals with the balancing.

If you know anything about an engine, you know that right over the main throttle valve, which lets the steam into the cylinder with the piston driving it backwards and forwards, there are two little governor balls running around. Sometimes they go fast, sometimes they go slow. And these control the condition of the pistons so that the engine doesn't run away and so that it keeps at an even motion.

That is exactly what the thirteenth chapter of 1 Corinthians is: to keep the gifts in perfect harmony till you do not turn away, get out of place. It shows that the wisdom that is from above lies in a human casket; it never loses its luster or glory or expression or force of character of divine origin.

So God has a plan for us to show us that without we understand the Scriptures for our life, though it may be wonderful—we may have prophecy, beautiful is prophecy, divine prophecy; though we have all faith to move mountains—if we lose the main factor, which shall produce the governing principles, we become nothing. But if we are so balanced by the power of the Spirit, every act would be an act with such divine quality that the people would know in a moment as they have perfect judgment, as they did that day when they saw Peter and John, although they were little and had not gone through college courses. They had something which expressed to them a fact. They had been in a place of changing character and language. They had been with the Master.

While I know many good things come out of colleges, you must not forget that you must occasionally go to the night school, as Nicodemus went, and see the Master.

A personal acquaintance with the Lord Jesus, by the revelation of the Spirit, can so move you that in an instant you may have revelation that would cause you to see that you are now encased by an enthronement or wisdom from on high.

Interpretation of Tongues:

The wisdom which is from above is first peaceable, easily entreated, without partiality, full of goodness and truth and the Lord of Hosts has us in His great pavilion of opening the avenue of our human nature, flowing forth through the natural lift, divine life, quickened from on high, because we are the children of the King.

Thank You, Lord. We are the children of the King. We belong to the Lord. Therefore, no other power has a right to us. We belong to Him.

Interpretation of Tongues:

From thy mother's womb I called thee. Though I have chastened thee and put thee through the fire, yet it was needful to bring out of thee and to bring thee out into a Land of Promise. It is true that thou hast passed through deep waters. The fire has many times seared thee. But it was all to chasten thee and to prove thee, to see if thou loved the Lord with all thy heart. And now the Lord has brought thee to the banquet. Eat, My beloved. Eat and be satisfied.

SPIRITUAL GIFTS

> *God does not intend you to be ignorant concerning gifts, spiritual gifts.*

We have gone carefully through a few verses in the twelfth chapter of 1 Corinthians, so I hope you are well established in the thought that you are not to be ignorant. God does not intend you to be ignorant concerning gifts, spiritual gifts; spiritual gifts which have revelation, which have acquaintance, which have within them power to deliver others, power to pray through.

The gift of intercession, the gift of laying hands on the sick, the gift of prophecy, the gift of the word of wisdom, the gift of the word of knowledge, the gift of discerning spirits, the gift of tongues, and the gift of interpretation—all these are mentioned in that one word, *"Now concerning spiritual gifts, brethren, I would not have you ignorant"* (1 Corinthians 12:1).

So I pray you to think seriously in your heart, because you have to be in the world, not of it, a personal manifestation of the living Christ just as Christ was walking about the earth, you have to walk about as a son of God, with power and manifestation, because the people have not time to read the Bible. So you have to be the walking epistle, *"known and read of all men"* (2 Corinthians 3:2).

Seeing that is so—and that you have to rightly see that Jesus is the Word, and you have to believe the Word of God and not change it because of the people who have other opinions—take the Word of God. Take the Word of God; it will furnish you in every good stand; it is there. You will find out you want nothing better; there is nothing better. It is there— you will find all you want: food for hunger, light for darkness, largeness of heart, conceptions of thought, inspiration.

I like the word of Paul. It is beautiful and it comes forth so often by the power of the Spirit, "The might of the Spirit in the inner man," which can fill everybody and which brings forth the revelation of the Word.

Jesus Is Not Trinity

I think we saw clearly in out previous studies that after we are really in the place God would have us, Jesus would be always the head of all things. We honor Him every way. We do not make Him trinity, because it is neither wise nor scriptural; it is foolishness, a great deal of ignorance and absolutely the height of folly to make three persons to come out in the Godhead of Jesus.

Father, Son, Holy Ghost is Trinity. Don't divide them. Keep them in their place and you will have a great deal of blessing.

THE GIVER, THEN GIFTS

We saw clearly, I believe, entered into it, why gifts were particularized, varieties of gifts, positions to hold gifts. We must not forget that the Giver is to be received before the gifts.

Salvation always precedes sanctification, and sanctification will always precede the baptism of the Holy Ghost. It is a body prepared for the Holy Ghost, and when the body is rightly prepared for the Holy Ghost, then it is the work of Jesus to baptize with the Holy Ghost.

The Holy Ghost then makes Jesus King in your life. You count Him as Lord and Master over all things, and you become submissive to Him unto all things. And you are not afraid to say, "Thou art mine! I love Thee!"

I love Him. He is so beautiful. He is so sweet. He is so loving. He is so kind! He never turns a deaf ear and He never leaves you in distress. He heals brokenheartedness. He liberates the captive. And to those which are down and out He comes right into that place and He lifts the burden.

It is truly said of Him, "*He came unto His own, and His own received Him not. But as many as received Him, to them gave He power to become the sons of God*" (John 1:11–12).

Thus I bring you again to the order of sonship, grace endued or enflowed or pressed through or over covering you, preserving you from all evil, this boundless grace, this capableness for your need of capability, till God has you in His own mind and purpose.

THE GIFT OF THE WORD OF WISDOM

In 1 Corinthians 12:8, we have the Word of God about wisdom: "*For to one is given by the Spirit the word of wisdom.*"

It does not say—and you must clearly understand it—it did not say, "the gift of wisdom," but the gift of "the word of wisdom." And you have to rightly divide the truth, because it will mean so much to us.

It is the gift of the word of wisdom when you want to build another temple—maybe larger than the one we are in—that everybody can speak and be heard without any trouble. There is needed a word of wisdom how to build the place for God's service.

A word of wisdom is when two ways meet, and it is a difficult problem for you to know what way to go. That word can come to you in a moment and prepare you for the right way.

The gift of the word of wisdom, at a needy hour when you are in great stress concerning some business transaction, provided it is a holy transaction, means you can ask God what to do and you will get the word on two lines.

This wisdom may be a gift or it may come forth because of the power of the Holy Ghost being upon you. I have been trying these last days to show to you that if you are filled with the Holy Ghost, the Holy Ghost could manifest any gift. At the same time, you are not to forget that the Word of God presses you to a place to desire earnestly the best gift. So while the best gift might be to you the word of wisdom, or some other gift, you should not come behind in any gift.

That is a great word for me to say this morning, but I declare to you that Scripture lends itself to me to be extravagant. When God speaks to me, He says, "Anything you ask." When God is speaking of the world's salvation He says, "Whosoever believes." So I have an extravagant God with extravagant language to make me an extravagant person—in wisdom.

If you have extravagances without wisdom, you will know very well it is going to be no profit. You have to learn not to leak out nor waste out, and you have to learn above all things that you have to be out and God in. The trouble with so many people is they have never got out so He could get in. But if ever God gets in, you will be first out, never to come in any more.

To this end we pray that God shall give us to understand now what is really the need of the word of wisdom and how we may be in a place that we shall surely know it is God. I am going to deal now with this word through an experience, and it will help you more than anything.

Money Borrowed through Word of Wisdom

One day, I went out of the house and met a friend who lived opposite me. They called him John. He came across the road from where I was, came up to me, and said, "Now, Smith, how are you?"

"Very well, John," said I.

"Well," he said, "my wife and I have been thinking and praying and talking together about selling our house, and every time we think about it in any way, your name is the only one we think about."

That was a strange thing to me.

"Will you buy it?" he asked.

Now, if you remember, when David got wrong, he only got wrong because he had to violate that holy communion and knowledge of what kept him. What was it? What was the word that would have saved him? *"Thou shalt not covet thy neighbour's wife"* (Exodus 20:17). He had to break that law to commit sin.

This was not a sin that I was dealing with, but there were many things that I knew, that if I thought for a moment, it would have saved many weeks of brokenheartedness and sorrow.

What was the first thing that I should have asked myself? "Can I live in two houses? No. Well, then, one is sufficient."

The next thing was, "Have I money to buy the house? No."

That is sufficient in itself, for God does not want any person in this place to be in debt. And when you learn that secret, it will save you from thousands of sleepless nights. But I was like many people. We are all learning; none of us is perfect. But I do thank God that we are called to perfection whether we come into it at once or not.

If you miss the mark of holiness ten times a day, brace yourself up to believe that God means you to be holy and stand afresh. Do not give in because you miss it.

GODLY REPENTANCE

No man, because he makes a blunder, fails to succeed in life, but it is when he makes the blunder twice. No person who fails once closes the high calling. Therefore, the Word of God says, when you repent, repent with godly repentance, that you will never do the same thing again.

You have not to give in. You have to brace yourself up. The day is young, the opportunities are tremendously large, and God helps you not to give in. Believe that God can make you afresh and turn you into another man.

Now, what was the trouble with me? I didn't communicate this transaction to God. Many of you are in the same place. What do we do afterwards? We begin working our way out. So I began working this thing out.

"How much will you take for it?" I asked.

He named the price. I thought to myself—this was human thought—now the society will give me all I want. They are well acquainted with me. That will be no trouble.

So the man came to look over the house.

"It is a beautiful house," he said. "It is very reasonable. You will lose nothing on this if ever you sell it. It is well worth the money. But I cannot give you within $500 of what you need."

I did not have $500—I couldn't get it out of the business I had at that time—so I tried still a human way. I did not go to God. If I had, I could have got out of it. But I tried to work my way out. Why? Because I knew I was wrong from the beginning.

TRIED RELATIONS

The first thing I did, I tried my relations. Have you ever tried them? What was wrong? They were all so pleased to see me, but I was either a bit too soon or a little bit too late; absolutely just missed it. They all wanted to do it, but I was there at the wrong time, I tell you, every time I saw a relation. I had a Turkish bath without paying for it.

I had another human plan: I tried my friends. The same thing.

Then I went to my lovely wife. Oh, she was a darling! She was holy! I went to her and I said:

"O, Mother, I am in a hard place."

"I know," she said. "I tell you what you have never done, my dear."

"What?"

"You have never gone to God once about this thing."

That is the secret. When you get out of the will of God, then you try your own way.

So then I knew she knew, and I knew if I went what I should get.

"All right, my dear, I will go."

It is lovely to have a place to go to, to pray. Oh! Those places to pray where you open your eyes to see if you can see Him. In reality, He is so near. Ah, to walk with God!

"Father," I said, "You know all about it. If You will forgive me this time, I will never trouble You again as long as I live with anything like this."

And then came the word of wisdom. He has it. And yet it was the most ridiculous word ever I heard in all my life. The Lord said, "Go see Brother Webster."

I came downstairs. I said, "He has spoken."

"I knew He would."

"Yes, but you see, He said such a ridiculous thing."

"Believe it," she said. "It will be all right. When God speaks, you know it means it is all right."

"But, Mother, you could hardly think it could be right. He has told me to go see Brother Webster."

"Go," she said.

EARLY BIRD

Brother Webster was a man that kilned lime. The most he ever got a week, to my knowledge, was $350. He wore a pair of big clogs and corduroy trousers. But he was a godly man.

Early in the morning I jumped onto my cycle, went to his house, and got there at eight o'clock.

"Why, Brother Wigglesworth," said he, "what brings you so early?"

"I was speaking to the Lord last night about a little trouble," I said, "and He told me to come and see you."

"If that is the case," he said, "we will go down to my house and talk to the Lord."

We went to the house. He locked the door.

"Now tell me," he said.

"Well," I said, "three weeks ago, I arranged to buy a house, found out I was short of a hundred pounds. I have tried everything I know and failed. My wife told me last night to go to God, and while I was there, God said, 'Go see Brother Webster,' and I am here."

"How long have you wanted it?" he asked.

"Three weeks," said I.

"And you have never come to see me before?"

"No," said I, "God never told me."

TRIED MAN

I could have got to know the next day, if I had gone to God, but I tried my way, went to every man possible without going straight to God. I hope you people won't do that now. You are to have the word of wisdom God is going to give you.

Then he said to me, "For twenty years I have been putting aside two and six pence a week (that is just over half a dollar) into a cooperative society. Three weeks ago they told me that I had a hundred pounds and I must take it out because I was not doing business with them. I brought it home I put it under the mattresses, under the floor posts, in the ceiling, everywhere. Oh, I have been so troubled with it! If it will do you any good, you can have it."

He knows it all; He knows it all.
My Father knows it all.
Your bitter tears, how oft they flow.
He knows; my Father knows it all.

I would like to change that somewhat. I will sing it the way God changed it to me:

> *He knows it all; He knows it all.*
> *My Father knows it all.*
> *The joy that comes and overflows,*
> *He knows; my Father sends it all.*
> *Yes, He knows. Glory to God!*

"I had so much trouble," he said, "I took it to the bank yesterday to get rid of it. If I can get it out today you can have it."

He went to the bank and asked, "How much can I have?"

"Why, it is your own," they said. "You can have it all."

He came out and gave it to me, and said, "There it is! If it is as much blessing to you as it has been trouble to me, you will have a lot of blessing."

Knows Need

Yes, brethren, He knows just what you need. Don't you know if I had gone to the right place right away, I never need have been in trouble? What I ought to have known was this: there was no need for the house at all.

I got rid of it and took the money back to Brother Webster and said, "Take it back; take the money back. It will be trouble to me if I keep that money. Take it."

Oh, to be in the will of God!

Don't you see, beloved, there is the word, the word of wisdom. One word is sufficient. You don't need a lot. One little word from God is all you require. You can count upon it. It will never fail. It will bring forth that which God has desired.

May the Lord give to you this morning wisdom so that you may rightly divide the word of truth, walk in the fear of the Lord,

———— ∞ ————

God can so reserve you for Himself that the whole of your body shall be in operation of the Spirit.

———— ∞ ————

be an example to the saints, never take advantage of the Holy Ghost, but allow the Holy Ghost to take advantage of you.

I have come to a conclusion which is very beautiful, in my estimation: once I thought I possessed the Holy Ghost, but I have come to the conclusion that He has to be entirely the Possessor of me.

God can tame your tongue. God can so reserve you for Himself that the whole of your body shall be in operation of the Spirit.

Interpretation of Tongues:

The Lord of Hosts is in the place, waiting to change the human race and fit it for a heavenly place.

PAUL'S SPEAKING IN TONGUES
Bible Study #5

There is a word here that has been very wrongly misunderstood.

I thank my God, I speak with tongues more than ye all: yet in the church I had rather speak five words with my understanding, that by my voice I might teach others also, than ten thousand words in an unknown tongue.

(1 Corinthians 14:18–19)

Here is Paul saying that he speaks in tongues more than any. Now, you can understand that he felt that he spoke more in tongues than they all, meaning to say that he lived in the utterances of the Spirit. Very likely, it would be lovely!

I remember one time in London, I asked a meeting to commence at 7:30. I was not well acquainted with London, and I knew I had two hours to spare before the meeting. I was walking in one of the busiest places in London. All the theaters were just getting ready for their big Saturday night.

"Now, Lord," I said, "let me just be enveloped in Thy glory for this two hours in the midst of the world."

And I went up and down Fleet Street and the Strand, lost in the Spirit, in tongues all the time. It was lovely. Yes, the world was filled with flesh—the lust of the flesh, the lust of the eye, and the pride of life—but God had His child in the midst of the blazing worldly affairs, lost in the Spirit.

Covet earnestly—we pray you, we desire you, beloved, to covet earnestly—to be in God's will so that at any time, wherever you are, you may pray in the Spirit, you may sing in the Spirit, you may have a good time thinking about the Lord. Remember, it is at those places and times and seasons when the Father and the Son come and make themselves known to you.

Now, a word in season as to the next thought. Paul was knowing that if the whole church turned to tongues—and tongues, only tongues! tongues! tongues!—there would be confusion and much distress, and there would not be that lift of divine power and acquaintance that Paul knew was a need.

So Paul's great heart was moved as a builder of churches. And he saw that the Lord was breathing through him this glorious attitude of forming these churches, and he said, "Think seriously and let your speaking be with carefulness. The people who have been filled with the Spirit and speak in tongues should not go on constantly with that, come to the meeting, and all the time have the meeting taken up with speaking in tongues." (See 1 Corinthians 14:27.)

You know, it is very lovely, the flow of the Spirit flowing through you; it is very lovely, but we must always be mindful that out brother and sister sitting next to us has to be helped. There are weak people in the church who need your careful attention. Then there are people of kinds of different nature and makeup. And we must always remember that we have to guard the church, look after it, keep it in sober-mindedness, till no person coming in should be taken up with the thought, "Why, those people are mad! There they are, all speaking in tongues."

Paul said, "I would rather speak five words with the understanding than ten thousand words that they couldn't understand." (See 1 Corinthians 14:19.)

Wasn't he right? Wouldn't I? Is there anybody that is really in wisdom who would dare to continue speaking in tongues without interpretation and without opening the knowledge of God to the people? Who would dare to do that? It would be foolishness, it would be madness, and you would lose the opinion of the people.

You must remember this, that whatever you do when you are in the church of God, you have to seek to excel to the edifying of the body of Christ.

TONGUES: A SIGN TO THE UNBELIEVER

There is a word here which says tongues are a sign for the unbeliever: "*Wherefore tongues are for a sign, not to them that believe, but to them that believe not*" (1 Corinthians 14:22).

We have a wonderful word there, and I know it will require some explanation. It is important, and I want to explain this to edification.

A friend of mine was attending a Wesleyan brotherhood meeting in England—a great, packed meeting. He saw a young man there who was full of desire for his people. He looked it, his frame looked it, and his face. My friend knew he was laboring there under great difficulty.

At the close of the service, he wrote him out a check. He said, "Take this check and go to Bradford to Brother Wigglesworth, a friend of mine, and have a rest in his home. All you have to do is to say that I have sent you. They will take you in and make you comfortable."

(If you want to know where I live, I will tell you Jesus sent seventy out, and they all came back in victory. I live at 70 Victor Road, Bradford. And I expect to go back to victory.)

When this man got this check, he was in need of a rest, and he said to the man, "Yes, I will go, and I thank you."

He arranged to go the next Friday. As soon as he got to Bradford, the first thing he did was to go to the Young Men's Christian Association to inquire if they knew anything about Wigglesworth.

"Oh, yes, we know everything about him. Why?"

"I have brought a letter of introduction to him and have been advised to go to his home for a rest."

"Now, you be very careful," they said. "This man is amongst those people that believe in tongues, and we believe it is of the devil. So you be careful lest you are taken in."

"Oh!" he said. "Don't be afraid; they will not take me in. I am too wise for that."

So he came.

I want you to notice the word we are dealing with now is tongues as an evidence to the unbeliever—not to the believer, but to the unbeliever.

This man came to my house full of unbelief. Great preacher, wonderful man, great abilities, and I tell you—I know him well—he is a godly man, but he was full of unbelief.

There are any number of people who are believers filled with unbelief. I have very little difficulty when I am dealing with a sinner about being healed. I scarcely ever see a sinner that knows nothing about Jesus fail to be healed when I pray for him. But if I pray for the believer, I find it very often he is not healed. Why? Unbelief in the believer it is a very astounding thing.

God speaks in the old prophetic language nine times as much to the backslider as He does to the sinner. So I want you to know *there is no place for you only believing what God says.* When you come to that place, God will bless you, and you will be amazed how much He will bless you.

Interpretation of Tongues:

For God hath not chosen thee that He might make thee as a waster, but He has chosen thee to bring thee on the hill of perfection, that thou mightest know that there shall not be weakness in thee, but strength and character, for God has chosen thee.

That message is for someone in the meeting, "God hath chosen thee." Be not afraid; God has chosen you.

When he got to my house, my wife was in the house alone. He went in and he talked and talked and talked and talked. When I got home, my wife came out and said to me, "We've got the strangest man we ever had in our house. He has been in there half an hour, and he has never stopped talking. You never heard such a talker."

"Let him alone," said I. "He will come to an end."

I was introduced to him, and he went on talking. He talked through the dinner hour and right through to nighttime.

That night, we were having a meeting at our house. He didn't stop talking. He knew if he stopped, there would be something in his mind, so he was going to talk and block everyone else that talked. He wasn't willing to be "taken in" with this.

The meeting began to fill up; the room was packed.

"Brother," I said, "you have talked ever since you came. We are going now to pray. It is our meeting night. You must cease to speak."

He got down before God. My, it was wonderful! The power of God fell upon us, and something happened that never happened before that I remember. We always began our meeting with a song, always, but this time we began it in the attitude of prayer.

At one side of the fireplace knelt one young woman; at the other side of the fireplace knelt another I have never known before nor since. But deliberately, instead of praying, those two began speaking in tongues.

As soon as they began speaking in tongues, this man jumped up, startled. He ran to the one nearest him, his hands on his ears, and bent down over the girl. Then, frantically, he ran to the other, then back to the first, then to the other one.

Finally, he came and said to me, "Brother, can I go to my room?"

"Yes, brother."

He was shown to his room.

We had a wonderful meeting. At about 3:30 the next morning, he came to my door and knocked.

"May I come in?" he called.

"Yes," I said, "come in."

As soon as he got in, he stammered, "Bl-bl-bl" with his hand to his mouth. "It's come! It's come!"

"Go back to bed, brother," I said.

Next morning, he came down to breakfast.

"Oh! Wasn't that a wonderful night!" he exclaimed.

"Which do you mean?" I asked. We had a wonderful time; I wanted to know what he had done.

"Oh!" he said. "I came here; I heard in Bradford that you had received the power of the working of evils, and I was warned to keep away, and I was filled with unbelief. I was determined that nothing of that should affect me. I made up my mind I would talk every moment. But when you told the people to go to prayer, that moment those people began speaking in tongues. I went to them. I know Greek and I know Hebrew, and one was saying to me in Greek, 'Get right with God,' and the other was saying in Hebrew, 'Get right with God.'"

Oh, yes, God has a way to do it and God can do it. *When we get unbelief out of the way, the baptism of fire, revelation, the gifts of the Spirit, the harmony, the comfort, the blessed unction will abound till there will never be a dry meeting. Every meeting will be filled with life and power and joy in the Holy Ghost.*

Continuing his story, this man said, "When I heard that, I knew it was for me. I went upstairs and I repented. I knew I had been wrongly interpreting what God meant, and I repented. As I repented, I found myself laid out. I tried to resist, but God was so dealing with me that He laid me out over and over, till God sanctified me. And at 3:30, the power of God fell upon me, and I found myself speaking as the Spirit gave utterance, and I came to your door."

That man is a wonderful man today. God has blessed him everywhere.

THE GIFT OF PROPHECY EXPLAINED

I want you to understand clearly that there are three classes of prophecy. Get it in your heart, because Paul would that we all prophesy. (See 1 Corinthians 14:5.)

1. *The prophecy which is the testimony of the saved person.* This prophecy we find described in Revelation:

And I fell at his feet to worship him. And he said unto me, See thou do it not: I am thy fellowservant, and of thy brethren that have the testimony of Jesus: worship God: for the **testimony of Jesus is the spirit of prophecy.**
(Revelation 19:10, emphasis added)

This is the same prophecy that Paul speaks about in the fourteenth chapter of 1 Corinthians: *"Follow after charity, and desire spiritual gifts, but rather that ye may prophesy"* (1 Corinthians 14:1).

Here, prophecy is chosen as more important than charity or other gifts. Think about that: prophecy is to be chosen and desired above faith, hope, charity, above all the other gifts. The greatest amongst all is prophecy.

Why prophecy? Because prophecy by the power of the Spirit is the only power that saves humanity. We are told in the Word of God that the gospel which is brought through in prophecy has power to bring immortality and light. Immortality is that which abides forever. Light is that which opens the understanding of your heart. Light—immortality—is by the gospel.

Prophecy is to be coveted above all things, and every person has to have it. Now, every person may have gifts, but there are very few that do. But everybody has prophecy.

Now, from that same reference in Revelation, let us see what prophecy is and how it comes forth.

"I fell at his feet" (Revelation 19:10).

"I?" Who is it? I would like all the people who have been so foolish—I call it foolishness because there is nothing that makes you so foolish as to turn aside from the Word of God. If ever you want to be a fool, turn aside from the Word of God, and you will find yourself in a fool's paradise.

The one speaking here is a man who has been in the earth. Lots of people are foolishly led of the devil to believe that they are asleep in the grave, absolutely contrary to the Word of God. Don't you know that even the body that you have, if you live to the Lord, comes itself to be put off and another put on because you cannot go into heaven with your body? This man has been in the earth in the body and is now in heaven in the Spirit, and he wants you to hear what he has to say. *"I am thy fellowservant, and of thy brethren that have the testimony of Jesus…for the testimony of Jesus is the spirit of prophecy"* (Revelation 19:10).

What is the testimony of Jesus? I am saved. What the world wants to know today is how they can be saved.

Testify that you are saved. Your knees may knock together; you may be trembling as you do it; but when you get it out, you enter into the spirit of prophecy. And before you know where you are, you are saying things that the Spirit is saying.

Now you come to a point where you say, "Is it the Holy Spirit?"

No, indeed.

What is it, then?

It is the Spirit of Jesus that you got when you were saved. There are thousands of people who never have received the Holy Ghost that have this wonderful spirit of prophecy. People are being saved all over by the testimony of people who have never been baptized in the Holy Ghost, but they have the spirit of prophecy.

John Wesley was moved by the power of God and created revivals all over the world. After the people were saved, they testified.

If you cease from testifying, you will be sorry when the accounts are made. You are the power of salvation to people. Testify wherever you are.

You are the power of salvation to people. Testify wherever you are.

Interpretation of Tongues:

You have not chosen Me, but I have chosen you and ordained you that you should go forth, your feet shod with the preparation of the gospel of peace. What lovely feet! What lovely desire! A desire in your heart, because you are saved, to get everybody saved. The spirit of prophecy!

You must all preach from this morning. Every one of you must be a preacher. You have a prophecy which has come from heaven to change you from vile inward corruption, transport your human evil nature, put within you a spirit of testimony, because you know where once you were dead, behold, you are alive!

Interpretation of Tongues:

Live in the place where the Lord thy God moveth thee, not to go from house to house, not speak from person to person, but where the Lord directeth thee, for He has the person which is in need of truth waiting for watering with your water can.

Oh, how the Lord wants to cheer you today! Do not forget that you are ambassadors for Christ. Don't forget you are in the place now where the prophets have a chance.

The Lord can bring you into a great place of splendor. He has His hand upon you. Whatever you do, covet to be holy, seek to be clean, so that you might always bear about in your body not only the dying of the Lord, but the life of the resurrection of the Lord.

Interpretation of Tongues:

Lift up your hands and never be feeble, for the Lord has said, "Lift up holy hands." Don't be afraid of coming into the treasury, of making thine hand clean, for they that bear the vessels of the Lord have to be only unto the Lord. So the Lord is bringing thee to this great place of His pavilion, that He may clothe thee upon with the Spirit, that thy water shall not fail. He shall give thee water and seed for thy ministry, for remember it is the same water and it is the same Sower. So don't forget, beloved, you are coworkers together with Him, and your ministry in the Lord is not to be in vain. See to it that you live so that your seed is well watered.

Now, that is one class of prophecy. General Booth knew it. He got the vision as clear as anything from Wesley. The greatest revival that has ever swept the earth yet that we remember is the revival the Salvation Army brought. I know they have lost the glory, the power, and the unction because they turned to philanthropic positions. But that does not mean that we have to lose it.

God revealed Himself unto Booth, every person was saved that would testify, and He moved the people that were saved—drunkards and harlots—into the streets to prophesy in the Spirit of Jesus.

This is the prophecy that you all have when you are saved. The spirit of prophecy is the testimony that you are saved by the blood of the Lamb.

2. *Every preacher that lives in unction has the second class of prophecy.* You will find that I mostly speak in prophecy. Why? Well, it has pleased the Lord to bring me into this order so that I do not come to the platform with thought, not thoughts of what I am saying.

I want you to know another thing: I never say what I think. It is very much below a prophet of the Lord to begin to speak to the people what he thinks. *The prophet must always say what he knows, because the people he is speaking to are the ones that have to think it out.* But he is in the place of knowledge.

The Holy Ghost takes the thoughts of Jesus and fills him with life divine till he speaks divine utterances, till he knows.

Sometimes I speak ever so much, never take any thought at all concerning what I am speaking, but it flows out like rivers—prophecy of divine power.

It is very important and very essential that the person who preaches should live in prophetic utterance. Then, a preacher should never be lamentable in his divine position. He is standing before the people as a chosen one of God. He has not in any way to bring his position in anything less than it is the Word of God. He is speaking, and there he is to be clothed with holiness like a garment of salvation.

Oh, this is true! The Spirit of the Lord is upon me now—I know it, I feel it. It is moving me. It chastens me. It is bringing me to a place where I know if you listen you will be blessed. The blessing of the Lord is upon you. Hear, for the Spirit speaketh to you.

This prophecy is as the Spirit gives forth, the illumination of truth by the Word of Life, the Holy Ghost having the chief position in the place, taking words, acts, everything, till he stands there complete—he the oracle of God, speaking words absolutely according as if the Lord were here saying them.

3. *The gift of prophecy.* There is another prophecy which I trust many of you people will have because it is the gift of prophecy.

What are the other two?

The other two prophecies are divine inspiration and Holy Ghost utterances.

Every person, in a very remarkable way by the Spirit of Jesus, can feel burnings and movings, chastening and thrillings. It is wonderful. All you have got to do is begin and you cannot stop.

There was something done on the cross which is truly wonderful. Don't you know you were made every whit whole? You were made holy. You were made a saint. You were absolutely cleansed from all unrighteousness.

The new birth is a revelation of God in the soul. You are made His forever when you are saved by His power. No one can estimate the new birth. It is beyond all human power to estimate. The new birth is larger than our human capacities. And, thank God, we have touches which make us on fire.

Now, the next, divine prophecy, as a gift. There are people who, like Isaiah, have this prophecy. Isaiah was so filled with this prophecy: *"Unto us a son is given"* (Isaiah 9:6).

It took five hundred years to bring it to pass, but there it was, definitely declared: *"And the government shall be upon his shoulder: and his name shall be called Wonderful, Counsellor, the mighty God, the everlasting Father, the Prince of Peace"* (Isaiah 9:6).

Oh, hallelujah! All the way down you will find you get the prophecy, so distinct. You will see Isaiah filled with prophetic utterances. Begin with Genesis and go right through, and you will find the golden or the scarlet thread right through all the prophecies. "He is coming, He is coming! He is on the way! He will surely come!"

The angels sang, "The Babe was born, and they called His name Jesus, for He saves His people from sinning." Prophecy fulfilled! "He shall in a manger lay; He should die on the cross; as Moses lifted up the serpent in the wilderness, so must the Son of Man be lifted up."

Ah, beloved, God can give you prophecy which shall fulfill the past to a perfect degree, chapter, verse.

He is coming! Glory to God! The saints shall be awakened; the prophecy shall appear. People will say, "Yes, He is coming! We know He is coming!"

And He will come!

THE GIFTS OF THE SPIRIT
Bible Study #6 – July 13, 1927

W e thank Thee, Lord, that Thou hast made sufficient atonement for sin, sickness, deficiencies, all our weakness, and everything.

As a groundwork for the study of the gifts of the Spirit, we should read the twelfth chapter of Romans. All that is done and said in these meetings is based upon the authority of the Word of God. I am sure it would not please God to turn aside to any human thing when we have such a valuable, wonderful display of wisdom and authority by this living Word.

Just as we become unmindful on human lines, clothed upon with the Spirit on divine lines, we shall be natural but supernatural. A lovely position, natural man, just the same physique, just the same expression, the same man only supernatural, inwardly displaying the revelation of the power of God through the same body, divine position.

Don't be afraid to understand that God meant that you are to be partakers of divine nature.

Don't be afraid to understand that God meant that you are to be partakers of divine nature: divine life in the human casket, divine thoughts, ever human mind. Human mind transformed, divine mind taking its place, that you should always be the children of the Lord and act as the people which are from above. You are from above. You are born of a new creation. You were planted with Him, you were risen, and you are to be seated with Him in the place of victory over the power of the enemy.

Don't forget that God is in all, over all, through all, in you all, that He might bring about in your daily ministry a divine plan as active and as perfect as the apostles at the beginning, as Jesus in His ministry. Jesus portrayed, showed forth, pressed in to His disciples this word: *"Be ye therefore perfect, even as your Father which is in heaven is perfect"* (Matthew 5:48).

We need not know people after the flesh anymore. From this day, let us learn that we have only to know the character of the people after the Spirit. Remember, the disciples came to a perfect place when they said, "We won't know Jesus anymore after the flesh." They wouldn't remember Him on the line of His fleshly ministry—not a fleshly power, but the fleshly body. There were any amount of things about Jesus on the natural line of His human need—of His wanting food from the tree, sitting by the well, and asking for water. We won't know Him that way anymore. We will know Jesus after the Spirit.

What is the difference? No weakness—perfect power over all weaknesses. May the Lord grant unto us in these days a divine acquaintance with the Master, that we begin from this day to be spiritual and more spiritual till we live in the Spirit, not fulfilling the lusts of the flesh, but in Christ.

Interpretation of Tongues:

The Lord Himself feed us with the finest of the wheat He seeks only to bring us into favor with the Father. He says, "Hitherto have ye asked nothing in my name: ask, and ye shall receive, that your joy may be full" (John 16:24). And as you ask, it shall be given you—a measure full, pressed down, shaken together, and running over—that there shall be no leanness in you, but you shall be full, overflowing, expressive; God manifest in the glory of the Lord upon you, and He bringing forth songs in the earth.

FRUITS AND GIFTS UNITED

Before we proceed with our discussion of the gifts, I want to speak a little about the dovetailing, the uniting together, of the fruits and the gifts. So I am going to just enumerate them so that we shall know. This will be very profitable to you, because you must be careful that whatever gift is manifested in you it has to coincide, have a joint fellowship, with a fruit of the Spirit, so that you would never miss the plan of God in this holy order. Any gift that God should give you should never go to waste; it will always be to profit.

For fruit of the Spirit, see Galatians 5:22. The first is the gift of wisdom, which must always be connected with love. Love is the first fruit; wisdom is the first gift.

The next is knowledge. You will find, if you work this out, that knowledge will always bring joy and will be accompanied with joy. Knowledge produces joy, and they coincide.

Faith. You never find that faith is to any profit without there is peace, so the gift of faith coincides with the fruit of peace.

Healings. You always find the person that is used in healing will be longsuffering. If he loses that, if the person who ministers to the needy does not enter in—remember in Philippians the words, *"The fellowship of his sufferings"* (Philippians 3:10). It doesn't mean that you have to go to the cross, but you have to be so in the Spirit with the needy sufferer that you enter right in.

DIVINE HEALING METHODS

In this behalf, remember you must be brought into a justification place, because it may be that many of you people are judging me and saying, "Isn't he rough!" Now we must understand every man in his own order. You can't fill my boat and I couldn't fill yours, but we can fill the boat God has made for us. And we cannot turn aside to please humanity because we have one Master, and that is Christ.

There came a woman before me in Australia, where thousands were looking on, and I ministered to her for healing. She was a very large woman. As she came to me, the Spirit of the Lord revealed to me that inwardly there was an adversary destroying her life. Instantly God helped me to rise up against the adversary, not against the woman.

In the name of Jesus, I dealt with this evil thing that had vexed the woman. With all the crowd looking on, she cried, "You're killing me! You're killing me! Oh, you're killing me!"

She fell down on the floor. "Bring her back again," I said. I knew I had not finished the work.

Then I went at it again, destroying the evil that was there, and I knew I had to do it. The people did not understand as again, she cried, "Oh, you're killing me!"

"Bring her back again," I said.

I laid my hands on her again in the name of Jesus, and the work was done. She walked five yards in the aisle and dropped her big cancer.

You people that are judging me, please leave your judgment outside, for I obey God. If you are afraid to be touched, don't come to me to pray for you. If you are not prepared to be dealt with as God gives me leadings to deal, keep away. But if you can believe God has me for a purpose, come and I will help you.

How we need to have the mind of Christ and to live for Christ. What a serious thing it would be for me at sixty-eight years of age to try to please people when I have my Father in heaven to please!

Interpretation of Tongues:

> *It is the way into the treasure house the Lord brings thee. It is not thy way of thinking, it is the way in which He brings thee through. Don't forget that Jesus said, "Strait is the gate, and narrow is the way" (Matthew 7:14). I brought you in to be the plan and place of redemption with fullness. Therefore, resist not the Spirit, judge not the things, even prophecy, but lay hold of it that God is in the midst of thee to bring thee to the place of thy desired health.*

Gift of Prophecy, Continued

We didn't exactly finish the word of prophecy yesterday morning, because I wanted you to see that there is a great deal of trouble through prophecy. There always has been. So I want you to guard this gift.

There are three classes of prophecy. The first position of prophecy everyone has, every newborn soul. Through the new birth unto righteousness, God has given an unction of the Spirit, a real unction of the Spirit of Christ. We felt, when we were saved, we wanted everybody to be saved. That has to be continuous. The whole world can be regenerated by the spirit of prophecy as we testify to our saving position in Christ.

The next type of prophecy is the preacher who delivers in prophetic utterances. My natural makeup is not full, but my supernatural makeup is an overflowing full. I depend upon an overflowing full that you may get something out of it, that you may overflow full.

I now turn to the prophecy which is the most wonderful of all prophecy and yet the most dangerous. What you have got to watch is this—the same in the gift of tongues, just the same in the gift of healing, just the same in prophecy—you have to watch this: because the gift has been received and the people been blessed through the gift, you are never to use this gift without the power of the Spirit brings into you a great thirst and longing to do it. It would be a serious thing for me to speak in tongues at any moment just because of the gift, without the unction of the Spirit, and it would fall to nothing.

All gifts are of no account at all without they are brought forth by the Giver of the gifts, and the Holy Ghost is the One who gives the nine gifts. And He has unction, fire, zeal, and expression until those that hear are moved, because when the Lord speaks, it changes and moves the natural, because it is supernatural. Supernatural always changes natural.

Prophecy is lovely because it makes the body very full of expressions of joy. It is lovely, for people all like to hear it. It is lovely when it is the Spirit moving.

You be careful, now, when the people are very pleased to hear you prophesy. Prophecy is like tongues; no man is to have advantage in a meeting that speaks and speaks and speaks and speaks in tongues. That is not what is advantage. Advantage is that when the Spirit is upon you, you will speak in tongues and you will close down the moment you know you are at the end. What spoils it is people going on and on, and the hearers are tired of it because they want something which God can bring in and move quickly.

Don't you think you will be heard by your mouth speaking, either by tongues or by praying or anything. You are not heard because of your mouth speaking. You are heard because you are definite. All your spiritual abilities are going to be acceptable with others as you learn how to obey the Spirit and never take advantage because you are in the place.

Another thing you have to learn: people rush up and down sometimes and say to you, "Oh, I was obliged to do that! I was obliged to jump up and to do that I was obliged to do that, and that, and that."

Don't believe them. It isn't true. There never was a man in the world as long as he was in the body that hadn't power over the Spirit. And so when people rush to you and say they are obliged to do this, that, and the other, don't you believe it. What have you to believe? You have to believe that when the Spirit is manifested in the order it should be, it will have three things with it: comfort, consolation, and edification. (See 1 Corinthians 14:3.)

If any of you find I do not speak by the Spirit of God and bring the Scriptures only, that which God desires, you meet me at the door and tell me. I have declared that this shall be my constant purpose. I have declared that as long as I live I shall never exaggerate. Exaggeration is lying. What God wants is a people that is full of truth. I want God to so have you that your word will be the bond; if ever you say a thing, the people will be able to believe. You have said it and you will do it.

When the unction is upon you, when the power of God is manifested through you, one thing that will be accomplished by prophecy is comfort. The Holy Ghost can so have you in prophecy that all the people will be comforted.

But if you get away from that prophecy because you begin and the people are delighted, go on till you come out with your human words, and you will lead people astray. People have been led to buy houses, to do all sorts of silly things, because of people who did not obey the Lord but brought in some human prophecy.

If anybody ever comes to you with human prophecy, say, "I know God, and without God gives me, I won't move."

Don't you be deluded by anybody. You can tell what is of the Lord. The Word of God distinctly says about this, "Do not despise prophecy." (See 1 Thessalonians 5:20.) Whatever you do, do not despise it. But in the next words, you are told to *"prove [judge] all things"* (1 Thessalonians 5:21). Say, "Well now, if that is of the Lord, I will see if it is of the Word of God." And you will have clear revelation as to whether it is the word of the Lord.

This is the day that we need comforting, and the power of the Spirit can comfort you and send you away from these meetings to know that you have been in the presence of God and heard the Word of God.

Gifts of Tongues and Interpretation

The gifts of tongues and interpretation we shall take for exploration and explanation at this time, in the name of the Father, Son, and Holy Ghost, to edification. These gifts are so primarily run together that it would be very difficult to deal with one without the other, and I believe that it will be very profitable for you if I take them two together.

> *I love the thought that God has all power over all the powers of the enemy in the heavenlies, on the earth, and under the earth.*

Why tongues? Why has God brought this gift into operation? There is a reason; if there were not a reason, it would not be there.

I love the thought of *"God…above all, and through all, and in you all"* (Ephesians 4:6). I love the thought that God has all power over all the powers of the enemy in the heavenlies, on the earth, and under the earth. Where are you going to get where He is not?

Why did God design it all? You must see with me that this gift was never in evidence before the Holy Ghost came.

Interpretation of Tongues:

> *The Spirit leadeth and will direct every thought and so bring into your hearts the fruit, till the fruit in your own life shall be a manifestation that God is in you of a truth.*

The Lord gave that to us. That is a very important word.

The old dispensation was very wonderful in prophetic utterances. No person received the Holy Ghost, whoever he is, but what will have prophetic utterances in the Spirit unto God or in natural order, supernaturally coming forth, that all the people will know that is the Spirit.

That is the reason why we want all the people filled with the Holy Ghost, because they are to be *prophetic*. Prophetic means to say that God has a thought, a word in season, that has never been in season before. Things new and old. The Holy Ghost brings it to pass!

So when God fulfilled the promise, when the time was appointed (and it is a wonderful appointment!), the Holy Ghost came and filled the apostles, and the gift which had never been in operation came into operation that wonderful day in the upper room. And for the first time in all history, men were speaking in a new order—not an old language, but language which was to be interpreted.

This is very profound, because we understand that God is speaking. No man understands it. The Spirit is speaking, and the Spirit opens the revelation that they shall have without adulteration of God's word flowing through the whole place.

Tongues are a wonderful display on this line: they are to revive the people; they are to give new depths of thought.

If ever you want to know why the Holy Ghost was of great need, you will find it in the third chapter of Ephesians. You will be amazed. The language is wonderful. Paul speaks. He says he is the least of all, and yet God has called him to be an apostle. His language is wonderful, and yet he feels in his heart and life that there is something greater, that the Spirit has him, and he bows his knee unto the Father. You cannot find in all the Scriptures words with such profound fruit, ringing through these verses from the fourteenth verse of that remarkable praying in the Holy Ghost: "*That ye might be filled with all the fulness of God*" (Ephesians 3:19), "*that ye…may be able to comprehend with all saints*" (Ephesians 3:17–18), and that you may be able to ask and think, and think and ask, and ask and think, and it will be not only abundantly but very "*exceeding abundantly*" above all you can ask and think (Ephesians 3:20).

There is a man closing down and the Holy Ghost praying.

Interpretation of Tongues:

> To this end He brings you together that He might pour into you the hidden treasure, for it is in thee God has refined thee, first cleansed thee, made thee just like a vessel that He might dwell in thee and make all His acquaintance with thee. But the Father, the Son, and the Holy Ghost should be primary over thee, and thou shouldst be just exalted in Him, not in thyself, but He should have the glory.

WHAT IS TONGUES FOR?

You may have heard three years ago, I was in Los Angeles. God's blessing was upon those meetings. Some of you remember blessings received. But since I left, you people do

not know what I have done. You are not living with me. You
have not been with me. I might have lost unction or favor with
God. And I might be like many people today who have lived
holy lives and got holy language and talked in holy language
but now are living in a backslidden condition, a life which is
not worthy of the language. There are people today who have
lived holy lives, preached sanctification, and their language has
been helpful, but something has come in the way. They have
kept their language. They have lost their zeal and fire, but they
still hold on to the language.

That can take place in any life. So I ask you that think you
stand, take heed lest you fall. You cannot play with this.

I would like you to know that the speaker is no good unless
he judges himself every day. If I do not judge myself, I shall be
judged. It is not sufficient for me to have your good word. I
must have the Master's good word. It is no good to me that I
should look good to you. If there were one thing between me
and God, I dare not come onto this platform without I know
that God has made me holy, for they *that bear the vessels of
the LORD"* must be holy unto the Lord (Isaiah 52:11). And I
praise God because I know:

> *His blood can make the vilest clean,*
> *His blood can make the vilest clean,*
> *His blood avails for me,*
> *His blood avails for me*
> *Holiness! Whiteness! Purity! Zeal!*

Interpretation of Tongues:

> *Grieve not the Holy Spirit whereby you are saved, but
> let everything be done decently and in order so that God
> shall have preeminence in all things and Christ shall reign
> over the house, even His house, which He says, "Whose*

house you are if you hold fast the profession of your faith without doubting."

So God is bringing us this morning to this holy place to bring us to see that we must only obey the Spirit.

You do not know what has taken place in my life since I was here. When the good people of the Angelus Temple wired to see if I could give them June or July, they did not know that I was still living in the center of God's holy will. Because I am only a man, it is possible I may have grieved the Spirit. When I got up to speak in this temple, what I said may have been only formal language, no unction, nothing moving the people. Then someone in the place—someone in the place who is hungry for God—cannot rest because they are not getting the cream of the truth, travailing and groaning in the Spirit and speaking in tongues; another person in the same way travailing, receiving the interpretation of those tongues, arises and gives that interpretation, thus lifting the people where the prophet could not do it because he was out of the will of God.

Then, you say, what about it when you are preaching and prophesying and we are all getting blessed and then we have tongues?

As I speak, from time to time, I am so full of the glory and the joy, and my body may be more full than my language can express, then instantly the Spirit pours forth His word in tongues. The power of God just lifts the whole place into revelation and the word of life far beyond where we were.

So the church is to come together so in the Spirit that the power of God can fall on Mary, on John, on William, or on Henry and move them, till the power of God moving through them the people get the mind of God.

In the fourteenth chapter of 1 Corinthians, we have very definite instruction about tongues:

If any man speak in an unknown tongue, let it be by two, or at the most by three, and that by course; and let one interpret. But if there be no interpreter, let him keep silence in the church; and let him speak to himself, and to God.
(1 Corinthians 14:27–28)

There are three positions of tongues, and there is laid down the spiritual law. But before we come to that, we must understand verse 32, else there will be no success in this place. *"And the spirits of the prophets are subject to the prophets"* (1 Corinthians 14:32).

Without you adhere to this word, every assembly where you are would be broken up and you would cause trouble. Until you come to a right mind upon the Scriptures, you will never be pleasing to God. You are not to consider under any circumstances that, because you have any gift, it is right for you to use that gift without the unction of the Spirit is upon you, and you have to be very careful that you never use it in confusion with prophecy. When the prophecy is going forth and the truth is being heard and all the people are receiving it with joy and being built up, there is no room for tongues or interpretation. But just at the time when language seems in my heart too big to bring forth the language, then tongues come forth and God looses the whole thing, and we get a new design in that.

Until you come to a right mind upon the Scriptures, you will never be pleasing to God.

So you people who have this wonderful gift, see to it that you never break in, in a place where the Spirit is having perfect right-of-way. But when the Spirit is working with you and you know there is a line of truth that the Lord has, then let the name of God be glorified.

You see, God wants it in perfect order by the Spirit. So He says, "*two, or at the most by three.*" You will never know me speak if there have been three speak before me. And you will never know me interpret any word in tongues if three have spoken already in order, to keep the bonds of peace in the body so that the people shall not be weary, because there are some people who have known nothing about right.

Except you come to the Word of God, you will be in confusion and you will be in judgment. God wants you to not be in judgment, neither in confusion. But He wants you to be built by the Scriptures, for the Scriptures are clear.

Whatever the Lord reveals to me, if I have said anything before which has not been absolutely scriptural, that is the last time I shall say it. I allow God's Word to be my judge. If I find anything I have said is not scriptural, I will repent before God. But God is my judge; I never say anything except I believe it is sincere truth. But if I find out it is not just in the most perfect keeping with the Word of God, I never say that anymore.

I believe there is a place to come to where we repent of a thing that we never have to repent of that thing anymore. I pray God will give us that kind of superabundant revelation of common sense. It is because there is not a superabundant revelation of common sense that everybody is using the nonsense. The Lord helps us to be true first to God; then, if we are true to God, we will be true to ourselves. Let God be first in the choice of our desires and our plans. Jesus must be glorified.

In the thirtieth verse of this Scripture, we read, "*If any thing be revealed to another that sitteth by, let the first hold his peace*" (1 Corinthians 14:30).

I hope someday the church will so come into its beauty that when I am preaching and you have a revelation on that very thing, a deep revelation from God, if you will stand, I will stop that moment. What for? Because the Scripture says if, when the prophets are speaking, anything is revealed to one in the audience, let the first hold his peace and then let that one speak.

Then, the Scripture says, *"For ye may all prophesy one by one, that all may learn, and all may be comforted"* (1 Corinthians 14:31). This refers to the one who is preaching. He may be led to hold his peace while one in the midst of the congregation speaks his line of thought, which is divinely appointed. Then, after he finishes, another has a line of thought on prophecy, and he gets up, until you may have several who have prophesied, and you have such revelations from this quarter until the whole church would be ablaze.

I believe God is going to help us that we might be sound in mind, right in thought, holy in judgment, separated unto God, and one in the Spirit. Fancy all the people in the place being comforted and edified and going away from the church feeling they have been in the presence of God, just because they have been obedient to the will of God.

Allow me to say this, and then you judge it afterwards. You are not in the right place if you do not judge what I say. You have not to swallow all I say. You have to judge all I say by the Scripture. But you must always use righteous judgment. Righteous judgment is not judging because of condemnation, but it is judging whether it be according to the Word of God. Righteous judgment is not a single eye to criticism, but righteous judgment is to judge it in its truth, that the church may receive edification, that all the people might be built according to the Word of God. That is the right judgment.

It may not be in the minds of all people to affirm and believe what I say about this, but I truly affirm and believe— because God has thus revealed it to me—that the words *"let it be by two, or at the most by three, and that by course"* (1 Corinthians 14:27) means to say that very often, the speaker does not finish his message by the first insight.

So often I have seen in the assembly that the first person has spoken, the Spirit of the Lord has been mightily upon him, but the unction is so that he did not finish the message by the first insight of truth and realizes he is not through with that message. Then, he comes on again, and we felt the tide was higher. Then, the third time again, he comes and it is higher still, and then he stops. This has led me to believe that *"and that by course"* means that one person may be permitted to speak in tongues three times in the one meeting.

In our conventions in England, we very often have nine tongues, but there would only be three persons speaking. You can have nine, but it is not necessary without the Lord is upon it. Sometimes I find that the Spirit will take us so through in prophecy that there will not be more than one, sometimes two. If I am in the right order—and I believe I am in the right order when I am saying this—when we are full of prophecy, the Spirit has taken the heart, moved the heart by the power of the Spirit, and I am speaking as fast as I can, giving no vent to thought. The Holy Ghost is the thought, the language, and everything. The power of the Spirit is speaking, and when the power of the Holy Ghost is speaking like this, there is no need of tongues or interpretation because you are getting right from the throne the very language of the heart and the man. Then, when the body gives out, the Spirit will speak and the Lord will give tongues and interpretation, and that will lift the whole place.

"Three at most"—don't you say four or five, but three at most. The Holy Ghost says it.

Three things are important before you go further.

There are three classes of tongues, and this is where the confusion comes. This is where the people judge you, and this is where the people have gotten wrong.

I know, and every person that interprets knows, there is an intuition of divine appointment at this time. Every person that has come into line when they have nothing before them except the glory of God will come into this line—you will know exactly one thing: you have to know never in a prayer meeting, when people are praying in the Spirit, never seek interpretation. The Scripture declares it clearly:

> For he that speaketh in an unknown tongue speaketh not unto men, but unto God: for no man understandeth him; howbeit in the spirit he speaketh mysteries.
>
> (1 Corinthians 14:2)

When they are receiving the Holy Ghost, that is one attitude. When you are in a prayer meeting is another attitude. You will find in a prayer meeting, when people will pray and speak in the Spirit, it will be unto God and not for interpretation. Do not try to seek interpretation, for if you do, you will find it is wrong.

Never under any circumstances expect tongues interpreted where it is continually routine, the same, the same, and the same. It is a Spirit language, but it is not a gift. What is it? You will find it is adoration. It is in the place where the soul has been in a real, definite position with God. Do not seek interpretation.

Now what is for interpretation? Diverse kinds of tongues. Now what is diverse kinds of tongues? Diverse kinds of tongues is languages with perfect syllables. When a person gets up with a perfect language by the Spirit, you will find it is decisive, it is instructive, it is lovely to hear, it is divine in its appointment. It is diverse kinds of tongues, and that has to have interpretation because God is speaking to us in language which is not understood, but it has to be interpreted.

Tongues are to bring forth in the church revelation and power and save from death and save it from being bound.

Tongues and interpretation are for liberty amongst the people, to lift the saints, fill the place with the glory. God will open this to you and you will see what it means to have people amongst you full of the Spirit, and you long to get the Spirit's mind.

Now, what is interpretation? Interpretation is the same spirit as the person with tongues. And they are so moved by the power of the Spirit that they are in a place where they know that that which God was burning within had to come out.

It is a common thing, when I give the interpretation to meet people at the door as I go out, that they say, "Oh, that interpretation was lovely! I had it."

Another will come, "Oh, that interpretation was beautiful! I had it, you know."

And I have had three in one meeting say that to me. "Oh, the interpretation was lovely! I had it."

Is it true? No. There is no truth in it at all. Why? No interpreter has the interpretation, not one I haven't got myself.

Then what have they got? They have got the spirit of it. They knew it was the spirit of it, and they knew it was according to the mind of God. They got the sense of the knowledge that God was speaking, and it was the Spirit, and they knew it was right. The interpretation never has it. Why? Because he is in the channel where the Spirit is breathing every word and he does not get the word; he does not get the sentences and everything made. The whole thing the Spirit breathes, and the interpreter speaks as the Spirit gives utterance.

So it is as divine and as original as the throne of God.

I want to show you the difference. There are some people that get up and are in tongues, and they give a little bit of tongues, then again, then again, and they repeat themselves. Never give interpretation to such foolishness.

There are other people who get up and profess to interpret it, and they stutter and stammer; they give a word now and then. Is that interpretation? No. Do you think that the Holy Ghost is short of language? If you are stammering and stuttering and giving a word of interpretation now and then, don't believe it. It is not of God. What is it? It is the waiting while some word in their mind comes forth, and they are giving you their mind. It is not interpretation.

I say all these things to save you from foolishness, save you from people that want to be somebody. The Holy Ghost has shown to me that all the time He is helping me; I have got to be nothing. There is not a place where any man can ever be anything. It is in the death, union, and likeness of Christ that He becomes all in all. And if we are not gone to death in the baptism of the Spirit, it shows to me that we are altogether out of order.

The Spirit of the Lord has been speaking to you for an hour. I have felt the unction. I have realized the power. I have been speaking as fast as I could get it out, and the Spirit has given everything. We have been, for once in our lifetime, in the presence of the Holy Ghost. We have been where there has been the manifestation of the glory, where God is speaking to our hearts, where He is bringing us to a place of inhabitation in the Spirit.

We have need to covet this meeting as a holy meeting with God.

See that you are built square on the authority of God. See that your testimony on salvation, sanctification, the gifts, the baptism is biblical. Then you cannot be troubled by the enemy. You will be above the enemy. You will be able to say to the enemy, "*Get thee behind me*" (Matthew 16:23), and he will get!

What are you ready for now? Are you ready for anything? Don't forget you have to go over the top this morning.

The top of what? The top of yourself, the top of your opinions and fancies and whims and foolish acts. You have to dethrone them; you have to have a biblical building; you have to be in the Scriptures.

"*For God hath not given us the spirit of fear; but of power, and of love, and of a sound mind*" (2 Timothy 1:7). When people say to me, "Oh, I have a nervous system, I have a nervous weakness," I know immediately that only one thing is wrong. What is it? It is a lack of knowing the Word, "*Perfect love casteth out fear*" (1 John 4:18). And there is no torment, no fear, in love.

I want you to get the Word of God in your heart till the demon power has no power over you. You are over the powers of fear. Then I want you to understand that the baptism of the Holy Ghost is a love beyond any ever you had. And you are to have power after the Holy Ghost comes, and it is power over the enemy, over yourself, and over your human mind.

You have to be dethroned and Christ enthroned and the Holy Ghost enlarging His position.

Go over the top and never slide down again the back way. If you go, you go forward, and you go onto victory from victory, triumphing over the enemy, having liberty in your captivity, rightly rejoicing in the triumph of God.

Faith is the victory. Faith is the operation in your heart. Faith is the stimulation of the life of the Master. Faith is the position where God takes you to the place where you are over all by the power of God.

Believe that no power of the enemy shall have power over you. Rebuke him. Stand on the authority of the Word. Go forth into victory. I want you to be saved, healed, and blessed through what God's Word says.

I want you to get the Word of God in your heart till the demon power has no power over you.

SONS OF GOD
Bible Study #7 – July 14, 1927

First John 3. This is a banquet of love, where Jesus is looking over us and making Himself known to us. It is surely the manifestation of love when we read in God's Word, "*As the heavens are higher than the earth, so are my ways higher than your ways, and my thoughts than your thoughts*" (Isaiah 55:9).

Surely beloved, God means to strengthen us by this coming near unto Him, to believe that our weaknesses shall be turned into strength, that out unbelief shall be made into living faith, that the dew of His presence, the power of His love, may be so active upon us that we are all changed by this wonderful Word.

I want to lift you to a place where you dare believe that God is waiting to bless you abundantly, beyond all that you can ask or think.

Are you ready? "What for?" you say. That you shall this day get before God with such living fairly to dare believe that all things are possible concerning you.

Are you ready? "What for?" That you may this day know that God's mercy never faileth. Though you are failing, He is still full of mercy.

Are you ready? You are? Then God will surely giant unto you a very rich blessing that *you shall forget all your poverty and come into a bountiful place of supply till you shall never know*—understand it, God means it—*you shall never know any barren thing concerning you, but you shall be brought into His treasures and He shall cover you with His bountifulness,* and you shall know that the God of the Most High reigns.

What Manner of Love!

The Lord has given me the privilege to bring before you another message this morning, a message that I trust will stir you all and change you in a very remarkable way.

The Lord is still leading me on the line of gifts, only there is just a little break this morning because we have been having so much on the line of the gifts, and now I want to put you in the place of a position where you are worthy of these positions, or divine appointments, with God.

To this end, let us consider the third chapter of the first epistle of John, the first to the tenth verses. This is one of the pinnacles of truth. A pinnacle of truth is that which leads you to a place of sovereignty of purity, a place where you cannot be moved by the situation. You have a fixed position. You take the position clearly on the authority of the Word of Jesus. God means to let it ring through our hearts distinctly, clearly, marvelously. Free from sin, children of God, heirs of the kingdom of His righteousness.

The opening word of this chapter is one of those words in which we find stimulation in Hebrews. You will find many words which have a lot to do with the opening of the Scriptures, such as *therefore* and *wherefore*. Here, we have a beautiful word, *behold*. Awake! Open! Listen! God is speaking.

What is He saying? *"Behold, what manner of love the Father hath bestowed upon us, that we should be called the sons of God"* (1 John 3:1).

What manner of love! It is one of those manifold—or much more; it is full of expression. It is God who looks past your weaknesses, your human depravities, all your makeups which you know were absolutely out of order, and He has washed you, He has cleansed you, He has beautified you, and He looks at you and says, "You are lovely! I see no spot of sin upon you. There is no spot. You are now My sons."

For the Lord is gentle, easy to be entreated, without partiality, full of goodness and faith. He seeth beyond all weakness, looks at the son of His love because of the shed blood, and opens unto us the treasures of His great love, and saith to us:

> *For the Lord is gentle, easy to be entreated, without partiality, full of goodness and faith.*

Interpretation of Tongues:

> *Thou art fair, My love, thou art fair. I have called thee into My banqueting house, I have decked thee with the jewels of the rarest, for thou shalt have gifts and the beatitudes shall cover thee, and My grace shall follow thee and I will give thee to understand the mysteries of the hidden things.*

THE ORDER OF SONSHIP

> *That we should be called the sons of God: therefore the world knoweth us not, because it knew him not.*
>
> (1 John 3:1)

The world knows us not in our sonship. We have to be strangers to the world's knowledge. We have to surpass all, even in the midst of it.

I want us to examine ourselves to see if this sonship is ours, if we are in the order of perfect sonship. And then, after that, you may strengthen yourself in God and believe for anything to come to pass. But you must examine yourself to see if you are in the Father.

The greatest blessing that can come to you will be that the Word of life in going forth will inwardly create in you a deeper desire for God.

If you are right, as the Spirit is giving the Word, it will make you long more for God, more for the holiness of God, more for the righteousness of God, for He has to make you this day to know that as *He is pure, you have to be pure.*

Don't stumble at the Word. If Jesus says anything, if the Word conveys anything to your mind, don't stumble at the Word. Believe that God is greater than you are, greater than your heart, greater than your thought, and that He can establish you in righteousness even when your thoughts and your knowledge are absolutely against it. He blotted out our transgressions in a thick cloud, and our sins, our iniquities, will He remember no more forever. (See Isaiah 44:22.)

Often, I find that people misunderstand God's Word because they bring their minds to the Word, and because the Word does not exactly fit their minds, they do not get liberty. They want the Word to come to their minds. It will never do it. You have to be submissive to God.

The Word of God is true. If you will understand the truth and right, you can be always on the line of gaining strength, overcoming oppositions, living in the world but over it, making everything subject to you.

LABOR LIGHTENED

One day, after holding a meeting, a man came to me and said, "Your ministry makes me feel that there is something radically wrong with me. I am a strong man to look at. There is apparently no weakness about me. I am ashamed of myself; I have three big lads and they are doing the work of men, and I know it is not right. And here I am, a big man, and if I do anything on the line of my business, I go down. I have just come out of three weeks in bed through working one day."

He had a business of carrying coal from house to house in bags of 112 pounds' weight. Every time he picked up a bag and carried it to a house, his whole frame gave way and he had to go to bed.

"Why," I said, "brother, you have never come into the line of truth. You are stranger to the truth of the Word of God."

There are any number of people who have not learned yet how they are masters of *their own bodies, masters of all kinds of work, masters of everything. You have to be a son of God in the earth, over your work, over your mind, over your body, over your life.*

Interpretation of Tongues:

> It is God who openeth the heart and gives us understanding, for without the Spirit gives life to the Word, you will be still held. But let the Spirit lift you by the Word and you will find you will come into perfect freedom today; for God taketh the Word, poureth it into thy heart, openeth thy understanding, and thou art in liberty, because the Word of God makes everybody free and the Word of God is not bound.

From Romans 7:25, we clearly see how we are over every manual labor of God: "*So then with the mind I myself serve the law of God; but with the flesh the law of sin.*"

There is the sequel to the position.

"My brother," I said, "you have carried those bags of coal with your body, and you have allowed your mind to come into your body, and you have gone down."

That is what people are doing all the time.

Now, what is the law of sin? Every kind of work there is today is the law of sin. Is it sin? No, it is not sin; it is what law brought. There was no work before the fall, but work of every description came because of sin, and through it you have to eat your bread by the sweat of your brow, and sweat is an emblem of sin.

Sweat, disease, weakness, calamity, and all kinds of depression the law of sin has brought.

Is it sin, then, to work? No, it is not sin to work.

I went to an asylum one day, and I said to the man, "What is the first indication when a man has come to reason and clear understanding?"

"Oh!" he said. "Are you a stranger?"

"Yes," I said.

"Well," he said, "are you...what makes you so intent about this thing?"

"I have someone in question," I said. "What is the first indication? Tell me."

"Why," he said, "it is marvelous that you should ask. You see that man over there? That man became perfect in a moment, and we had six men in charge of him. In a moment he came right. We agreed together to pray at a certain time, and that man was as free as possible."

"What is the first indication?" I asked.

"The first indication," he replied, "is that when a man is coming sound in his mind, he wants to work."

And the first indication you are getting unsound is when you will not work!

There is nothing wrong in work. It is an institution that came through sin. There is nothing wrong in it. *But it is wrong when we do not know how to live in it and over it.*

This coal carrier said, "I see!"

What did he see? He saw that he could go on to his work, get hold of those bags of coal, put them on his back, keep his mind on the Lord, and every hour he was stronger. And he carried a hundred bags out and finished promptly.

That is what God wants us to learn: whatsoever we do, do it to the glory of God.

If you listen to the Word of God this morning, it shall make you strong. *You will find out that whatever work you have to do will be made easier if you keep your mind stayed on the Lord.* Blessed is the man that has his mind stayed upon the Lord! We must see to it that in the world, we are not moved.

Kept in Perfect Peace

One day, God revealed to me that if I had any trouble in my body, in my heart, I had missed it. He showed me that if I had trouble in my heart, I had taken on something that did not belong to me, that I was out of the will of God. So I investigated it and found it was true, on this line: they that keep their minds stayed on God shall be kept in perfect peace. (See Isaiah 26:3.)

Interpretation of Tongues:

> *God in His great love towards us has so distributed the power of His righteousness through our human bodies that the very activity now within us is a lift of praise. We adore Him, we thank Him, we praise Him, because He has delivered us from the power of evil and surrounded us by the power of light.*

ATTRIBUTES OF SONSHIP

...that we should be called the sons of God. (1 John 3:1)

What to do? Be as a son of God. A son of God...

+ must have powers over the powers of the devil.
+ must behave himself seemingly.
+ must be temperate in all things.
+ must have the expression of the Master.
+ should be filled with tenderness and compassion and should have a body filled with bowels of mercies.
+ must excel in every way.

> *God says to you more than you dare say about yourself, "Behold, ye are sons of God."*

God says to you more than you dare say about yourself, "Behold, ye are sons of God." (See Galatians 4:6.)

So do not be afraid. Take the stand, come into line, and say, "I will be that."

God spoke and the heavens gave place to His voice, and He cried, "*This is my beloved Son: hear him*" (Mark 9:7).

And afterwards, Jesus always said, "*I am the Son of God*" (John 10:36).

God comes to you this morning and says, "Behold, you are the sons of God!" Oh! That we could have a regiment rising, claiming their rights, standing erect with a holy vision and full of inward power, saying, "I am, by the grace of God, a son of God!"

"*Wisdom is justified of all her children*" (Luke 7:35). The man or woman that takes the place of God this morning, do not fear; I stretch out my hand to you. You may have in many ways felt that you were never wet thy, but God makes you worthy. And who shall say you are not worthy?

It is the will of God to choose you. It is not your choice; it is the Lord's choice. Hear what He says:

Interpretation of Tongues:

I have chosen you, I have ordained you, that you should go forth bearing much fruit, and that your fruit should remain. For herein is your Father glorified: When you bring forth much fruit, so shall you be My disciples.

Sons of God Now

Beloved, now are we the sons of God, and it doth not yet appear what we shall be: but we know that, when he shall appear, we shall be like him; for we shall see him as he is.

(1 John 3:2)

I am not dealing with the second coming of Christ. I am dealing with the life in the believer. I am dealing with sonships in the earth. I am dealing with sonship, sonlikeness, what we are to be like and what will take place, how we shall overcome the world.

"*Every man that hath this hope...*" (1 John 3:3). This hope of sonship; this hope of ministry; this hope of life-giving, transmitting life.

One thing that the saints need to get to know is not how to quote Scripture, but how the Scripture should be pressed out by the Spirit, that the Spirit should impart life as the Word is given. Jesus says, "My word is the spirit of life" (see John 5:24), so we need the Spirit to bring life into the believer, imparting life.

Imparting life? Why? How? There is a deep secret right in the midst of this: "*Every man that hath this hope in him purifieth himself*" (1 John 3:3).

There is a lovely word along this line in 1 Corinthians:

If we would judge ourselves, we should not be judged. But when we are judged, we are chastened of the Lord, that we should not be condemned with the world.

(1 Corinthians 11:31–32)

Peace—Not Hysteria or Nervousness

In the classroom this morning, a student asked a very important question. I hope someday to deal especially with how to discern evil spirits and how to deal with voices, because many people today are troubled with voices, and some people run hither and there through voices. Some people are so much unhinged by voices that instead of being the sons of God, they seem to be gripped with a condition of hysteria or nervous prostration.

Beloved, *God wants to make you sound. God wants to make you restful. God wants to give you peace. He wants to cause you to live in the world with peace.*

The very first message the angel gave was, "*On earth peace, good will toward men*" (Luke 2:14). Jesus had to bring peace on earth and goodwill to men.

If you are not at peace, there is something wrong. If you are not at rest, something has taken place. You must know that *God means you to be so at peace as if you were in heaven.*

It is true, God hears me say it: I am as much at peace as if I were in the glory. I declare unto you also that on the line of the fact of the faith of the Son of God in me, I have no knowledge of the body, am free from everything that means weakness.

There is a redemption in Christ, a fullness of redemption, that shall make us free from powers of sin, powers of thoughts of evil, and powers of evil thoughts, so that we reign in the world over the powers of the devils, not being subject to but making everything subject to us. It is a real royal place that I want you to come into this morning: purified as He is pure. (See 1 Peter 1:16.)

Most people fail to come into perfect line with God because they allow their own reasoning to defeat the power that God has.

Why should I always bring up the past? Why, there is not a man in this place that can forgive himself. You would give the world if you could forgive yourself. The best men in this place would give anything if they could forgive themselves for what they have done. But you cannot; you feel ashamed.

One thing is, you cannot forget the evil things that you have done. Another thing is sure, that the devil will not let you forget. But there is another thing which is true: God has forgot, and it is whether we will believe ourselves or the devil or God. Which are you going to believe? When He forgives, He forgets.

On the authority of your believing God's Word, I can bring you onto another line. There are wonderful things to achieve this morning on the line of faith that dares to believe God. Only believe! *"According to your faith be it unto you"* (Matthew 9:29).

MASTER OVER EVIL THOUGHTS

The question the young woman asked was this: "What is the condition of a person that is always troubled with evil thoughts? How is he going to stand? What position is he in when these evil thoughts are always following him?"

Evil thoughts are from Satan. Satan does not know your thoughts. Satan does not know your desires; God hides from him these things. God can search the heart and try the reins [kidneys], but a stranger never interferes with it. Nobody knows you, only God. The devil has never a chance of knowing you.

> *Nobody knows you, only God. The devil has never a chance of knowing you.*

But what does he do? He came to Jesus. And when he came, all his suggested evil things could not arouse a single thing in Him. He came and found nothing in Him.

When does he find anything in you? When he suggests a thought—the devil suggests it—in order to bring out of you some thought. And he gets you the moment he does. But if you are so delivered by the blood and made holy, the devil cannot arouse you.

Nevertheless, if you are troubled because he suggests an evil thought, you are in a good place. But if you are not troubled, you are in a bad place.

Supposing he is continually after you like that. Is there a way? Of course there is. How can you deal with it? Say to him, "Did Jesus come in the flesh?"

And the evil one will say, "No." There is not a demon power out of hell or in hell that has ever been willing to say Jesus came in the flesh. (See 2 John 1:7.)

And when he says no, you can say, "Get behind me, Satan! I rebuke you in the name of Jesus."

Oh, it is wonderful! The child of God brought into liberty, power, blessing, strength, till he lives in the earth purified like the Lord.

Do you believe you can ever be like Him? Cheer up, now. Don't measure yourself by the Lord, for *"every man that hath this hope in him puriefieth himself, even as he is pure"* (1 John 3:3). And there you are in a wonderful place of dominion over it.

A Dance Turned into a Prayer Meeting

There are wonderful things about this. I would like to bring you to a place where it is so easy to triumph over the powers of the devil right in the midst of them.

When I was traveling on the ocean between England and Australia, about the third day out, they were seeking me while seeking everybody to join with them in their entertainment. We had a mission on holiness lines, and we would not allow a teacher in our Sunday school that went to questionable amusements. So we never had what they call "entertainments." But these people came around me and said, "We want to know if you will join us in an entertainment."

So I had to go quietly to the Lord. "May I?" I had the sweetest rest about it. It was all right.

So I said, "Yes, I will be in the entertainment."

They said, "What can you do?"

"I can sing," said I.

Then they said to me, "Well, we have a very large program, and we would like to put you down, and we would like to give you the song."

"Oh!" I said, "My song will be given just before I sing. So you cannot put it down until I am to sing."

They did not care for that so much, but they passed it on.

They came again to me and said, "We are very anxious to know what place you would like to be put down in the entertainment."

"What are you going to have?" I asked. "How are you going to finish up?"

"Oh!" they said. "We have all kinds of things."

There wasn't a thing the devil could arrange, but it was all there.

"Well, how are you going to finish up?" I asked again.

"We are going to finish up with a dance," they replied.

"Put me down just before the dance," I said.

My turn came. There were some parsons there. I felt so sorry when I went there to find these parsons trying to satisfy a giddy, godless lot of people and trying to fall in.

A young woman, half dressed—no sleeves, no skirts— came up to play for me. I gave her the music.

"Oh!" she said. "I never—I never could play that kind of music."

"Don't be troubled, now," I said. "I have music and words."

And I sang:

> *If I could only tell it as I know it,*
> *My Redeemer who has done so much for me;*
> *If I could only tell you how He loves you,*
> *I am sure that you would make Him yours today.*

Could I tell it? Could I tell it?

I never could tell it. The people were weeping all over. The dance was off. They couldn't have a dance. But we had lots of prayer meetings. We had some fine young men give themselves to Jesus.

Oh, beloved, be in the world, not of it. What a lovely thing He said to the Father: *"I pray not that thou shouldest take* them out of the world, but that thou shouldest keep them from the evil" (John 17:15).

Can He do it? He can do it. He has a way to do it.

You say, "How does He do it?"

> Let the waves wash me;
> Let the waves cleanse me.
> Lord, in Thy power
> Let them roll over me.

How the blood can cleanse! How He can make us clean in a meeting like this! How He can stimulate faith and change our prostrate position!

SIN DETHRONED

Now I want to put before you some difficult things. There are some things so difficult and so easy. Their difficulty rises and brings perplexity because we do not see that the Lord is greater than all. So we have to see that the Master's hand is so much greater than our hand, and His ways over our ways.

First John 3:4–5 says, "Whosoever committeth sin transgresseth also the law: for sin is the transgression of the law. And ye know that he was manifested to take away our sins; and in him is no sin."

No sin is in us, purifying ourselves as He is pure. Sin is destroyed.

Do not be afraid to claim your place. "Sin shall not have dominion" (Romans 6:14).

Do not be afraid to see the Word of God. It is true. "Reckon ye also yourselves to be dead indeed unto sin, but alive unto God" (Romans 6:11). The same thing.

As sin had reigned unto death, so now Christ comes and reigns in life over you. And you reign in life over sin, disease, and the devil. You reign over principalities and powers—in Christ reigning.

He is manifested. Where? In our flesh, to destroy the emotions of our body, to bring carnality to an end, to bring everything of human depravity to a place of nonplus. Christ is in the body; sin is dethroned. Sin shall not reign over you.

Believe that God is bringing you to this place. *This place is a dethronement of human helplessness. It is an enthronement of Christ's righteousness in us.*

He comes in and begins to rule over our human bodies by another plan. How is it? *"Every man that hath this hope in him puriefieth himself, even as he is pure."* How come?

There are one or two stepladders to go up.

Whosoever sinneth hath not seen him, neither known him. Little children, let no man deceive you: he that doeth righteousness is righteous, even as he is righteous.

(1 John 3:6–7)

Listen to the eighth verse, another climb up higher: *"He that committeth sin is of the devil; for the devil sinneth from the beginning. For this purpose the Son of God was manifested, that he might destroy the works of the devil."*

Manifested? Where was he manifested? In your flesh, that He might destroy the works of the devil.

Where? Outside? No, in your flesh, where there was no good thing. He destroyed everything that was not good, came and ruled there, and is there this morning.

Now I give you one of the hardest problems of the Scriptures, and yet the most beautiful position of the Scriptures. It is a keynote of prospectiveness. It is like being on the Mount of Pisgah looking over into the Promised Land, and all the fruits of Canaan are at your feet. God will make the grapes of Eshcol very beautiful as you enter into this sublime position of faith.

> *And every man that hath this hope in him purifieth himself, even as he is pure....Whosoever is born of God doth not commit sin; for his seed remaineth in him: and he cannot sin, because he is born of God.*   (1 John 3:3, 9)

Now I want to explain that to help you. Many people, on the authority of God's Word, will be made strong over the powers of sin today. You will not meet it any longer as a master; you will meet it as a conqueror, dethroning it. Here is your conquering position: *"Every man that hath this hope in him purifieth himself."*

This is the seed of life—the seed of the Son of God. The nature of the Son of God is purity. And he that has obtained this possession of the life of the Son of God, the eternal seed, the purifying position, the incorruptible power—he that purifieth himself—this seed remaineth in him and he cannot sin.

Many people, on the authority of God's Word, will be made strong over the powers of sin today.

The purifying seed makes you hate sin. The salvation of the world is for people to hate sin. No one who hates sin ever commits sin.

Look at the Master. Have you ever seen Jesus? God highly exalted Him and gave Him a name above every name. Why? He hated iniquity.

What is the difference between hating sin and knowing sin is there, passing it by without seeing it or speaking to it?

The latter position will never save you. You have to have a righteous indignation against the powers of evil and the devil. And all the time you are being purified, and you get to the place where you cannot sin.

This is a glorious position of advent. This is a blessed place of exit. This is a glorious place of overcoming. This is a place of rest for your feet. This is a great place for enduement of power; for *holiness is power, and sin is weakness and defeat.*

God Claims You as His Own

You are so intense. Your hearts are longing. Your souls are athirst. You are waking up to the fact that *God has chosen you for sons, for purity, for power, for righteousness.*

Sin shall not have dominion. Disease shall be dethroned. God shall claim you as His own. You shall be the sons of God, with power. Who says so? Your Father in heaven.

Sons of God!

Sins dethroned!

Hearts aflame!

Look at where God brings you. I will read the words to you to strengthen your hearts to go away in a new place. This is the place, wonderful place, of covenant blessing:

> *Hereby we know that we are of the truth, and shall assure our hearts before him. For if our heart condemn us, God is greater than our heart, and knoweth all things. Beloved, if our heart condemn us not, then we have confidence toward God. And **whatsoever we ask, we receive of him, because we keep his commandments, and do those things that are pleasing in his sight.*** (1 John 3:19–22, emphasis added)

DISCERNMENT
Bible Study #8 – July 15, 1927

P raise the Lord! The Word of God is very clear on this line. *"Let everything that hath breath praise the LORD. Praise ye the LORD"* (Psalm 150:6).

If ever you get to the place where you cannot praise the Lord, it is a calamity in your life and it is a calamity in those people round about you. If you want to take blessing into homes and make all the people round about know that you have something more than an ordinary life, you must know that God has come to supplant you and put within you a perfect praise.

God has a great place for us this morning, that His will may be done and we may be subject to His perfect will. When that comes to pass, what may happen no one can tell, for Jesus reached the highest place when He said, *"I came down from heaven, not to do mine own will, but the will of him that sent me"* (John 6:38). So there is something in a yielding place this morning where God can have us for His own.

God has a choice for us all that we might lose ourselves in God in a way we have never done before. I want to provoke you to love that you might come into a place of blessing, for God wants you to be blessed that you might be a blessing.

> *God has a way beyond all your ways of thought. He has a choice and a plan for you.*

Beloved, believe that God today has a way for you. Perhaps you have never come that way before. God has a way beyond all your ways of thought. He has a choice and a plan for you.

There is a great need today. People are hungry for truth. People are thirsting, wanting to know God better. There are thousands in the valley of decision, wanting someone to take them right into the depths for God.

Are you ready to pray? You say, "What shall I ask for?"

You may not know what to ask; but if you begin, the Spirit knoweth the desire of your heart, and He will pray according to the mind of God. You do not know, but God knows everything, and He is acquainted with you altogether and desires to promote you.

So, this morning, I say, "Are you ready?"

You say, "What for?" That you may come promptly into the presence of God, that you may ask this day as you have never asked. Ask in faith, nothing doubting, believing that God is on the throne, waiting to anoint you afresh today.

Are you ready? "What for?" That you may be so brought into the banquet house of God, even as Esther came in, and God will put out the scepter, and all that thy heart shall desire, He shall give it thee.

PRAYER

Father, in Jesus' name we come before Thee this morning, believing in Thy almightiness that the power of Thy hand does move us. Chasten us. Build us. Let the Word of God sink in our hearts this day. Make us, O God, worthy of the name we bear, that we may go about as really holy saints of God. Just as if You were on the earth, fill us with Your unction, Your power, and Your grace. Amen.

FIRST CORINTHIANS 13

We find one of the most marvelous passages of all Scripture in 1 Corinthians 12:27–13:13. I am so thankful that God in His wonderful mercy placed this beautiful chapter right in the midst of these gifts, right in the middle—gifts and then workings of gifts, and right there in the middle, like a diamond shining forth in all its glorious luster, to save us from going toppling over on every line, and that we become nothing.

What a serious thing it would be after waiting for the enduement of power for months and months and months, and then after that, failing God because we turned to some human desire because we liked it.

I want to say at the beginning that there is no unction like the unction that comes out of death, when we are dead with Christ. It is that position that makes us live with Him. If we have been conformed to His death, then in that same death, like Paul, we shall be made like unto Him in His resurrection power.

But do not forget that Jesus was coequal with the Father and He made Himself of no reputation. He did not come out and say He was this or that or the other. No, that was not His position. Jesus had all the gifts. He could have stood up and could have said to Peter and John and James and the rest of them, when they brought that dead person out of the gate, "Stand on one side, Peter. Clear out of the way, John. Make room for Me, Thomas. Don't you know who I am? I am coequal with the Father. I have all power; I have all gifts; I have all graces. Stand on one side. I will show you how to raise the dead!"

Is that how He did it? No! Never. What made it come to pass?

He was observant. The disciples were there, but they had not the same observance. Observance comes from an inward holy flame kindled by God.

What did He see? He saw the widow and knew that she was carrying to burial that day all her help, all her life. Her love was bound up there in that son. There she was, broken and bowed together with sorrow, all her hopes blighted.

He had compassion upon her, and the compassion of Jesus was greater than the death. And in that order of His compassion, being so marvelous, it went beyond the powers of death and all the powers of demons.

"*Bless the* LORD, *O my soul, and forget not all his benefits*" (Psalm 103:2). Isn't He a lovely Jesus! Isn't He a precious Savior! Don't you see that if we bear in the body the marks of Jesus or the life of the manifestation of Jesus, if we live only as Jesus is manifested—if they take knowledge of us that we have been with Jesus as they took knowledge of Peter and John—oh, that would pay for everything; it would surely be beautiful!

"I Can Cast Out Devils!"

Let me give you an illustration that will help you in thought. These meetings are not ordinary meetings. The Holy Ghost is amongst us. Jesus is being glorified. We are not seeking our own in these meetings, but we are seeking to provoke one another in holiness and character, that they may be likeminded to Jesus. The same manifestation that was in Him has to be in us.

So I want to draw you a picture. One day, a young man got so elated because he had received his baptism, and he got in a place where most people seemed to fail to see was the wrong place.

I have never, under any circumstances, as long as I live, to take advantage of God or of Jesus or of the Holy Ghost. I have to be subservient to that power.

Here this young man was on the platform, and he said, "I am baptized with the Holy Ghost. I can cast out devils. Come, I can cast them out!"

There was a poor man who had been bound by the devil for many, many years, so bound that he was helpless. He could not help himself; he was bound in every way. He had never heard such words before. And when he heard them, he was so moved that he struggled out of the seat, took hold of the chairs, and went down amongst the people in the aisle, a poor, helpless man, seeking the first time he heard that he could be delivered.

He went up and stood before the preacher and cried out, "Cast them out! Please cast them out! Help me! Please cast them out!"

The young man did all he could, but could not do it. The church was broken; the whole place was brought into travail. Oh, they wept and they cried because it was not done.

A More Excellent Way

It never will be done that way. It isn't the way to do it. But there is a way, and it is the way which is in the Scriptures, and we shall look into this perfect way.

> *Though I speak with the tongues of men and of angels, and have not charity, I am become as sounding brass, or a tinkling cymbal.*　　　　(1 Corinthians 13:1)

Did you ever read a verse like this? It is a position of being brought into a treasury. Do you know what a treasury is? A treasury is to hold or handle the priceless things.

God puts you into the treasury to hold or handle the precious gifts of the Spirit. So in order that you may not fail to handle them aright, He shows you the picture of how you may handle them.

What a high position of authority, of grace, the Lord speaks about in this verse! "*Speak with tongues of men and of angels.*" Oh, isn't that wonderful?

There are men with such wonderful qualifications of speaking. Their knowledge on the natural order is so surpassing that many people go to hear these eloquent addresses because they are so beautiful in language. God puts you right in the midst of them and says He has given you these capabilities of speaking like men, with power of thought and language at your disposal, so that you can say anything.

People are failing God all the time, all over the world, because they are eloquent and taken up with the eloquence, and God is not in it. They are lost with the bombacity of their great authority over language, and they use it on purpose to tickle the ears and the sensations of the people, and it profits nothing. It is nothing. It will wither up and the people that use it will wither up.

God has said there is a way. Now, how would language like men and like angels come to prosper? When you went through before, you could get in to do anything. When you were so undone that without God helped you to do it, you couldn't do it. When you were so broken in the spirit that your whole body seemed to be at an end without God reinstated you.

Then the unction came, and every word was glorifying Jesus and every sentence lifted the people, and they felt as they listened, "Surely God is in this place! He has sent His Word and healed us," and they saw no man there save Jesus. Jesus was so manifested that they all said, "Oh, wasn't Jesus speaking to out hearts this morning!"

Never think for a moment that the Acts of the Apostles are complete. It is an incomplete book. When you read Revelation, it is complete. You cannot add to nor take from this wonderful position of prophecy. It is complete. And so when you are used only and desire only for the glory of God, your acts and life, ministry, and power will be an endless recording in the glory of heaven, for the Acts of the Apostles are being recorded in the glory.

So let the Lord help us to know how to act in the Holy Ghost.

Interpretation of Tongues:

Set thy house in order for, except thou die, thou canst not live. For God is coming today and taking us—others may be left, but we are taken—taken on with God, taken into God, moved by the power of God, till we live and move in God; and God has us as His channel, breathing through, divinely fixing, bringing forth words new and old. And God is moving in the midst, and His people are being fed with the finest of wheat.

SAVED ONCE, SAVED ALWAYS?

Let us look at the second verse. It is like the first, only the Word of God is very remarkable. It starts like this, brings you to a place where there is no condemnation, and then fills you up where there is no separation. That is God's plan. We have a great salvation, but some people limit it. I believe in eternal salvation.

W e are a very wealthy and a very privileged people to be able to be gathered together this holy morning. I count it a very holy thing that we are gathered together to think of Him, because it is impossible to think of Him and be in any way unholy. *The very thought of Jesus will confirm truth and righteousness and power in your mortal bodies.*

There is something very remarkable about Him. When John saw Him, the impression that he had was that He was as a Lamb without blemish and without spot. When God speaks about Him, He says, "He came forth in the brightness of the expression of the countenance of God." (See Hebrews 1:3.) When revelation comes, it says, "In Him is all fullness." (See Colossians 1:19.) Lovely character of beauty, loveliness of display of meekness, compassion beyond all humanity, feelings of infirmities, succoring them which pass through trial. And it is to be said about Him that is not said about anyone else, that in all points He was tempted as we, yet without sin.

I want you, as Paul describes it wonderfully in the Hebrews, to consider Him when thou art weary and tempted and tried and all men against you. Consider Him who hath passed through it all, that He might be able to succor thee in the trial as thou art passing through, and He will sustain thee in the strife. When all things seem as though you have failed, the Lord of hosts, the God of Jacob, the salvation of our Christ, will so reinforce thee that thou wilt be stronger than any concrete building that was ever made.

Interpretation of Tongues:

> *Thy God, thy Lord, in whom thou trusteth, shall make thee so strong in the Lord and in the power of His might that no evil thing shall befall thee. As He was with Moses, He will be with thee. As He stood by Daniel, He will cause the lions' mouths to close. He will shut up all that is against thee and the favor of heaven, the smile of the Most High, the kiss of His love, will make thee know thou art covered with the Dove.*

This word which we have this morning is so beautiful: "*I therefore, the prisoner of the Lord, beseech you that ye walk worthy of the vocation wherewith ye are called*" (Ephesians 4:1).

The one who is speaking to us is exercised for the church, is filled with the loveliness of the character of the Master that is breathing through by the power of the Spirit, and is zealous that we may walk worthy. This is the day of vocation he speaks about. This is the opportunity of your lifetime. This is the place where God increases strength or opens the door of a new way of ministry, that you shall come into likemindedness with this holy apostle, who was a prisoner.

Further it says, "*With all lowliness and meekness, with longsuffering, forbearing one another in love*" (Ephesians 4:2).

Jesus made emphasis of the new commandment when He left us, and inasmuch as we miss it, we miss all the Master's provocation. If you miss that commandment, you miss everything. All the future summits of glory are yours in the very fact that you have been recreated in a deeper order by that commandment He gave us: "*A new commandment I give unto you, that ye love one another, as I have loved you*" (John 13:34).

When we teach this attitude, then we have no mistake about lowliness. We shall submit ourselves in the future for usefulness to one another. The greatest plan that ever Jesus showed forth in His ministry was the ministry of service. He said, "*I am among you as he that serveth*" (Luke 22:27). And when we come to a place where we serve for our love's sake, because it is the divine hand of the Master upon us, we shall find out that we shall never fail. Love never fails when it is divinely appointed in us, but this is not so in our human nature and has not been from the beginning.

> *The greatest plan that ever Jesus showed forth in His ministry was the ministry of service.*

EPHESIANS 4:1–16

A man has written to me trying to establish a relationship. The only thing I shall have to say in answering him is, "Brother, all I know about Wigglesworth is bad." There is no good thing in human nature. But all I know about the new creation in Wigglesworth is good. And it is whether we are living in the old creation or the new creation.

So I beseech you to see that there is a lowliness, a humbleness, which leads you to meekness, which leads you to separate yourself from the world, which leaves you so in touch with the Master that you know you are touching divine kind.

Purity of heart character has purity over the mind character and has purity over the blood character, and the blood of Jesus in this character cleanses you from all sin and all pollution. And there is something in this holy position that makes you know you are free from the power of the enemy.

We have yet to see the forcefulness of the Word of God. I give you reference to it in passing in Hebrews 4:

> *For the word of God is quick, and powerful, and sharper than any twoedged sword, piercing even to the dividing asunder of soul and spirit, and of the joints and marrow, and is a discerner of the thoughts and intents of the heart.*
>
> (Hebrews 4:12)

The Word is the life, the presence, the power in your body, in the very marrow of your bones, and absolutely everything else must be discharged. Sometimes we do not take it in the fullness of reflection. The Word, the life, the Christ which is the Word, separating in you soul from spirit—what a wonderful work! The Spirit dividing you from soul affection, from human weakness, from all depravity, from the human soul in the blood of the man. And the blood of Jesus can cleanse your blood till the very soul of you is purified, and your very nature is destroyed by the nature of the living Christ.

I speak to you precisely on resurrection touches. We have come into divine resurrection touches in Christ, the greatest work God ever did on the face of the earth. He had to use His operation power. Christ rose from the dead by the operation of the power of God. And the operation in our hearts of the resurrection of Christ will dethrone, and at the same time as it dethrones, it will build. Callousness will have to change; hardness will have to disappear; all evil thoughts must be gone; and instead of that, lowliness of mind.

What beautiful cooperation with God in thought and power and holiness! The Master made Himself of no reputation, absolutely left the glory with all its wonder, left it, submitted Himself, humiliation, down, down, down into death, for one purpose only: that He might destroy the power of death, even the devil, and deliver those people who for all their lifetimes have been subject to fear—deliver them from the power of death and the devil. (See Philippians 2:5–8.)

This is a wonderful plan for us. But how will it come to pass? Transformation, resurrection, thoughts of holiness, intense zeal, desire with God for all of God, till we live and move in the atmosphere of holiness.

If I say *holiness* or *baptism* or *resurrection* or *rapture*, remember all these words are tremendous. And there is another word I would like to say: after that, you were illuminated. Have you been there? What does it mean? Illumination means this: that your very mind, which was depraved, is now the mind of Christ; the very nature which was bound has now a resurrection touch; the very body that you have has come in contact with the life of God, till you which were lost are found, and you which were dead are alive again by the resurrection power of the Word of the life of Christ. What a glorious inheritance in the Spirit!

Are you there? Don't forget the ladder that Jacob saw. When I was going over the hill and saw Jerusalem for the first time, a person said to me, "See that place there? That is where the ladder from earth to heaven was seen."

Brother, if you have not reached all, the ladder is from heaven to earth to take you from earth to heaven. Do not be afraid of taking the steps. You will not slip back. Have faith in God. Resurrection life divine, more divine in thought, more wonderful in revelation, living in the Spirit, wakened into all likeness, quickened by the same Spirit!

Interpretation of Tongues:

He rose, and in His rising He lifted us and He placed us in the place of searing, and then gave us a holy language, and then began to entertain us and show in us that now the body is His and that we become members in particular of the body. Sometimes He chastens us that all the dross might go and all the wood and the stubble might be burned in the testing, that He might get purer gold, purer life, purer soul, that there should be nothing in the body that should be defiling, but He should take us out of the world and make us like a ripe shock of corn, ready for the dawning of the morning.

Are you lowly and meek in your mind? It is the divine plan of the Savior. You must be like Him. You desire to be like Him? There is nothing but yourself that can hinder. You are the one who stops the current, or you are the one who stops the life. The river and current is coming just now; I feel it all over me.

I do like children to speak. They say such wonderful things.

While ministering in one place, we had a banquet of all people distressed, people who were lame and weary, blind, and withered in every way. We had a big crowd of people, and we fed them all. After we got them well filled with all the good things that were provided, we said, "Now we are going to give you an entertainment."

A man who had spent years in a wheelchair but who had been healed came on the platform and told how he was loosed. A person with a blood issue many years came and testified. A blind man came and told how he got his eyes opened. For one hour, people entertained them.

Then I said to the people, "Are you ready?"

Oh, they were all so ready! A man got hold of a boy who was encased in iron from top to bottom, lifted him up, and placed him on the platform. Hands were laid upon him in the name of Jesus.

"Papa! Papa! Papa!" he said. "It's going all over me! Oh, Papa, come and take these irons off!"

And he took the irons off—and it had gone all over the boy!

This is what I feel, the life of God going all over me, the power of God all over me. Don't you know this is the resurrection touch? This is the divine life. This is what God has brought us into. Let it go over us, Lord, the power of the Holy Ghost, the resurrection of heaven, the sweetness of Thy benediction, the joy of the Lord!

> *If our fellowship below with Jesus be so sweet,*
> *What heights of rapture shall we know*
> *When round His throne we meet?*

Interpretation of Tongues:

> *The Spirit sweetly falls like the dew, just as still on the grass, and as it comes it is for a purpose, God's purpose. It may be withered grass, but God calls it to come forth again. And the Spirit of the Lord is right in the midst of thee this morning, and though thou mightest been withered, dried, and barren for a long time, the dew is falling. God is in the midst of us with His Spirit of revival, and He is saying to thee, "All things are possible; only believe," and He shall change thee.*

KEEPING THE UNITY OF THE SPIRIT

> *Endeavoring to keep the unity of the Spirit in the bond of peace.*
> (Ephesians 4:3)

You are bound forever to loyalty to God to see that there is no schism come into the body, the church, to see that nothing comes into the assembly, as they came into the flock where David was, to tear and rend the body. You have to be careful if a person comes along with a prophecy and you find it is tearing down and bringing trouble. Denounce it on this line: judge it by the Word. You will find that all true prophecy will have perfect lines of hopefulness. It will have compassion. It will have comfort. It will have edification.

So if there is anything that comes into the church that you know is spoiling the flock or disturbing the assembly, you must see to it that you must get to prayer so that this thing is put to death and brings unity in the bonds of perfection, so that the church of God shall receive edifying. And the church will begin to be built up in the faith and the establishing of truth, and they will be one.

> *God means us to be very faithful to the church, that we do not allow anything to come into the church to break up the body.*

Do not forget: God means us to be very faithful to the church, that we do not allow anything to come into the church to break up the body. You cannot find anything in the body in its relation to Christ that has schism in it. Christ's life in the body—there is no schism. When Christ's life comes into the church, there will be no schism. There will be perfect blending of heart and hand, and it will be lovely. Endeavor to keep the unity of the Spirit in the bond of peace.

Now I come to a very important point: "There is one body" (Ephesians 4:4).

There is one body. Recognize it. When schism comes into the body, they always act as though there were more than one. For instance, there is the Wesleyan Church, there is the Baptist Church, and there are many other churches. What have I to notice about them? I have to see that right in that body, right in that church, God will have a remnant belonging to His body. They may not all be of the body, but God will have a remnant in that body. I have not to go out and denounce the Baptists, the Wesleyans, nor any other church. What I want to do, I have to so live in the Spirit of Christ that they shall see that I am one with them. It is the Holy Spirit in the new church, in the body, the mystical body, which is uniting, binding, and mightily moving. In every church, whether they baptize or not, there is a place where the Spirit is.

There is a difference between the Spirit being in you and the Spirit being with you. For instance, we are getting light now from outside this building. This is exactly the position of every believer that is not baptized with the Holy Ghost. It is a true picture of John 14. The Spirit is with every person that is not baptized, and they have light from outside. But let me take the sun, which is giving all the light outside, and put it inside this morning, and what will be the effect? Suppose all the light that is coming through the windows was inside. That is exactly what is to be taking place. We have revelation from outside—revelation in many ways by the Spirit—but after He comes inside, it is revelation from inside, and it makes things right outside.

The epistles never talk about water baptism, excepting to refer to it in the past tense. Water baptism belongs to the Gospels, and it is placed also in the Acts of the Apostles. We are baptizing people in remembrance of placing them into death, because every believer ought to be covered, because when he is planted in death, the believer should not expect to go that way, but the believer expects to go up. So every believer must be put into death.

Now, the baptism of the Spirit is to be planted deeper until there is not a part that is left, and there is the manifestation of the power of the new creation by the Holy Ghost right in our mortal body. Where once we were, now He reigns supreme, manifesting the very Christ inside of us, the Holy Ghost fulfilling all things right there.

Jesus has been wonderfully ordained, incarnated of God, and God has given Him preeminence. He has to be preeminent in us. And someday, we shall see the preeminence of this wonderful Savior, and we shall take our crowns and place them at His feet. Then He will come to a place where He will put the Father in all preeminence, and will take all our crowns and us also and present us to the Father, with Himself, that the Father shall be all in all, forever and ever.

That will take ten million years to get through. In thinking about it, my calculation is that the Supper of the Lamb and the Marriage will take fifty million years.

"What do you mean?" you say.

One day with the Lord is as a thousand years, and the glory in our supernatural body in its infinite relationship will so live in the bliss of all things that time will fly, and the Supper and the Marriage and everything will be supremely delightful and full and refreshing, pure and glorious and light. Oh, hallelujah! It's coming! It is not past; it is on the way. It is a glory we have to enter into.

> *There is one body, and one Spirit, even as ye are called in one hope of your calling: one Lord, one faith, one baptism.*
> (Ephesians 4:4–5)

"*One Lord.*" Oh, it is lovely! One Lord, one heart, one love, one association. "*One Lord, one faith, one baptism.*" Not water baptism; the baptism of the Holy Spirit, the baptism of the new creational order, the baptism into divine life, the baptism with fire, the baptism with zeal, the baptism with passion, the baptism with inward travail! Oh, it is a baptism! Jesus had it. He travailed. He moved with compassion.

One Lord—all one, all in Christ Jesus, all one in Christ. One faith, stimulation, laying hold of the immensities, daring to believe, holding fast that which thou hast till no man shall take thy crown, for we are being quickened by this resurrection and now faith lays hold.

Contend for it. Lay hold of it. Lay hold of eternal life, something you cannot handle, something you cannot see, yet more real than we. Eternal life! Lay hold of it. Let no man rob thee of it. It is a crown. It is a position in the Holy One. It is a place of identification. It is a place of Him bringing thee into order. Only He can do it—and He does it.

Let us look at the next verse, which is very beautiful, for here is our position in this world: *"One God and Father of all, who is above all, and through all, and in you all"* (Ephesians 4:6).

"Who is above all." Think of that! It does not matter what the enemy may bring into you or try to bring. Remember: one Father, above all, over you. Anything else? Yes. The next thought is larger still: *"through all."* And the next: *"in you all."*

The God of power, of majesty, and of glory. Who can bring you to a place of dethroning everything? The Father of all, above all, through all, in you all.

Do you dare believe it? You should go away with such inspiration on these lines of faith that you will never have a doubt again, and I want to take you there above all things.

Remember that God our Father is so intensely desirous to have all the fullness of the manifestation of His power that not one thing do we have to have but His Son came to bring. We have to have perfect redemption. We have to know all the powers of righteousness. We have to understand perfectly that we are brought into line where He is with us in all power, dethroning the power of the enemy.

It is real. Greater a thousand million times to you is God over you—not the devil, not the powers of evil, not the powers of darkness. How do I know? Hear what the devil says to God about Job: "*Hast not thou put an hedge about him?*" (Job 1:10). This means to say that the devil was unable to get near Job because there was a hedge. What was the hedge? It was the almighty power of God. It was not a thorny hedge. It was not a hedge of thistles. It was the presence of the Lord round about Job.

And the presence of the Lord is so round about us, the almightiness, that the devil cannot break through that wonderful encasement.

If you are afflicted in any way, do not for a moment under any circumstances come to the conclusion that the devil has enmity against you. No, he never has. The devil has nothing against you. But the devil is against the living Christ and wants to destroy Him. And if you are filled with the living Christ, the devil is anxious to get you out of the way, thereby to destroy Christ's power.

Say this, "Now, Lord, look after this property of Yours."

Then the devil cannot get near. When does he get near? When you dethrone Christ of the rightfulness of the position over you, in you, through you.

You will be strong if you believe it. I preach faith, and I know it carries you through if you dare believe it. Faith is the victory always. Glory to Jesus!

Notice here that the apostle is having revelation about Jesus after this, speaking about the grace and the gifts of the Christ— not the gifts of the Holy Ghost, but the gifts of Christ.

But unto every one of us is given grace according to the measure of the gift of Christ. (Ephesians 4:7)

The gifts of Christ are so different from the gifts of the Holy Ghost that I want to get you into this place for a moment.

Wherefore he saith, when he ascended up on high, he led captivity captive, and gave gifts unto men....And he gave some, apostles; and some, prophets; and some, evangelists; and some, pastors and teachers; for the perfecting of the saints, for the work of the ministry, for the edifying of the body of Christ. (Ephesians 4:8, 11–12)

We are now reading the epistles. The Gospels are the Gospel of the kingdom; the Acts of the Apostles is the position where believers pass through and repent, are saved, baptized, and become eligible to come into the epistles, that they might be in the body in the order of the epistles. The body is not made up after you get into the epistles. You are joined to the body the moment you believe.

For instance, some of you may have some children, named differently, but the moment they appeared in the world, they were in the family. The moment they were born, they were in the family.

The moment you are born of God, you are in the family, and you are in the body as He is in the body, and you are in the body collectively and particularly. After you come into the body, then the body has to receive the sealing of the promise, or the fulfillment of the promise—that is, Christ shall be in you, reigning in you mightily. The Holy Ghost shall come to unveil the King in all His glory that He might reign as King there, the Holy Ghost serving in every way to make Him King.

You are in the body. The Holy Ghost gives gifts in the body. Living in this holy order, you find that revelation came to you and made you a prophet. Some of you may have a clear knowledge that you have been called into apostleship. Some of you may have perfect knowledge that you have been made a pastor in this order. When you come in to be sealed with the Spirit of

Promise, then you will find out that Jesus is pleased and gives gifts in order that the church might come into a perfect position of being so blended together that there could be no division—perfect body, perfect statute, perfect oneness in Christ.

To this end I have been speaking that you may see the vocation Paul is speaking about—humility of mind, meekness of spirit, knowing that God is in you, through you, knowing that the power of the Spirit is mightily bringing you to the place where not only the gifts of the Spirit, but also the gifts of Christ have been given you, making you eligible for the great work you have to do.

This is not to tell what God has for you in the future. Press in and claim your rights. Let the Lord Jesus be so glorified that He will make you fruit bearers—strong in power, giving glory to God, having no confidence in the flesh, but being separated from natural things; now in the Spirit, living fully in the will of God.

Testing of Spirits
Bible Study # 10 – July 20, 1927

God has never changed His mind concerning His promises. They are yea and amen to those that believe. God is the same yesterday and forever. To doubt Him is sin. All unbelief is sin. So we have to believe He can heal, save, fill with the Holy Ghost, and transform us altogether.

Are you ready? "What for?" That you might be so chastened by the Lord, so collected by Him, that as you pass through the fire, as you pass through all temptations, you may come out as Jesus came out of the wilderness, filled with the Spirit.

Are you ready? "What for?" That you may be so brought in touch with the Father's will that you may know that whatsoever you ask, believing, you receive. This is the promise, this is the reality God brings to us.

Are you ready? "What for?" That you might know yourself no more after the flesh; that you not yield to the flesh, but be quickened by the Spirit, living in the Spirit without condemnation, your testimony bright, cheerful, and full of life. This is the inheritance for you today.

Testing of Spirits

The message the Lord wants me to speak about to you is in the fourth chapter of 1 John.

I would like the day to come that we would never come to a meeting without having the Word of God with us. The great need today is more of the Word. There is no foundation apart from the Word. The Word not only gives you foundation, but it puts you in a place where you can stand and, after the battle, keep on standing. Nothing else will do it. When the Word is in your heart, it will preserve you from desire of sin. The Word is the living presence of that divine power that overcomes the world. You need the Word of God in your hearts that you might be able to overcome the world.

> *The Word not only gives you foundation, but it puts you in a place where you can stand and, after the battle, keep on standing.*

FIRST JOHN 4:1–19

"Beloved." That is a good word. It means to say we are now in a place where God has set His love upon us. He wants us to hearken to what He has to say to us because when His beloved are hearing His voice, then they understand what He has for them.

This is an exhaustless subject. We should get a great deal out of this message that shall serve us for an evil day and the day of temptation.

God is dealing with us as sons, as *"beloved,"* He calls it. We are in the truth but we want to know the truth in a way that will keep us free. I want to help the people who have been so troubled with voices and with things that have happened that they felt they had no control over them. And I want to help those people who are bound in many ways and have been trying in every way to get free. I believe the Lord would have me very definitely deal with things that will be of an important character to you as long as you live.

This Scripture is a definite place how to deal with evil powers, evil voices; how we may be able to dethrone them and be in a place where we are over them; how we may live in the world not subject to fear, not subject to bondage, not subject to pain, but be in the place of defeating them, ruling over them, reigning in the world by this life of Christ, so that we are from above and know it; not subject to the world, but reigning over the world, so that disease, sin, and death shall not have dominion.

There is a keynote running through the whole of the Scriptures that Jesus has vanquished and overcome all of the powers of the devil and destroyed his power, even the power of death. Whether we are going to believe it or not, that is for us. God sends out the challenge and He says, "If you believe it, it shall be so."

What shall hinder us? Human nature. That has a lot to do with hindering God—when the human will is not wholly surrendered, when there is some mixture, part of spirit and part of flesh, when there is a division in your own heart.

Do not forget the Word of God is very clear on this line. The Scriptures distinctly say there are children of obedience and children of disobedience, and they are both children, both saved. Both know it. Both can tell when it happened. One lives in obedience, another in disobedience, and the disobedient always gets the whip.

In a house where there are two children, one may be desirous to obey the father and mother, and it is loved and is very well treated. The other is loved just the same, but the difficulty in the way is this: the wayward boy who will have his own way does many things to grieve the parents, and he gets the whip.

They are both children in the house; one is getting the whip, the other is getting the blessing without the whip.

There are any number of God's children that are getting the whip that know better than they do. So I want you to wake up to do what you know ought to be done, because there are stripes for those who won't obey.

Sin is never covered by your appearance, your presence, your prayers, or your tears. Sin can be removed only by repentance. When you repent deep enough, you will find that thing goes forever. Never cover up sin. Sins must be judged. Sins must be brought to the blood.

When you have a perfect confidence between you and God, it is amazing how your prayers rise, you catch fire, you are filled with zeal, your inspiration is tremendous, and you find out that the Spirit prays through you and that you live in a place of blessing.

> *Beloved, believe not every spirit, but try the spirits whether they are of God: because many false prophets are gone out into the world. Hereby know ye the Spirit of God: every spirit that confesseth that Jesus Christ is come in the flesh is of God: and every spirit that confesseth not that Jesus Christ is come in the flesh is not of God: and this is that spirit of antichrist.* (1 John 4:1–3)

There are today many people living who are called spiritists. I call them 'devilists." I never give any quarter on these lines. If I see a spiritist meeting advertised, I say, "There is a devil-possessed meeting." I never meet Christian Science people but that I know they are also working the powers of darkness and they are on the devil's side. I never meet a Russellite but I know that he has changed the Word of God, and I know that God has moved him from the blessing.

Interpretation of Tongues:

> On the housetop things will be declared. God will bring everything to light that has been in darkness. There is not one thing but what will have to be judged, and in the present time the believer in Christ is in the position of judging the devil. The prince of this world is judged, and God is fulfilling His divine power when He is bringing us into perfect order through the Spirit, so that we voice the power of the Word of God, so that we deal with satanic influences, satanic power. In this world we are to overcome till we deal with every demon power, so that Christ comes at the top and reigns over us, because He has given us power and authority over all the power of the devil.

So God, by the power of the Spirit, has given us in this a revelation of our position. Whatever happens in the world, we must see that every demon power must be dislodged, cast into the pit forever.

We must see that God's Son is placed in power over the power of the enemy, and we must see that anybody that deals with the Word of God falsely takes away the position that Christ put.

What did Christ say? In a very definite way, He said, "Beware that you be cast into hellfire, where the worm dieth not and the fire is not quenched; it is better for you to go into life with one eye, one foot, or one arm rather than having two eyes, two feet, and two arms, and be cast into everlasting fire. Better to go into the presence of God half, than to go into hell with all your faculties." (See Mark 9:42–48.)

Jesus knew that hell was a reality, and He gave no quarter for it. And when He was dealing with the devils, He rebuked a *"foul spirit"* (Mark 9:25), meaning that there is no clean demon power. All demon powers are unclean.

God wants a clean people. He is cleansing us from all the filthiness of the flesh so that when the devil comes, he shall find nothing filthy in us.

THE SPIRITLESS BLASPHEME

One day, we were having a meeting after the Holy Ghost came upon us, and it was noised abroad that we had received the baptism of the Spirit, as we called it, and we were speaking in tongues. Many people said we had received satanic power and were speaking in tongues through the power of the devil. So the whole city was awakened.

At this meeting, we had two rows of spiritists—these demon-possessed people. The power of the Spirit was upon me and I began speaking in tongues, and these demon powers began muttering, shaking, rolling, and all kinds of things.

I went off the platform, stood at the end of the two rows, and said, "Come out, you devils, in the name of Jesus!" And the two rows filed out of the seats, went down the aisle and outside. And when they got outside, they cursed and blasphemed and said all evil things. But thank God they were outside!

ONE MAN'S PRESENCE HINDERS MEDIUMS

One day, I met a friend of mine in the street, and I said, "Fred, where are you going?"

"I am going—oh, I don't feel I ought to tell you," he said. "It is a secret between me and the Lord."

"Now, we have prayed together, we have had nights of communication, we have been living together in the Spirit,"

I said, "Surely there is no secret that could be hid from you and me."

"I will tell you," he said. "I am going to a spiritualistic meeting."

"Don't you think it is very dangerous?" I asked.

"No," he said. "They are having some special mediums from London."

He meant to say they were having some people from London that were more filled with the devil than what we had in Bradford. They were special devils.

"I am going," he said, "and I am going with the clear knowledge that I am under the blood."

"Tell me the results, will you?"

"Yes, I will."

The séance meeting began, the lights went low. Everything was in dismal position. These more possessed devils were on the platform. They tried every possible thing they could to get under control for one hour and over, and then the lights went up and they said, "We can do nothing tonight. Someone here believes in the blood."

Interpretation of Tongues:

> See that thou keepest thine heart in a place where the blood is covering thee, where the wicked one toucheth thee not, for has He not given charge over thee to keep thee in all thy ways? He shall send His angels and they shall bear thee up lest thou shalt dash thy foot against a stone. It is the Lord thy God that overshadows, it is the Lord thy God that protecteth, for He will not slumber or sleep, but He keeps thee in the perfect place, like the apple of His eye in perfection.
> (See Psalm 91:11–12; Matthew 4:6; Luke 4:11.)

JUDGE YOURSELF BY GOD'S WORD

There are two ways of being in the place of God. One is that you see you obey. The next is that you examine yourself to see that you are in the faith.

If you do not judge yourself, you will be judged. But if you judge yourself by the Word of God, you will not be condemned by the present evil world.

BE NOT MISLED BY SATANIC VOICES

There are a lot of people who are very much troubled with voices. Some people are so troubled that they get very distressed. Some people take it as a great position. They think it is very remarkable and they go astray.

Lots of people go astray by foolish prophecy, and lots of people are foolish enough to believe that they have tongues and interpretation and they can be told what they should do. This is altogether outside the plan of God and close on the range of blasphemy.

I am preaching not what I am thinking. I never come on this platform and tell you what I think, because everybody can think I come on this platform to tell you what I know. So what you have got to do is listen to what I know, that you may get to know and tell others what you get to know, so that they will get to know what you know.

How may I be able to dislodge the power of Satan? How can I deal with satanic power? How may I know whether a voice is of God or not? Are there not voices of God? Yes.

I am here believing I am in the right place to build you on the authority of the Word of God. I believe I am in the right place to build you so that you will be able to deal with the things that I am getting through, because I am come this morning with a knowledge of how to deal with these things, because I have been dealing with them.

Hereby know ye the Spirit of God: Every spirit that confesseth that Jesus Christ is come in the flesh is of God: and every spirit that confesseth not that Jesus Christ is come in the flesh is not of God. (1 John 4:2–3)

The grace of the Lord Jesus Christ, and the love of God, and the communion of the Holy Ghost, be with you all. (2 Corinthians 13:14)

Here we have how to deal with satanic power not of God. And then we have within us a decisive position by God, made that we may have the communion of the Holy Ghost, who has all the latest designs, thoughts, and language from heaven. You know an executive is one who has a right to declare everything on the board. And the Chief Executive in the world is the Holy Ghost. He is here today as a communicative to our hearts, to our minds, to our thoughts, what God wants us to know. So this Holy Executive, who is in us, can speak wonderful words. In fact, you will find the Holy Executive will speak most of the language in this sermon.

I am dealing now with what you may know when you are fully in the Holy Ghost. The Spirit will teach you, bring all things to your remembrance, and you need not know that any man shall teach you. But the unction abideth and you need not teachers, but you need the Teacher, which is the Holy Ghost, to bring all things to your remembrance.

> *The Spirit will teach you, bring all things to your remembrance, and you need not know that any man shall teach you.*

This is the office of the Holy Ghost. This is the power of His communication. This is what [John] means when he says, *"God is love"* (1 John 4:8, 16). Jesus, who is grace, is with you. But the Holy Ghost is the speaker, and He speaks everything concerning Jesus.

There may be people here who have been hearing voices, and it has put them in a place that they have been moving from place to place. I am dealing with voices which have caused tremendous issues in the life, brought very much distress, brokenheartedness, led you into confusion and trouble. Why? Because you knew not how to judge the voice.

If a voice comes and tells you what to do, if a person comes and says they have a special prophecy that God has given them for you, you have as much right to ask God for that prophecy as they had to give it to you, and you have as much right to judge that prophecy according to the Word of God. If you do not, there are people going about pretending to be tremendous people, and they are sending people nearly off their wits' end because they believe their damnable prophecies, which never are of God but of the devil. I am very severe on this thing; God won't let me rest. But I have to deal with these things, because I find people all over in a terrible state because of these voices.

How shall we get to know? The Scripture gives it to us.

Interpretation of Tongues:

> God brings liberty and fruit, precious fruit, holy fruit, inward piety, holiness, entirety, separatedness from the world, chastened by the Lord, filled with light, admiration of Jesus, and you see Him above all, full of light and truth, bringing forth into your hearts perfect peace and joy. This is tranquility. This is God's desire for you, every one of you, to be filled with the joy of the Lord.

The Spirit Gives Joy and Gladness

The difference is joy, gladness, and expression instead of sadness, sorrow, and depression. When Jesus comes with joy into the soul and lifts them higher and higher, it is the Spirit that giveth light. When satanic power begins to rule, then there is weariness; then their faces are like a tragedy; then their eyes glare as though they had passed through terrible trial.

You are always right to "*try the spirits whether they are of God*" (1 John 4:1). If you do not do it, then you will be sure to be caught napping.

Misled by a "Voice"

I want to deal with some of these cases before I further explain it.

We had two sisters saved in our meetings, very lovely characters. Their expression was good. No one could look at them without admiring them. They were saved, and then they were filled with the Holy Ghost.

Both of them worked in a telegraph operating room, and they were both desirous to be missionaries. They were so zealous to be missionaries that they were laying aside money and everything they could in order to be prepared to be missionaries. They were zealous for God. Their very lives would tell in a meeting or anywhere. They were so zealous for God they would do anything.

One of them was operating a machine when a voice came, a voice on this line: "Will you obey me? If you will obey me, I will make you the most wonderful missionary that ever lived."

Only the devil promises such a thing, but she did not know. She did not understand.

She was so excited that her sister noticed it and went to her.

"What is it?" she asked.

"Oh! God is speaking to me," she said, "saying wonderful things to me."

She became so excited that her sister asked if she could leave the place for a time, because she saw she would have to protect her. So the overseer allowed them both to be free for a time, and they went into a room.

She became so excited with these messages, so believing it was of God, so full of excitement, that her white blouse became spotted with blood as she pricked her flesh with the nails of her hand.

That is never of God. What do I read about the Word of God? I read that it is full of peace and gentleness, it is easy to be entreated, it is without partiality, it is full of goodness and truth. And remember, if ever you know anything about God, it will be peace. If ever you know anything about the world, it will be disorder. The peace of God that passeth all understanding comes to the heart after you are saved. We are justified by faith and we have peace with God through our Lord Jesus Christ. And the peace continues until it makes us full of the hope of the glory of God.

God showed me a long time ago, and it has not been taken out of my mind, that if I was disturbed in my spirit and was at unrest, I had missed His plan.

How can you miss it? In three ways:

First of all, you can miss it because you have taken on someone else's burden. All the time you are told to cast your burden on the Lord. Any number of people are over-surfeited with sorrow because they are taking on someone else's burden.

That is wrong. You must teach them and teach yourself that you have to cast your burden on the Lord.

Second, if you have not peace, you have gotten out of the will of God in some way. You may not have sinned. You can be out of the will of God without sinning. You can be out of the will of God if you are not making progress. If you have not made progress since yesterday morning, you are a backslider. Everybody is a backslider who is not going on with God. You are a backslider if you do not increase with all the increasing of the divine character and likeness of Christ. You have to move from state to state, from glory to glory, by the Spirit of the Lord.

Interpretation of Tongues:

> The Spirit quickeneth, moveth, chasteneth, buildeth, buildeth, buildeth, and makes you free.
>
> This is like heaven to me;
> This is like heaven to me.
> I've crossed over Jordan to Canaan's fair land,
> And this is like heaven to me.

You won't be down in the dumps then.

You know what Jordan represents? Jordan represents death, and you have crossed over death. Do not drop into it again.

You can lose your peace by missing some divine plan of God, and then you can lose your peace because you may have gotten your mind on something natural. A natural thing is a carnal thing. The Word of God says that the carnal things have to be destroyed because they are not subject to the law of God and cannot be. Every carnal thing must be destroyed. (See Romans 8:5–8.)

So you can miss the plan.

Now, what is the plan? "They that keep their minds stayed upon God shall be kept in perfect peace." (See Isaiah 26:3.) Examine yourself to see where you are. If you are not in perfect peace, you are out of the will of God.

So these voices, if they take you out of peace, you will know it is not the will of God. But if the Spirit speaks, He will bring harmony and joy, because the Spirit always brings three things: comfort, consolation, and edification. And the Spirit will make you sing songs in the night. It will cause you to rise in high places, and you will not be afraid of declaring the works of the Lord. When the Spirit of the Lord is upon you and greatly active, you may go from strength to strength, praising the Lord.

My wife and I were at the house when these two young women came in from work. We saw the distress. We saw the wild condition. If you are wild, that is the devil. If you go breathlessly to the Bible, looking for confirmation of the voice, that is the devil. The Word of God bringeth light. I must use it as the Word of Light. I must see it as the Light of light. I must have it as the Light. I must not run up and down the same as if I had been hit with a stick.

I must be wise, because if I say I am baptized with the Holy Ghost, if I say I am a child of God, I must act so that people will take knowledge that I have been with God.

If there is anything I would resound through this meeting like a trumpet, it is this: *Let not your goodness be evil spoken of!*

Who is speaking? It is the Spirit speaking to us that He wants us in the world, that we should not have anything— neither tongues, interpretations, prophecy, discerning; neither acts in any way—but what should commend us that we have been with Jesus and now the light had come, the truth had fallen upon us, and now we have come into the wisdom of the

Most High God, and therefore the people will take knowledge that we have been with Jesus.

If ever you find a person who has given prophecy and he will not allow that prophecy to be judged, as sure as anything, that prophecy never was right. Everybody that has the true prophecy is willing to come to the light, that everything shall be made true according to the Word of God. Son, don't you receive these things.

What happened? The moment this girl was so possessed with this position, what did the devil say?

"You keep this a secret. Don't you tell anybody; if you confide in anybody, let it be your sister, because she seems to understand you."

Now that is as surely satanic as anything you ever heard in your life, because every true thing, every holy thing, need not be kept under any circumstances.

So they confided in each other. We tried to help them.

"Oh, God is speaking to me!" she said.

And we could not change her.

That night, she said the evil power continued speaking, saying to her, "Tell no one but your sister. Go to the station tonight, wait for the train. The train will come in at thirty-two minutes past seven. Buy two tickets for Glasgow. After you have bought your tickets you will have sixpence left."

This could be confirmed, and no one had to know but the sister. They went to the station. The train came in, exactly at the right time, and they had just sixpence left after they had bought the ticket. Marvelous! Wonderful! Sure to be right.

"See! I have just the money left after I have bought the tickets that the voice said."

The train came in. A gentleman had to sit in one of the carriages with all the money ever she would want, and he would give her all the money, and they had to take it to a certain bank at a certain street corner in Glasgow and right opposite this gentleman there was to sit a woman with a nurse's bonnet on.

The train came in. They rushed from one end of the train to the other. No such person in the train. Then the voice came: "On the next platform, the next train."

And they rushed over.

Would you believe, those two young women were kept moving from platform to platform by those voices till half past nine at night. And then the same power said, "Now that I know you will obey me in everything, I will make you the greatest missionary in the world."

How could they have known at the moment? Why, according to the Word of God. What does it say? *"Many false prophets are gone out into the world"* (1 John 4:1).

Who are these false prophets after? Sincerity, earnestness, zeal, and purity. Who knows? These evil powers know.

What is it necessary to keep in our mind all the time? This: What am I living for? What is the hope of my life? Have I to be the best missionary in the world and a wonderful worker, or has Jesus to be glorified in my life to do as He wills with me for the world?

The ripe grape is never so pure and perfect as it is just before it decays. The child of God is never so near God, just at the summit, as he is when the devil can come and say, "You are wonderful!"

It is satanic to feel you are different from anybody else, that God has a special message for you, and that you are someone very particular.

Every place that God brings you to in a rising tide of perfection is in humility, brokenness of heart, fullness of surrender, where only God can rule in authority—not where you are somebody, but where God is everything, and where you will be living for the exhibition of the glory.

It took months and months of pleading, of crying bitterly. It was three months before these two young women were delivered of this delusion. But God did deliver them, and they have been really wonderful missionaries in China. The devil's plan was defeated, but it was at tremendous cost, almost of their lives.

> *Every place that God brings you to in a rising tide of perfection is in humility, brokenness of heart, fullness of surrender, where only God can rule in authority.*

How could they have got to know it was a false voice? How can you know? When a voice comes, no matter how it seems, you test it. When a voice comes, it is strange, it is persistently pressing you to do something, and you are taken to a hard place and you know the difficulties are such that you can hardly conceive how this thing is, you have a position in the power of the Word of God to say to this evil power, *"Did Jesus come in the flesh?"* (1 John 4:3). And the satanic power will say no. Never yet was there a Spiritist, anybody that was under satanic power, anybody in a fit, anybody losing their mind, who has ever said that Jesus came in the flesh. Satanic forces will not do it.

But the Spirit of the living God, the Holy Spirit, always says yes. And so you can get to know. You have to listen. The Scriptures are there. We have to live in the place of knowing so that we are able to spiritually, divinely discern whether these things are of God or not.

Did Jesus come in the flesh? Yes, and the living Christ is in this body. Christ came in the moment you believed. There is a manifestation of it. You may so live that the Christ is greater than you. You may so live that your language, your expressions, your actions, and everything speak of Christ. "*They took knowledge of them, that they had been with Jesus*" (Acts 4:13). You can so live that the personality of Christ is exactly what Paul said: "Not I—I don't live anymore; Christ liveth in me." (See Galatians 2:20.)

The Christ life, the Christ power, the personality of His presence could be so in you that you could not doubt the Word of God. If you prayed, it would always be in faith, and as you preached, it would always be in faith. You "*live by the faith of the Son of God*" (Galatians 2:20) till your whole body is aflame with the faith of God. This is a divine position of a living attitude where we will live and reign in this beautiful place with Jesus.

A RUINED LIFE

Lots of people are thrown over with that which ruined the life of a young Christian I want to tell you about.

After I was baptized, for many years the Lord graciously helped me. I laid hands upon people and they received the Holy Ghost. I thank God that that power has not stopped. I believe in asking God, lifting up holy hands, and saying, "Father, grant me that it shall be that whosoever I place my hands upon, they shall receive the Holy Ghost."

They called me from place to place to come and help them when they had people they wanted to receive the Holy Ghost. So they sent from York, saying that they had fourteen people that they wished to receive the Holy Ghost. Would I come? They had all been saved since I was there the last time.

I went there. I have never in all my life met a people that were so intoxicated with a certain thing that was come since I had been there. In the open-air preaching, the power of God had been upon them and all these people had been gathered from the marketplace. And right there in the midst of them, they had caught a young man who had developed such a gift of teaching and such a gift of power of the Spirit of leading the people on with God that they said they did not believe there was another man like him in all England. They were intoxicated beyond anything; they were drunk.

Did I rejoice with them? Certainly.

If there is anything in this place of Angelus Temple that I love, it is the young men and young women. When Jesus began His ministry, He laid hands upon eleven that turned out to be the most marvelous men, and yet they were all younger than He. When Paul was brought into the knowledge of the truth, he was a young man. So Jesus began the great ministry of the worldwide revival with young life.

The first World War showed us that no man over forty years of age was good enough for that way. They had to have young blood, young life, that could stand the stress of frost, of heat, and all kinds of things.

God wants young life filled with the power of God to go into the harvest field because they can stand the stress. And Jesus knew, and He got all young men around Him.

Wouldn't it be a lovely lot? Yes, when He was in the midst of them. You are a lovely lot of people because Jesus is in the midst. You will be more lovely still if you refuse to live except He is in the midst.

Moses said, "Except Thou go with us, take us not hence." (See Exodus 33:15.) And we have a right today to live in the presence of the power of the Holy Ghost.

As soon as I got there, the people came around me and said, "Oh, we've got him! We've got him! The only thing that is needed now, we want him to receive the Holy Ghost, and as soon as he receives, we know we have got him."

Was anything wrong about that? No, I rejoiced with them.

Then the power of God fell. You know, we allow anything in a meeting before people receive. Don't you be afraid when people are on the floor. Lots of people roll about the floor and get their black clothes made white. Any number of things take place when the flesh is giving way to the Spirit. But after the Holy Ghost has come in, then we do not expect you to roll again on the floor. We only expect you to roll on the floor till the life of the personality of the Holy Ghost has got right in, turned you out, and you will be able to stand up and preach then, instead of rolling on the floor.

There they were, all lying on the floor. It was a wonderful sight. They came to me, and they said, "Oh! Oh! We've got him now!" Oh, it was so lovely! And when he spoke in tongues, they almost went wild. They shouted, they wept, they prayed. Oh, they were so excited!

One woman came up and she said, "I shouldn't wonder but what you had another John the Baptist."

And they were all round about him, shaking hands and saying, "Oh, now we've got him! Now we know you are the best teacher that has ever been in Pentecost yet."

Thank God, the young man was able to throw it all off, and he was in a beautiful place.

Again, before we left, this woman came up and said, "Will you believe it is a prophecy? I have got that you have to be John the Baptist."

Thank God, he put it off again. But how satanic, how devilish, how unrighteous, and how untrue!

That night, as he was walking home along the country road, another voice came, louder than the woman's, right in the open air.

"You are John the Baptist!"

Again the young man was able to guard it off.

In the middle of the night, he was wakened up out of sleep and this voice came again: "Rise, get up. You are John the Baptist. Declare it!"

And the poor man this time was not able to deal with it. He did not know this truth. With sorrow of heart I tell you, for hours that morning he was walking about York shouting, "I am John the Baptist!" Nothing could be done. He had to be detained.

Who did it? Why, the people, of course.

You have no right to come around Wigglesworth, Mrs. McPherson or anybody, and say, "You are wonderful!" That is satanic. I tell you, we have plenty of the devil to deal with without your making a thousand devils to come and help them. We need common sense.

How could that young man have been delivered? He could have said, "Did Jesus come in the flesh?" This demon power would have said no, and then the Comforter would have come.

These are days when God wants you to build. God does not want to take away your glory; He wants you to have the glory, for Jesus came and said, "I have given them the glory which Thou gavest me." But what is the glory for? To place on the Master. Give Him all, let Him have all—your heart's joy, your life. Let Him have it. He is worthy. He is King of Kings. He is Lord of Lords. He is my Savior. He died to deliver me. He should have the crown.

PREPARATION
FOR THE RAPTURE
Bible Study #11 – July 21, 1927

Our hearts are moved. God is moving us to believe that He is on the throne, waiting for us to make application. Stretch out your hands to God to believe that the almightiness of His grace is for us in a most marvelous way. Whatever yesterday was, today is to be greater.

Are you ready? "What for?" To come to a place where you will not give way, a place where you will dare believe that God is the same today as He was yesterday and will surely make you satisfied, because He longs to fill you. Those who believe shall be satisfied.

Are you ready? "What for?" To so apply your heart to the will of God, to so yield yourself to the purposes of God, that God will work a plan through your life that has never been before.

Are you ready? "What for?" To come into such likemindedness with Christ today that you have no more human desire, but you will be cut short from all human bondages and be set free. The shoreline must never again know you. Come to God in all the depths of His fullness, His revelation, His power, that you may today be clothed upon with God.

I believe that you believe in the coming of the Lord and the rapture which is to take place. I am going to deal with the position that leads you right up to the rapture. To that end, we will be reading the fifth chapter of 2 Corinthians.

This is one of those divine propositions; it is one of those openings to the heart that brings enlargement and conception. It is one of those moments that we enter into by faith to see that we can be so occupied, so changed, so in Christ, so ready, so clothed upon, so filled with Him, that the very breath of the life of that which is causing it would cause us to leave this earth.

DEAD TO SIN; ALIVE UNTO GOD

As you listen to the Word, do not allow natural to interfere with supernatural evidences. You will never be what God has ordered you to be until you are willing to denounce your own failings, unbelief, and every human standard.

You must be willing to denounce them so that you might stand in place, complete, believing that you are a new creation in the Spirit; and that God, in a mighty way, can so fill you with life and destroy all that is natural that would interfere with the process of change, until you are alive unto God by the Spirit, ready for the coming of the Lord.

Now, we have here a definite position, as Paul had received much revelation which was clear to him, but not as cleat to others. In fact, Peter said that Paul said many things which are hard to understand. "Nevertheless," Peter said, "we know that these things are of the Lord." (See 2 Peter 3:15–16.)

Paul wrote many things that are hard to understand. Unless you are spiritually enlightened, you will not be able to comprehend the attitude of the place of ascension he had reached.

All your spiritual acquaintances should come into the place of ascension. Always keep in mind that to be conformed to this world is loss, but to be transformed from this world is gain. The transforming is the working of His mighty power in the mind.

The body and the soul can be so preserved in this wonderful life of God that nothing can hinder us from living as those who are dead to sin and alive unto God. We find that sin has been destroyed, disease absolutely put aside, death abolished in the life of the resurrection of Christ in the body!

> *Always keep in mind that to be conformed to this world is loss, but to be transformed from this world is gain.*

The Spirit of the Lord is giving us revelation that will teach us a plan which is so supernatural, you will live absolutely in a new creation, if you dare believe. You will go by leaps and bounds into all the treasury of the Most High as you believe.

Nothing will interfere with you but yourself. And I believe God can change even your mind. He can give you much aspiration, holy-inflating life divine in human order, filling you with great ambition for purity, holiness, and transformation (which means "transportation").

God often has to cause revolution in the body before He can get the throne in a heart. He causes you to come to death, and then to death, and then to death, so you will see that sin violates, or hinders, progress, that anything of the natural order is not divine, that you have to have a divine mind (a new mind, a new will), that everything about you must be in the line of consecration, or separation unto perfection.

Believe it. Maybe as you examine yourself, you will believe it never could happen in your life. Get your mind off yourself. That is destruction. Get your mind on the Lord.

No building could be built without a plumb line and a straight edge. The Word of God is a true plumb line. God has given us a plumb line and a straight edge, causing us to be built in supernatural lines so that we may be an edifice in the Spirit, and causing us to be strong against the devil.

Interpretation of Tongues:

> *Weakness may be turned into power, feeblemindedness into the mind of Christ. The whole body, fitly joined together in the Spirit, can rise and rise until it is an edifice in the Holy Ghost. It is not what it is; it is what it is going to be. God has made preparation for us to be freed from the law of sin and death. He has gained the victory. He has overcome and vanquished the enemy, and the last enemy that shall be destroyed is death.*

Yes, deeper, deeper and higher, higher we are to go; holier, holier and purer, purer we are to be, all until God sets His seal upon us. We are His forever, bought with a price—not with silver and gold, but with the precious blood.

Let the Spirit move thee, chasten thee, bring thee to naught. Thou must be chastened by the Lord in order to have the fruits of His holiness. He observes thee today to see if you live by the position, "Except thou die, thou canst not live." (See John 12:24–25.)

While you are in the very attitude of death, He causes resurrection force to come into thy life until thou dost come out of all things into the living heart; until Christ is over thee, nourishing thee in the mind and in the body, and causing thy spirit to live; until thou dost feel the very breath of heaven breathing upon thee and the wings of the Spirit moving within thee.

GETTING READY FOR THE FUTURE EXIT

> *For we know that if our earthly house of this tabernacle were dissolved, we have a building of God, an house not made with hands, eternal in the heavens. For in this we groan, earnestly desiring to be clothed upon with our house which is from heaven.* (2 Corinthians 5:1–2)

These verses speak of a present-tense lesson which makes us ready for a future exit. Present-tense lessons are wonderful. You miss a great deal if you do not live in the present tense. You must never put anything off until tomorrow. Believe God to work today! He can do it. The Word of God says, *"Jesus Christ the same yesterday, and to day, and for ever"* (Hebrews 13:8).

Don't say, "'Tomorrow I will be healed."

Don't say, "Tomorrow I will be baptized."

Don't say, "Tomorrow I will have more light."

"To day if ye will hear his voice, harden not your hearts" (Hebrews 3:15), for the hearing of faith is wonderful! God wants you to believe and have everything today!

We all wish that from this day on, no one would die. Speaking of death, the Scriptures say of the natural body, *"It is sown in corruption* [dishonor]*"* (1 Corinthians 15:43). We know that God is going to raise us in power, but there is a state we can go on to where we see that sin, disease, and death are destroyed, and we will live forever with the Lord.

SURPASSING JOY

I want to help you today. If you are not moved in some way by this message, God is not with you. One of two things has to be: either you have to be moved until you cannot test, or you have to be made so glad, you cannot remain in the same place.

I cannot believe that anybody filled with the Spirit could speak to an assembly of people and they would be the same after he had finished. I take it for granted that God has me preaching to move you, to make you very thirsty, or to cause a gladness to come into your heart that will absolutely surpass everything else on the line of joy!

THE BODY MUST BE CHANGED

No flesh can come into the presence of God. If you do die, a process occurs to get rid of all that is in the body. The very body that you are in must be disposed of. It must come to ashes.

There is no such thing as your body being in the presence of God. But if no flesh can come into the presence of God, then what is going into the presence of God? Your body has to give place *to a resurrection order, to a resurrection life.*

The Scriptures speak about dissolving if your body does not go through the process of death and lose all the elements of earthly cabbages, potatoes, corn, wheat, and such. If it does not get rid of all its earthly acquaintances, but simply goes up, God will cause the old body to be turned into gases. There will not be a bit of it left.

In that moment, the very nature of Christ, the life of God in you, will be clothed upon with a body that can stand all eternity.

Be ready for a change. You say, "How can I be ready?"

I am going to answer that. Follow me very closely.

"For in this we groan," 2 Corinthians 5:2 says. There should be a groaning attitude in us. We must reach a place where we see that there is some defect, that there is not a perfect purifying going on in our lives. When we come to that attitude, knowing we are bound, we will groan to be delivered.

What is this deliverance? Shall it come in this present world? Certainly I am not in heaven yet; I am on the earth. I am dealing with people who are on the earth, people who can be on the earth and have supernatural power abounding within them.

The very nature that came into you when you were born again is of a spiritual quality of the nature of knowledge. It can understand supernatural things. It has power to compare spiritual things with spiritual things. And only those who are born of God can understand spiritual things. The world that has never been saved cannot understand them.

But the moment we are quickened, born again, made anew, this nature, taking on its supernatural power, begins travailing, groaning to be delivered from the body. And it will go on, and cry on, and cry on, until the saints will be seen in large numbers, crying, *"Come, Lord Jesus"* (Revelation 22:20).

The consummation will be most remarkable! But I believe God has a plan for us even before that occurs. Carefully and thoughtfully enter with me into more of the fifth chapter of 2 Corinthians.

> *If so be that being clothed we shall not be found naked. For we that are in this tabernacle do groan, being burdened: not for that we would be unclothed, but clothed upon, that mortality might be swallowed up of life.*
>
> (2 Corinthians 5:3–4)

I am dealing with clothing again. The first time, it was about being clothed with flesh; this time, it is about being clothed with the Spirit.

Being *"clothed upon"* in this way is not desiring to go, but desiring to stop because we realize we are not exactly ready to go. We want to be so clothed upon while we are in the body, clothed upon with the life from heaven, that no natural thing would be in evidence in us. We then would be absolutely made alive in Christ, living only for the glory and the exhibition of the Lord of life.

This is the clothing we want, that we might not be naked. You know exactly what nakedness is. They knew when Jesus walked about, for their nakedness was made bare.

Nakedness is a sense of consciousness that there is something that has not been dealt with, that has not been judged; hence, the blood has not had its perfect application.

Nakedness means that you are inwardly conscious that there is some hidden thing, something that has not been absolutely brought to the blood, something that could not possibly stand in God's presence, something that is not ready for the absolute glory.

Second Corinthians 5:4 also speaks of "*life.*" The Word of life is preached unto you through the gospel, and it has a wonderful power in it. It brings immortality into that which is natural in a person, until he realizes the first spring in his heart of supernatural power. And from that moment, he knows that he is in the earth, but he belongs to heaven, and that this life which is in him is a life which has power to eat up mortality.

LIFE THAT EATS UP MORTALITY

Two verses from the eighth chapter of Romans will help us here.

> *There is therefore now no condemnation to them which are in Christ Jesus, who walk not after the flesh, but after the Spirit. For the law of the Spirit of life in Christ Jesus hath made me free from the law of sin and death.*
>
> (Romans 8:1–2)

The "*law of...life*" is that law which came into you and which is incorruptible and divine. It is the very nature of the Son of God.

Suppose I was dealing with the subject of the coming of the Lord. The revelation that I have about the coming of the Lord is that all those who are going to be caught up are going to be eaten up. Their old nature, their old desires, their old life, is going to be eaten up by the life of Jesus Christ. When He comes, the life will meet *the* Life, but the process we are going through now is for building us on the lines of readiness.

Yes, there is a life that has power to eat up mortality. What is mortality? When I speak about mortality, you no doubt think of your physical body and say, "That is mortality."

But that is *not* mortality. That is not what will be swallowed up or eaten up. As long as you are in the world, you will want the casket, and the body is the casket! But it is that which is in the body which is mortal. What is in the body will be eaten up with immortality.

If I would go through Romans, Galatians, Timothy, Luke, Mark, and Peter, I would find sixty-six different descriptions of mortality.

I would find sedition, heresy, envy, strife, malice, hatred, murder, emulation, witchcraft, covetousness, adultery, and fornication included among them. All these are mortality. But there is also a life in the supernatural which can eat them *all* up, devour them *all*, destroy them *all*, until there is no condemnation in this body at *all*.

The Scriptures are very clear: we must allow ourselves to come in touch with this great life in us, this wonderful life divine, this Christ-form, this spiritual revelation.

> *The Holy Ghost is not a cleanser. The Holy Ghost is a revealer of imperfection, which takes the blood of Jesus to cleanse.*

Do not forget, the Holy Ghost did not come as a cleanser. The Holy Ghost is not a cleanser. The Holy Ghost is *a revealer of imperfection*, which takes the blood of Jesus to cleanse. After the blood has cleansed the imperfection, you need the Word of God, for the Word of God is the only power which creates anew. Life comes through the Word. The Word is the Son. He that has received the Son has received life; he that has not received the Son has not life. (See 1 John 5:12.)

Millions of people living today don't have life, eternal life. Only one life is eternal life, and that is the life of the Son of God. One is the life of eternal death, the other of eternal life. One is the life of destruction, the other of eternal deliverance. One is a life of bondage, the other of freedom. One is a life of sorrow, the other of joy.

I want you to see that you are to live so full of the life divine that you are not moved by any wind of doctrine or anything which comes along.

People make the biggest mistake in the world and miss the greatest things of God today by turning to the letter instead of the Spirit.

How many people have spoiled their life because they "went mad" on water baptism? You cannot prove to me through any part of Scripture that water baptism can save you, as they say. Baptism is only a form, yet people are mad, being firm that if you are not baptized, you are lost. These people get the letter, and the letter always kills. *The Spirit always gives life!*

The person, whoever he is, who would turn you from the baptism of Matthew 28 to any other baptism is a thief and a robber and is trying to destroy you. Do not be carnally minded. Be spiritually minded, for then you will know the truth, and the truth will make you free.

See to it that you know and affirm that it is Christ who gives life. Division in your thinking gives sorrow; it brings remorse, trials, and difficulties. Let Christ dwell in your hearts richly, by faith.

Don't go mad on preaching only on the baptism of the Holy Ghost. You will be lopsided.

Don't go mad on preaching water baptism. You will be lopsided!

Don't go mad on preaching healing. You will be lopsided!

There is only one thing that you will never go lopsided on, and that is the preaching of salvation. The only power is the gospel of the kingdom. Men are not saved by baptism, not even by the baptism of the Holy Ghost, and especially not by the baptism in water. They are saved through the *blood* and preserved by the *blood*.

The Lord wants to bring us to the place of real foundation truth. Build upon the foundation truth. Don't be twisted aside by anything. Let this be your chief position: you are living to catch more of the Spirit, only the Spirit!

I clearly know that the baptism in the Holy Ghost is not the only thing that makes me eligible for the coming of the Lord. People have gone mad thinking it is. They have gone mad because they have gotten baptized with the Spirit and think no one is right with God but those who are baptized with the Spirit. It is the biggest foolishness in the world. Why is it foolishness? Because the Truth bears it out. The thief on the cross went right up to meet Jesus in Paradise, and he was not baptized with the Spirit!

But just because a thief missed some good things, shall you miss them? No! It was the great grace of the Lord to have mercy upon him who didn't have them.

There is not a gift, not a grace, not a position that God will not give you to loosen you from your bondages. He wants you to be free in the Spirit. He wants to fill you with the Holy Ghost and the Word until He brings you to the place of sealing of the Spirit.

The Sealing of the Spirit

You say, "What is the sealing of the Spirit?"

The sealing of the Spirit is when God has put His mark upon you and you are tagged.

Some people are troubled if they are "tagged" in the street when a man comes by them on horseback! But it is a wonderful thing to have the tag of almightiness. It seals you. The devil cannot touch you. It proves the Lord has preserved you for Himself. There is a covenant between you and God, and the sealing of the Spirit keeps you in that covenant, where evil powers have no more dominion.

Don't go away with the idea that I am preaching a perfection where you cannot sin. There is a place of perfection, of being purified as He is pure, so that we cannot commit sins. No man can commit sin if he is being purified. But it is when he ceases from seeking a deeper experience, a holier vocation, a deeper separation, a perfect place where he and Christ are one, that sin comes in.

Only in Christ is there security.

Let no man think that he cannot fall because he stand. No, don't think that. Remember this: you need not fall. Grace abounds where sin abounds, and where weakness is, grace comes in. Your very inactivity becomes divine activity.

Where absolute weakness is, so that you feel you cannot stand the trial, God comes in and enables you to stand. Life is ministered to you; Christ takes the place of weakness. You can say, *"When I am weak, then am I strong"* (2 Corinthians 12:10), for God touches you with His strength.

This is ideal. This is divine appointment. This is holy installation. This is God's thought from the throne. The Lord is speaking to us, and I would speak His words with a trumpet-voice to the whole world: "Be ye holy!" (See 1 Peter 1:15–16.)

Don't fail to see that God wants you ready for translation. Holiness is the *habitation* of God.

Spiritual Drunkenness

There is a place to reach in the Holy Ghost which is mystifying to the world and to many people who are not going with God. It is remarkable: we can be so filled with the Spirit, so clothed upon, so purified within, so made ready for the rapture, that we are drunk in the Spirit all the time!

> *For whether we be beside ourselves, it is to God: or whether we be sober, it is for your cause.* (2 Corinthians 5:13)

Oh, to be so filled with the Spirit of life that you are absolutely drunken, completely beside yourself!

Now, when I come in contact with people who would criticize my drunkenness, I am sober. I can be sober one minute and drunk the next. But I tell you, to be drunk is wonderful! Ephesians 5:18 admonishes us, *"Be not drunk with wine, wherein is excess; but be filled with the Spirit."*

A drunk man stops at a lamppost, and he has a lot to say to it. He talks the most foolish things possible. The people say, "He's gone."

Pray, "O Lord, that I may be so drunk that it makes no difference what people think!"

I am not concerned about what people think. I continue to speak to the Lord in hymns and spiritual songs, making my boast in the Lord. The Lord of hosts is round about me, and I am so free in the Holy Ghost that I am ready to "take off." But He does not take me.

Why doesn't He take me? I am ready to "take off," and it is better for me to go, but for the church's sake, it is preferable to stop. It is preferable to be clothed upon, living in the midst of the people with no nakedness, full of purity full of power, full of revelation, for the church's sake.

Yes, it is far better to go. But for the church's sake, to stop, that I may be helpful by telling the people how they can have their nakedness covered, how all their imperfections can be covered, how all the mind can be clothed, how all their inward impurities are made pure in the presence of God, and how to be living, walking, and acting in the Holy Ghost. This is wonderful—living, walking, and acting in the Holy Ghost. This is wonderful, and this is the height God would have us to be at.

> *When Christ is in your heart, enthroning your life, and sin is dethroned, righteousness abounds, and the Holy Ghost has great liberty.*

Here is a keynote verse to many positions we are holding in this subject of preparing for rapture.

And if Christ be in you, the body is dead because of sin; but the Spirit is life because of righteousness.

(Romans 8:10)

There is no such thing as having liberty in your body if there is sin there. Only when righteousness is there does righteousness abound. When Christ is in your heart, enthroning your life, and sin is dethroned, righteousness abounds, and the Holy Ghost has great liberty.

My, what triumphs of heights, of lengths, of depths, of breadths there are in the holy place! And where is the holy place? Right inside us! Right inside the children of God, the heirs of God, the joint-heirs with Christ!

Interpretation of Tongues:

> *He that is dead is free from sin, but alive unto God by the Spirit, and is made free from the law of sin and death. And he had entered into a relationship with God. Now God is his reward.*
>
> *He is not only a son, but joined in heirship because of sonship. In purity, he is joined together with Him. And no good thing will He withhold from him, because he walks uprightly. Every good thing is for us on the holy line, walking uprightly, being set free, being made God's property.*

RECONCILIATION IN CHRIST

> And all things are of God, who hath reconciled us to himself by Jesus Christ, and hath given to us the ministry of reconciliation; to wit, that God was in Christ, reconciling the world unto himself, not imputing their trespasses unto them; and hath committed unto us the word of reconciliation.
>
> (2 Corinthians 5:18–19)

What is reconciliation? To be absolutely joined to Christ and blended with Him in atonement. Reconciliation is a glorious thing! We remember the blessed Son of God, taking our place in reconciliation, becoming the absolute position of all uncleanness, of every sin God laid upon Him—the iniquity of all—that every iniquity might go, every bondage might be made free. Sin, death, disease leaving; resurrection, re-creation entering!

When He comes, we shall not be naked, but clothed upon, separated, filled within, made like Him in every way.

I come to you only in the living fact of this testimony. To me, it is reality. I am living in it. I am moving in it. I am acting in it. And I am coming to you with the joy of it!

> *It is joy unspeakable and full of glory,*
> *And the half has never yet been told.*

I know that this life divine, which is free from bondage, free from the power of Satan, free from evil thoughts, free from thoughts of evil, is for us. God is reconciling us in such a way to Himself that He abounds to us. In Him, we have

Freedom!

Purity!

Power!

Separateness!

We are ready for the great trumpet!

Temptation Endured
Bible Study #12—July 22, 1927

*L*et the Spirit cover you today that you may be intensely in earnest about the deep things of God. You should be so in the order of the Spirit that you may know that your will, your mind, your heart may be so centered in God that He may lift you into the pavilion of splendor where you hear His voice, lift you to the place where the breath of the Almighty can send you to pray and send you to preach, the Spirit of the Lord being upon you.

You are at the banquet of multiplication, banquet of no separation, a banquet where you have to increase with all increasing, where God has for you riches beyond all things—not fleshly things, not carnal things, but spiritual manifestations, gifts, fruits of the Spirit, beautiful beatitudes—the blessing of God always being upon you.

Are you ready for this glorious place where you are dismissed and God takes place, to send you on your eternal race to win thousands of people that they may enter into eternal grace?

For our study this morning, the Lord has led me to select the first chapter of James. This is a marvelous subject in itself. This is the Master's subject, and He will be able to manage it. I would have to give in if it were my subject, but seeing it is the Master's subject, I will begin.

Interpretation of Tongues:

> *The Spirit moveth and changes His operation, bringing the soul into the place of hunger and desire till the whole of the being cries out for the living God. Truly the creature must be delivered from this present evil thing. So God is operating through us by these meetings and letting us know that all flesh is grass. But He is bringing the Spirit of revelation that we may know that this inheritance we are having is to endure forever and ever, for we belong to the new creation of God, clothed upon with the Spirit, made like unto Him, because our whole hearts now are bringing forth that which God has established, and it is out of the fullness of the truth of the hidden heart that God flows forth His glory, His power, His might, His revelation, and His power in association, and makes us one, and says, "Ye are mine."*

VICTORIOUS IN BATTLE

> *James, a servant of God and of the Lord Jesus Christ, to the twelve tribes which are scattered abroad, greeting. My brethren, count it all joy when ye fall into divers temptations.* (James 1:1–2)

> *There is no person ever able to talk about the victory over temptation without he goes through it. All victories are won in battles.*

There is no person ever able to talk about the victory over temptation without he goes through it. All victories are won in battles.

There are tens of thousands of people in the old land and also in America and other parts of the world who are wearing badges to show they have been in the battle, and they rejoice in it. They would be ashamed to wear a badge if they had not been in the battle; it is the battle that causes them to wear the badge. It is those people that have been in the fight that tell about the victories.

It is those people who have been tried beyond all things that can come out and tell you a story. It is only James and Peter and Paul, those who are in the front of the battle, that tell you how we have to rejoice in the trial because there is wonderful blessing coming out of the trial. It is in the trial that we are made.

Tribulation, Patience, Experience

You people want an experience, do you? I will read you something that will give you an experience; I know nothing like it.

> *Therefore being justified by faith, we have peace with God through our Lord Jesus Christ: by whom also we have access by faith into this grace wherein we stand, and rejoice in hope of the glory of God. And not only so, but we glory in tribulations also: knowing that tribulation worketh patience; and patience, experience.* (Romans 5:1–4)

And out of the experience, we tell what is being done. Do you want to have a big story to tell? Well, it is here. Count it all joy in the midst of temptations. When the trial is severe, when you think that no one is tried as much as you, when you feel that some strange thing has so happened that you are altogether in a new order, the trial is so hard you cannot sleep, you do not know what to do, count it all joy. He has something in it, something divine, something of a divine nature. You are in a good place when you do not know what to do.

After Abraham was tried, then he could offer Isaac—not before he was tried. God put him through all kinds of tests. For twenty-five years, he was tested, and he is called "the father of the faithful" because he would not give in. We have blessing today because one man dared believe God without a move for twenty-five years.

Twelve Months' Experience of Faith

A woman came up to me in a meeting one day and said, "I have come for you to heal me. Can you see this big goiter?"

"I can hardly see anything else," I said.

She told her father and mother and the family before she came that she believed she was going to be healed because Wigglesworth was going to pray for her.

As soon as she was prayed for, we had a testimony meeting. Her testimony was wonderful.

"Oh!" she said. "I thank God because He has perfectly healed me!"

She went home, and they were all glad to hear what she said.

"When I was prayed for, I was perfectly healed!" she exultantly exclaimed.

For twelve months, she went all up and down amongst the assemblies, telling how God had healed her.

The next twelve months, I was in the same place, and she came, filled with joy. When she came in, the people said, "See, oh, how big is that goiter!"

They were all looking on. By and by, we had a testimony meeting.

"Oh!" she said. "Twelve months ago, I was prayed for here, and I was marvelously healed. I have had twelve months of the most wonderful time on earth because God so wonderfully healed me twelve months ago."

She went home. When she got home, she said to her mother, "Oh! If you had been there and seen the people, how they were moved when they heard me tell how God healed me."

"Look!" the mother said. "You don't know—you don't seem to know—but the people are believing there is something wrong with your mind, and they believe all the family is touched with it, and you are bringing disgrace upon all the family. We are disgusted with you. It is shameful. The whole thing is rolled onto us because you are touched in your mind. Why don't you go look in the glass? Then you will see the thing has not moved at all."

She went to her room. She said, "Lord, I do not want to look in the glass. I believe You have done it, but let all the people know that. You have done it. Let them all know. You have done it just the same as You have let me know. You have done it."

The next morning, she came downstairs as perfect as anybody could be, and the family knew the Lord had done it.

More Precious Than Gold

Some of you people, because you are not healed in a moment, wonder what is up. God never breaks His promise. The trial of your faith is much more precious than gold.

God has you in the earth trying to bring out His character in you. He wants to destroy the power of the devil, wants to move you so that, in the face of difficulties and hardships, you will praise the Lord and *"count it all joy"* (James 1:2).

You have to take a leap today. You have to leap into the promises; you have to believe God never fails you. You have to believe it is impossible for God to break His Word. He is from everlasting to everlasting.

> *Forever and ever, not for a day,*
> *He keepeth His promise forever;*
> *To all who believe,*
> *To all who obey,*
> *He keepeth His promises forever.*

There is no variableness with God; there is no shadow of turning. He is the same. He manifests His divine glory.

To Mary and Martha, He said, *"If thou wouldest believe, thou shouldest see the glory of God"* (John 11:40). We must understand that there will be testing times, but they are only to make us more like the Master.

He was tempted in all points like as we, yet without sin. He endured all things. He is our example.

Oh, that God shall give us an earnest, intent position where flesh and blood have to yield! We will go forward. We will not be moved by our feelings.

The man who is prayed for tonight and gets a blessing, but tomorrow—because he does not feel exactly as he ought to do—begins murmuring, what does he do? He changes the Word of God for his feelings. What an awful disgrace it is for you to change the Word of God because of your feelings. Let Him have His perfect work.

"My brethren, count it all joy." It does not mean to say, "Count a bit of it joy," but "Count it *all*."

It doesn't matter on what side it comes, whether it is your business or your home or what—count it all joy.

Why? For *"all things work together for good to them that love God, to them who are the called according to his purpose"* (Romans 8:28).

A great word, that means that you have a special position where God is electrifying the very position of you, so that the devil will see there is a character about you and he will have to say something about you as he said about Job. (See Job 2:3–6.) "Satan, what is your opinion about Job?" Then, the Lord goes on and says, "Don't you think he is wonderful? Don't you think he is the most excellent of all the earth? Isn't he beautiful?"

"Yes—but, You know, You are keeping him."

Praise the Lord! I am glad the devil has to tell the truth. And don't you know, He can keep you?

"If You touch his body," the devil said, "he will curse You to Your face."

"You do it, but you cannot touch his life."

The Scripture says that Jesus was dead, but He is alive again and hath power over death and hell. And then, there is a big "Amen." So the devil cannot take your life without the Lord allows it: "Thou shalt not touch his life." (See Job 2:6.)

He thought he could do it, and you know the calamity. But Job said,

> *The Scripture says that Jesus was dead, but He is alive again and hath power over death and hell.*

> Naked came I out of my mother's womb, and naked shall
> I return thither: the LORD gave, and the LORD hath taken
> away; blessed be the name of the LORD.   (Job 1:21)

Oh, it is lovely! The Lord can give us that language. It is not language of the head. This is divine language; it is the heart acquaintance.

I want you to know that we can have heart acquaintance. It is far more for me to speak out of the abundance of my heart than out of the abundance of my head. I learned a long time ago that nothing but libraries make swelled heads. And nothing but the Library of the Word makes swelled hearts. You are to have swelled hearts, because *out of the heart, full of the fragrance of the love of God, there issues forth the living life of the Lord.*

Interpretation of Tongues:

> *It is the Spirit that giveth liberty. The prophet is nothing, but the Spirit brings us into attainment where we sit at His feet and seek with Him and have communications of things divine, for now we are not belonging to the earth. We are transformed by the renewing of our mind and set in heavenly places with Christ Jesus.*

You must cease to be. That is a difficult thing for you and me, but it is no trouble at all when you are in the hands of the Potter. You are only wrong when you are kicking. You are all right when you are still and He is forming you afresh. So let Him form you afresh today and make another vessel so that you will stand the stress.

BE PERFECT

"*But let patience have her perfect work, that ye may be perfect*" (James 1:4). Oh, is that possible? Certainly it is possible. Who is speaking? It is the breath of the Spirit, it is the hidden man of the heart which has a heart like his brother—this is James, the Lord's brother. He speaks very much like his brother. Likely enough we might expect when we read these wonderful words that we have a real touch with kindred spirit.

James had to learn patience. It was not an easy thing for him to understand how his Brother could be the Son of God and be in the same house with Judas, his brother, and Josiah and the others. It was not an easy thing for him, and he had to learn to be patient to see how it worked out.

There are many things in your life that you cannot understand, but be patient, for when the hand of God is upon the thing, it may grind very slowly, but it will form the finest thing possible if you dare wait till the end of it. Do not kick until you are through, and when you are dead enough, you will never kick at all. It is a death come to death that we might be alive unto God. It is only by the deaths we die that we are able to be still.

"The cross? I can despise the cross. The shame? I can despise it. The bitter language spoken round, 'If thou be the Christ, come down and we will believe.'" (See Matthew 21:40, 42; Mark 15:30.)

He stood it. They smote Him, but He reviled not again. He is the picture for us. Why did He do it? He was patient. Why? He knew that as He came to the uttermost end of the cross, He saved the Los Angeles people forever.

You cannot tell what God has in mind for you. As you are still and pliable in the hands of God, He will be working out a greater vessel probably than you can imagine in all your life.

ENTIRE, WANTING NOTHING

"Let patience have her perfect work, that ye may be perfect and entire, wanting nothing" (James 1:4) Entirety means to say you are not moved by anything, only living in the divine position of God. Entirety means to say you are not moved, you are not changed by what people say. There is something about divine acquaintance which is instilled—intuition, in-wrought by the mighty God.

The new life of God is not surface. It builds the character in purity till the inward heart is filled with divine love and has nothing but the thoughts of God alone.

"That ye may be perfect and entire, wanting nothing."

They came to me in New Zealand and said, "We would like to make you a Christmas present if you can tell us what you would like."

"I haven't a want in the world," I said. "I cannot tell you. I have no desire for anything, only God."

One day, I was walking down the street with a millionaire, I was feeling wonderfully happy over the way the Lord was blessing in our meetings.

As we walked together, I said, "Brother, I haven't a care in the world! I am as happy as a bird!"

"Oh!" he said. "Stop! Say it again! Say it again!" And he stood still, waiting for me to repeat it.

"Brother, I haven't a care in the world. I am as happy as a bird!"

"Oh!" he said. "I would give all my money, I would give everything I have to have that!"

Wanting nothing. Hallelujah!

The Spirit of the Lord is moving us mightily to see this is resurrection power. We were planted with Him, we have been risen with Him. We are from above. We do not belong to beneath. We reign in life; it is the life of God's Son manifest in this human body.

Ask God for Wisdom

If any of you lack wisdom, let him ask of God, that giveth to all men liberally, and upbraideth not; and it shall be given him.
(James 1:5)

This is a very remarkable word. Many people come to me and ask if I will pray for them to have faith. I want to encourage them, but I cannot go away from God's Word. I cannot grant people faith. But by the power of the Spirit, I can stimulate you until you dare to believe and rest on the authority of God's Word. The Spirit of the living God quickens you, and I see that "*faith cometh by hearing, and hearing by the word of God*" (Romans 10:17).

This is a living word of faith: "*If any of you lack wisdom, let him ask of God, that giveth to all men liberally.*"

One thing you cannot find is that God ever judged you for the wisdom He gave you or for the blessing He gave. He makes it so that when you come again, He gives again, never asking what you did with the last. That is the way God gives. "*God…giveth liberally and upbraideth not.*" So you have a chance today to come for much more. Do you want wisdom? Ask of God.

Interpretation of Tongues:

> It is not wisdom that you get from the earth; it is divine wisdom. It brings a peaceful position. It ruleth with diligence, and it causes you to live in quietness. You know the difference between the wisdom which is from above and the wisdom which is from beneath, and so the Spirit breathes through our Brother to show you that you have to be so in the perfect will of God in asking for these things till one thing must be fulfilled in your heart. If you ask, you must believe, for God is only pleased when you believe.

You have to be in the order of asking. This is the order: "*But let him ask in faith, nothing wavering*" (James 1:6).

I am satisfied that God, who is the builder of divine order, never brings confusion in His order. It was only when things were out of order that God brought confusion. When they asked for bricks, they were given straw. God brought confusion in the whole thing because they were out of order. They were trying to get into heaven some other way, and they were thieves and robbers. So He turned their language to confusion. There is a way into the kingdom of heaven, and it is through the blood of the Lord Jesus Christ.

If you want this divine order in your life—if you want wisdom—you have to come to God believing. I want to impress upon you the fact—I am learning it more every day—if you ask six times for anything, it shows you are an unbelieving person. For if you really believe, you will ask God only once, and that is all you need, because He has abundance for your every need. But if you go right in the face of asking once and ask six times, He knows very well you do not mean what you ask, so you do not get it. God does not honor unbelief; He honors faith.

If you would so get to business about the baptism of the Holy Ghost and ask God definitely and once to fill you, and believe it, what would you do? You would begin to praise Him for it because you knew He had given it.

If you ask God once for healing, you will get it. But if you ask a thousand times a day till you did not know you were asking, you would get nothing. If you would ask God for your healing now and begin praising Him, because He never breaks His Word, you would go out perfect. *"Only believe"* (Mark 5:36).

God wants to promote us. He wants us to get away from our own thoughts, our own foolishness, and get to a definite place, believing that He is and that He is a rewarder of them that seek Him diligently.

Have you got to the place that you dare? Have you got to the place that you are going to murmur no more when you are in the trial? Are you going to be weeping around, telling people about it, or are you going to say, "Thank You, Lord, for putting me on the top"?

There are any number of people who do not get checks sent to them because they didn't thank the donor for the last. There are any number of people who get no blessing because they did not thank God for the last. A thankful heart is a receiving heart. God wants to keep you in the place of constant believing.

Keep on believing, Jesus is near,
Keep on believing, there's nothing to fear;
Keep on believing, this is the way,
Faith in the night, the same as the day.

> *There are any number of people who get no blessing because they did not thank God for the last. A thankful heart is a receiving heart.*

ENDURED TEMPTATION BRINGS THE CROWN

Blessed is the man that endureth temptation: for when he is tried, he shall receive the crown of life. (James 1:12)

People do not know what they are getting when they are in a great place of temptation. Temptation endured brings the crown of life, *"which the Lord hath promised to them that love him"* (James 1:12).

Let no man say when he is tempted, I am tempted of God: for God cannot be tempted with evil, neither tempteth he any man: but every man is tempted, when he is drawn away of his own lust, and enticed. Then when lust hath conceived, it bringeth forth sin: and sin, when it is finished, bringeth forth death. Do not err, my beloved brethren.
(James 1:13–16)

There is nothing outside of purity but what is sin. All unbelief is sin. God wants you to have a pure, active faith so that all the time, you will be living in an advanced place of believing God, and you will be on the mountaintop and singing when other people are crying.

I want to speak now about lust. I am not speaking about the menial things, the carnal desires. I am not speaking so much about adultery, fornication, and such things. But I am speaking about that which has turned aside to some other thing instead of God. God has been offering you better things all the time, and you have missed it.

There are three things in life, and I notice any number of people are satisfied with one. There is blessing in justification, there is blessing in sanctification, and there is blessing in the baptism of the Holy Ghost. Salvation is a wonderful thing, and we know it. Sanctification is a process which takes you on to a higher height with God. Salvation, sanctification, and the fullness of the Spirit are processes. Any number of people are satisfied with "good"—that is salvation. Other people are satisfied with "better"—that is a sanctified life, purified by God. Other people are satisfied with the "best"—that is the fullness of God with revelation from on high. I am not satisfied with any of the three; I am only satisfied with the best with improvement. So I come to you not with good, but better; not with better, but best; not with best, but with improvement, going on with God. Why? Because *"when lust hath conceived, it bringeth forth sin; and sin, when it is finished, bringeth forth death"* (James 1:15). When anything has taken me from God, it means death in some way.

When Jesus said to the disciples, "The Son of Man will be put into the hands of sinners and crucified" (see Matthew 26:45; Mark 14:41), Peter remonstrated with Him, but Jesus said, *"Get thee behind me,…for thou savourest not the things that be of God, but the things that be of men"* (Mark 8:33).

Anything which hinders me from going to death is the devil. Anything which hinders me from being separated unto God is the devil. And anything which hinders me from being purified every day is carnal, and it is death.

So I pray you today that you must see there is no lustful thing in you that would rob you of the glory, and God will take you to the very summit of the blessing, where you can be increased day by day into all the fullness of God.

Another word I want you to have; I understand clearly by this that God has wrought out the whole plan of our inheritance, and He is showing us that the whole thing is so beautiful that we are brought into existence in the spiritual order through the Word.

Wherefore, my beloved brethren, let every man be swift to hear, slow to speak, slow to wrath: for the wrath of man worketh not the righteousness of God. Wherefore lay apart all filthiness and superfluity of naughtiness, and receive with meekness the engrafted word, which is able to save your souls.
(James 1:19–21)

Do not neglect the Word of God. Take time to think about the Word of God. It is the only place of safety.

THE GLORY OF
THE INCORRUPTIBLE
Bible Study #13 – July 26, 1927

God has wonderful things for us in this present tense. I wish to enlarge your capacity of thought, and also your inward desire after God, so that you may claim richly all things God has for you today.

God has, before the foundation of the world, made a provision for us all, and many are coming into the knowledge that they have been pre-thought about, predestined, wonderfully changed in the operation of the Spirit.

Are you ready? "What for?" To change strength with God by a living faith.

Be ready for the enduement of power, the enrichment of His grace, the oil which makes the face of you to rejoice and be glad. Be full of expectation. Be earnest. Make your supplications without fear. Be bold in the presence of God. Dare believe that you enter in through the blood into a very large place today.

Are you ready? "What for?" That you may be lost in God, wholly swallowed up in His divine plan; that you might be enriched above all enrichment of earthly things with divine capacity, with the knowledge of His sovereign grace; that you may be filled with all His fullness.

Our subject this morning is belonging to the deep things of God. We need in these days groundwork, inward knowledge, of greater things. We need to be supernaturally built, changed by a living authority, to come into a divine construction where the mind is operated by the Spirit and where we live not, but another mightier than us liveth in us.

Oh! For a revelation that we may be taken on with God—not left, but taken on with God into all His divine arrangement for us. This meeting, however beautiful it may be, is all arranged, divinely. There is nothing out of order with God. God is so large in all of His providences, providing, arranging, that these meetings are not just happening. God has had these meetings in His mind since the foundation of the earth. All things are in His perfect order.

Occasionally, I see one of my hairs drop out of my head, but He keeps the number that are left. I am not troubled about my hair, whether it grows white or remains its natural color. Some people try to change the color of the hair. They have forgotten that God has said you cannot make one hair black or white.

How we ought to see that God wants us a supernatural order, not conformed to the world with powder and all kinds of paint. Don't you know that you have to be pretty in the sight of the Lord? That prettiness is a meek and quiet spirit. It is where the Lord has the right-of-way of your heart. It is where you are not troubled about the natural physique, knowing that the supernatural physique is being made like Him. We have borne the image of the earthy, but we are going to bear the image of the heavenly.

Oh, that we could be lost to these things, set apart for the glory of God, brought into the resurrection order, filled with audacity, divine appointment, where the Lord is taking us on, heights, depths, lengths, breadths, yea, everything in the mind of God, higher, higher, higher!

For our study this morning, I want to take the first chapter of the first epistle of Peter. This chapter has a foundation line of truth. We cannot cover it all, but I want to deal with the incorruptible Word, the incorruptible seed, and the incorruptible life in the body, which has all lines laid down on an incorruptible plan, so that you may be able to understand how the mind of the Lord has to be so extravagantly in you, even to deny your own personality before you deny the power of the Word of the living God.

The days will come when your ministry will be tested on all lines and your own life will be. If you can get beyond your nature, beyond your natural line of thought, and beyond yourself into a place of almighty provision for you in the flesh, quickened by the Spirit, you shall survive. As the Word of God says, *"Having done all, to stand"* (Ephesians 6:13). When the trial is on, when everything comes to a point that it seems the last strand in the rope, then the Lord will very mightily bring you into a land of plenty. Lord, let it please Thee this morning to keep us in that place.

When the trial is on, when everything comes to a point that it seems the last strand in the rope, then the Lord will very mightily bring you into a land of plenty.

In order to reach this climax in divine order, let us read the first verse of the first epistle of Peter:

Peter, an apostle of Jesus Christ, to the strangers scattered throughout Pontus, Galatia, Cappadocia, Asia, and Bithynia. (1 Peter 1:1)

Peter, like James, is speaking to us on this line because of a trying time. James is edifying us in a trying corner. Here, we have the same things.

PERSECUTION COMES AFTER BAPTISM

The people are scattered, persecution is come in. They had a good time at Jerusalem, and God knew—I say it reverently—*God knows that we never make progress in an easy time.* You may settle down to ease and miss the great plan of God. God allowed strange things to happen in Jerusalem after the Holy Ghost came.

A man may be saved for many years without knowing anything much about persecution. A man may be sanctified for many years without knowing anything much about persecution. But it is impossible to be baptized with the Holy Ghost without entering into persecution.

The disciples had a wonderful time when they were with Jesus. They had no persecution. But there was One in the midst of them whom they tried to throw over the brow of the hill. The priests joined together to kill Him. After the devil entered into Judas, the only people he could have conversation with were the priests. The priests were willing to talk to the devil after he got into Judas.

Interpretation of Tongues:

> Guard the door of thy lips. See to it that thy heart is perfect, that thou hast no judgment, that thou dost not stand in the way and condemn everybody that is in the way, for there are lost today like the priests in their day. They will neither go in themselves or let anybody else. But don't let this spirit be in thee, for God wants to guard thee, purify thee, and present thee as a chaste virgin, made ready for every good work.

Let us see to it, whatever happens, that there is no harsh judgment in us, no bitterness. We must see that we have been quickened, brought into, changed by, a new authority; incorruptible in the corruptible; divine life where death was; love where hatred was; the power of God reigning in the human; the Lord lifting upon us the light of His countenance; right in the midst of death, life breaking forth like rivers in the desert.

May the Lord bring us to a place that hard judgment is past, make us meek and lowly in heart. This is the principle of the Master.

Satan Cannot Be Made Holy

There is no such thing as purifying the impure. Evil things never get purer but more vile. All impurity, all evil, must be cast out. You never can make Satan holy. He will be hellish and fiendish forever. And when the brightness of God comes by the express image of the Father, the very brightness against uncleanness, he will be glad to get in the pit and be there forever and ever.

There are some fools in this day. There are some absolute asses, who foolishly say that the devil will be saved, and they will go arm in arm. You will never purify sin. Sin cannot be purified. *"The carnal mind...is not subject to the law of God, neither indeed can be"* (Romans 8:7). Carnality has to be destroyed. Evil propensities must be rooted out.

God's plan is this: "A pure heart will I give thee, and a right spirit" (see Psalm 51:10). And this is the order of the new creation in God.

As sure as the Holy Ghost fell, James was beheaded, Peter was put in prison, they had a tremendous row at Jerusalem, and the saints were scattered. The scattering of the saints meant to say the proclamation of the gospel. So, here, Peter is writing to the people which are scattered.

SANCTIFICATION OF THE HUMAN SPIRIT

Elect according to the foreknowledge of God the Father, through sanctification of the Spirit, unto obedience and sprinkling of the blood of Jesus Christ: Grace unto you, and peace, be multiplied. (1 Peter 1:2)

Notice that there is a sanctifying of the human spirit. It does not matter what you say; if your human spirit does not get wholly sanctified, you will always be in danger. It is that position where the devil has a chance to work upon you.

Therefore, we are taught to come into sanctification where the rudiments—the uncleannesses, the inordinate affections, corruption—passes away because of meet corruption abiding; where all kinds of lusts have lost their power.

This is the plan. Only in the ideal of pursuit of perfection and holiness and understanding the mind of the Spirit and the law of the Spirit of life are we brought into a very blessed place.

For instance, it is the place of holiness, the place of entire sanctification, the place where God has the throne of the heart. It is the place where the mind is so concentrated in the power of God that he thinks about the things which are pure and lives in holy ascendancy, where every day is an exchange into the power of liberality with God. God highly honors him, but He never exalts him. The devil comes to exalt him, but it cannot be under the lines of the sanctification of the Spirit. The blood is all for rudiments of evil.

There is a sanctifying of the human spirit where the human spirit so comes into perfect blending with the divine mind of Christ that he cannot be exalted. You can live in the body with all the glorious unction, revelation, and power, and the Spirit can sanctify your spirit until you will never vaunt yourself and will never say "I, I, I," but it will be "Christ, Christ, Christ," and He will be glorified.

Interpretation of Tongues:

> *Into this death within, this inward deepening of all human weaknesses and human powers that would assert themselves, deeper into and on with God, learning only the principles of Christ, as He is, to be like Him in holiness, in righteousness, and in purity, till you reign with Him, gloriously reigning in Him, through Him, by Him, over the powers of the devil. Holiness is power; sin is defeat. Sin is weakness; holiness is strength.*

"Transformed in the spirit of your mind" (see Ephesians 4:23) is a place where you are always being lifted into clearer light, always seeing more the hideousness of sin, always having a consciousness of the powers of evil and a consciousness of the powers of God over evil. May the Lord grant unto us by His mighty power this spiritual intuition of divine association with the Father.

Interpretation of Tongues:

> *He is exalted far above all, and we are united in Him, closer than all, till there is no division. Holy as He is, pure as He is, life, truth revealed in us. Because of truth in us, He becomes Alpha, Omega. He has the last thought; He is all in all. We love Him! We say, "Thou art altogether lovely!"*

THE INCORRUPTIBLE SEED

Consider now the thirteenth to fifteenth verses of the first chapter of 1 Peter.

Wherefore gird up the loins of your mind, be sober, and hope to the end for the grace that is to be brought unto you at the revelation of Jesus Christ; as obedient children, not fashioning yourselves according to the former lusts in your ignorance: but as he which hath called you is holy, so be ye holy in all manner of conversation; because it is written, Be ye holy; for I am holy. (1 Peter 1:13–15)

It is settled in the canon of Scripture that what came into you at the new birth had no corruption in it, no defilement in it, and it could not desire evil. That incorruptible seed, that divine life of the Son, that quickening of the Spirit, that regenerative power, that holy creative power within thee, that divine position which caused thy very nature to bring forth a likeness to the Son of God—even thy very bowels yearned with desire after its purity. You loved to sing of the holiness of Him.

I remember, when quite a little boy, I used to lie on my back singing, until heaven seemed to be let down, till it seemed like glory. It was wonderful. What was it? The new creation longing, waiting. Oh, hallelujah! Sixty years ago, and still greater desire, more longing for that which came then to be met with the very life that gave it.

There is something about it so remarkable that it was so concentrated in my human life that, from that day to this, I have never lost that holy knowledge that I am His, wholly His.

I want all the people in this place to be created anew after this fashion till they will become. Don't be afraid of being called saints. Don't be afraid of the word *holiness*. Don't be afraid of the word *purified*. Don't be afraid of the word *perfect*. Believe that, in you, there is a power which has in it no corruption, which has no desire to sin, which hates uncleanness, which is born of an incorruptible power, which has no evil in it. It is godlike. It is Sonship order, and it has to grow up in you till

He is manifested in you, perfect—perfect sight in God, perfect feeling after God, holy feelings, no carnal desires, yearning after purity, longing after cleanliness, desiring after God. This is the inheritance of the saints—in the world, not of it—over it.

He who has this faith, he who has this life, overcomes the world. Who is he that overcometh the world but he that believeth that Jesus is the Son of God?

What does it mean for Him to be the Son of God to you and me? God is holy, God is light, God is love. Jesus was the fullness of the expression of the purpose of all fullness.

The same fullness, the same life, the same maturity, after a perfect standard of life, has to be in you till you are dead indeed unto the world and alive unto God in the Spirit.

Believe that in you, there is a power which has in it no corruption, which has no desire to sin, which hates uncleanness, which is born of an incorruptible power, which has no evil in it.

Holy, Holy, Holy, merciful and mighty,
God in Three Persons, blessed Trinity.

Trinity, boundless affinity, holy, transforming power, the very nature of the Son of God, the very powers of the world to come, the very nature of the wonderful Son, formed in us.

There are five senses in the world. When He is come, there are five senses of spiritual acquaintance: the hearing of faith, the feelings after God, the seeing supernaturally, the speaking after the mind of the operation of the Spirit, the tasting after God's plan.

Yet God wants us to be so triune, perfectly joined, till the very Christ is formed in us, His very life manifested in human, till we know we have no questions. No matter what other people say, we know in whom we have believed and are persuaded. (See 2 Timothy 1:12.)

There are things that can be moved, and there are things that cannot be moved. There are things that can be changed, and there are things that cannot be changed. We have within us an incorruptible place which cannot be moved. It does not matter who is moved or what is moved, the things that God has given us remain.

Some things can be wrapped up and folded like a garment. The heavens may be rolled up like a scroll and melted with fervent heat. The very earth we are standing on may be absolutely melted. But we are as endurable as He is, for we have the same life, the incorruptible life, the eternal power. The Everlasting King is moving in the natural things to cause the natural to know that this is eternal, this is divine, this is God! Hallelujah!

Seeing that these things are so, we must build in this order, for it is in this order that nothing can contaminate us. You are perfect over sin, if you will believe it. You are perfect over disease, if you will believe it. You are perfect over death, if you will believe it. You are perfect in the order of Enoch's translation, if you dare believe it.

There are always three things which are working silently but powerfully: the blade, the ear, the full coin in the ear. *God is developing us in a righteous line to know we are of a royal aristocracy. We belong to a new company. We belong to the firstborn. We have the nature of the Son. We belong to eternal workings.* God, who is greater than all, has come through all and is now working in all to His glory, to His power.

You may not be able to take these things in because you know so much about gravity, and I am speaking so much about gravity being removed. There is no gravity to the spirit. There is no gravity to thought. There is no gravity to inspiration. There is no gravity to divine union with Christ. It is above all. It rises higher. It sits on the throne. It claims its purposes.

God has brought us to a place where all manner of evil powers are subdued. Reigning over them, being enriched by the new creation of God in the Spirit, you are not timid and afraid; you meet these things with joy, you triumph over them in the place of blessing.

There are people in this place who are saying, "If I could talk to you, I should have to say so many things that I know are in me that are not in that."

You must allow the Lord to remove you out and bring you into the right place. Unbelief is the great dethroning place. Faith is the great rising place. Many people lose great confidence in the Spirit and cease to be going on to perfection because they allow their own minds and lives, their own knowledge, their own associations, to continually bring them into a deplorable, low estate.

God says you are not of this world. You have been delivered from the corruption of the world. You are being transformed by the renewing of your mind. God says that you are a royal priesthood, a holy people, belonging to the building, and Christ is the great cornerstone.

The Holy Spirit is coming forth to help you to claim your inheritance. Do not be afraid of getting rich this morning. Do not be afraid of coming in, but be very afraid if you do not come in. Have God's mind on this, that God says you have to overcome the world, that you have to have this incorruptible, undefiled position now within the human body, transforming your mind —even your very nature—realizing the supernatural power working through you.

It is lovely for me to be here speaking about this knowledge of this glorious incarnation of the Spirit, and I want you to know I would be the last man to speak about these things without I knew they can be attained to. This is our inheritance; this where God wants to make you His own in such a way that you will deny yourself, the flesh, and the world, that you may rule over principalities and powers and over spiritual wickedness in high places, so that you may reign in life by this lovely place in Christ Jesus.

I want to stir you up today. If I cannot make a diseased person that is suffering righteously indignant against that place, I cannot help him. If I can make every sufferer know that suffering, disease, and all these things are the workings of the devil, I can help him.

Let me give you a Scripture for it: *"The thief cometh not, but for to steal, and to kill, and to destroy"* (John 10:10). That is the devil. And if you know that, believe the other, that Jesus has come to give you life—live eternal and life abounding.

If you can see that the devil is after you, for all he is worth, to kill you, believe that Christ is enthroned in your heart to destroy the very principles of the devil in every way.

Have the reality of this; build upon it by perfect soundness till you are in the place of perfect bliss. For this is perfect bliss: to know Him. Be so built in Him that you be not afraid of that which comes on the line of all evil. You must have a fullness that presses out beyond. You must have a life which is full of divine. You must have a mind which is perfectly Christ. You must cease to be natural and begin to be supernatural.

God is on His throne and can take you a thousand miles in a moment. Have faith to jump into His supernatural plan.

Are you ready? "What for?" To be so changed by the order of God that you will never have this human order of fear anymore. Remember that *"perfect love casteth out fear"* (1 John 4:18).

Step into the full tide of the life of the manifestation of God. Your new nature has no corruption in it. Eternal life is not just during your lifetime; it is forever. You are regenerated by the power of the Word of God, and it is in you as an incorruptible force, taking you on from victory to victory till death itself can be overcome, till sin has no authority, till disease could not be in the body. This is a living fact by the Word of God.

> *You are regenerated by the power of the Word of God, and it is in you as an incorruptible force, taking you from victory to victory.*

You say, "How can I come into it?"

Read carefully the first two verses of Romans 8:

There is therefore now no condemnation to them which are in Christ Jesus, who walk not after the flesh, but after the Spirit. For the law of the Spirit of life in Christ Jesus hath made me free from the law of sin and death.

(Romans 8:1–2)

Right in this present moment, there is no condemnation. This law of the Spirit of life is a law in the body, it is a law of eternity, it is a law of God, a new law. Not the law of the Ten Commandments, but a law of life in the body, changing you in the body till there is no sin power, no disease power, and no death power.

Believe it! It doesn't matter if a thousand people die today. You believe you have to live forever. It does not matter how many people die after I have prayed for them; I am not going to change my order because I do not know what the order was with them. God speaks to me. And I have to believe His Word. His Word cannot change.

You who desire to go a thousand miles through faith, beyond what you have ever gone before, leap into it. Believe the blood makes you clean. Believe you have come into resurrection order. Believe you are young again. Why should you die? Believe you are young. He will renew thy youth (see Psalm 103:5). Believe it!

You say, "I will try, anyhow." All right, only "trying" is an effort. "Believing" is a fact. Don't join the endeavor society, but come into the faith society, and you will leap into the promises of God, which are yea and amen to all that believe. (See 2 Corinthians 1:20.)

Don't look down your nose and murmur anymore. Have a rejoicing spirit, get the praise of God in your heart, go forth from victory to victory, rise in faith, and believe it. You must not live in yourself. You must live in Christ. Set your mind upon things above. Keep your whole spirit alive in God. Let your inheritance be so full of life divine that you live above the world and all its thoughts and cares.

PRAYER

O Lord, move away disease, move away blind eyes, move away imperfect vision. Give the Word, let us understand the blood, let us understand the spirit of prophecy, of testimony. Let us understand, O God, that Thou art still building the foundation on the prophets and on the apostles and on all that worketh Thy wonderful Word.

So build us till every soul is filled with divine grace.

QUESTIONS AND ANSWERS:

Q: After the baptism of the Holy Spirit, you claim there is no shaking of the body?

A: I maintain that after anyone has received the Holy Ghost, there is no shaking and no falling on the ground. Shaking and falling on the ground is a very limitable position instead of unlimitable position. There may be a manifestation, but it is not to edification, and the manifestation you are to have is to be to edification. (See 1 Corinthians 14:12.)

If anybody were to stand up now and shake and shake till her hair came down, no one in the place would be edified and no people would want it. If the person knew it was not edification, he or she would seek a place which was better. What is it? Seek a gift.

I declare unto you that no man can shake and do all these things and speak in tongues. The Spirit has a way out, and no man, when giving interpretation, has these manifestations because the Holy Ghost has a way out, and you want to seek that you may excel and not be doing things that rather bring discord and discredit to your position.

Q: Is it true that tongues and interpretation are not for personal guidance at any time?

A: Tongues and interpretation are never for guidance. There is no such thing in the Scripture. Tongues and interpretation are on the line of prophecy to edify the church.

Q: If you do not receive the baptism of the Holy Spirit, will you be lost?

A: Certainly not. You are not saved by the Holy Ghost. You are saved by the Word of God and the blood.

Q: Can satanic influences come to us in thought, as well as in word, audibly?

A: Any number of people are troubled with thoughts. There are two classes of thoughts: there are evil thoughts and thoughts of evil. Evil thoughts are suggestive powers of the devil to see if he can raise in you any evil thought. If he can, it shows you have never been changed of your corruption and sin. If he cannot raise anything, it shows you are pure; the blood has cleansed you, and carnality is defeated. This is what Jesus meant when He said that when the devil comes, he finds nothing in you. (See John 14:30.)

The devil does not know your thought; he does not know the desire of your hearts; he does not know your language. So the devil always suggests in order to get something from you. If we would only realize that, we could come into meetings and bind this power so that he would have no chance at all. *"I give unto you power…over all the power of the enemy"* (Luke 10:19). We have a right to bind his power.

If a person is troubled at evil thoughts, he is safe; if he is not troubled, he is in danger.

If you are troubled with evil thoughts, test them and say, "Did Jesus come in the flesh?" (See 1 John 4:2.) That demon will go. You have a right to know these things, because they will keep you in a place of real victory. If you are not troubled at evil thoughts, you need to get to the penitent form and ask God to purify your hearts.

Until you voice anything on any line, the devil does not know it. You people have desired to have converts, you have desired to have a glorious time in your meetings, and you have voiced it. And then you have had to fight for life and death to get it. Why? Because all the adversary's power came. Why?

Because you declared it. They would not have known if you had not.

Q: Should you ask for inspirations of God in secret so that the devil cannot know?

A: No. Always pray aloud so the devil will clear out of the window. When Jesus said go in the closet and pray in secret, He did not mean to say that you are to pray silently. He meant you are to go in the closet and shout aloud. If you do not, you will find the devil will battle all around the ground, you will fall asleep, et cetera. Pray aloud.

> *Always pray aloud so the devil will clear out of the window.*

Q: If a person has made the mistake of declaring his position against the devil so that the forces of hell are arrayed against him, what will be effective in destroying Satan's power?

A: It is no mistake to declare yourself against the devil. There are two positions mixed here. You declare a thing such as this, "Now, we are going to have the biggest time on earth. Now, we will have a revival. Now we will have a fasting time," et cetera. You have proved that those will be difficult times, because Satan will assail himself against you. But he cannot dethrone you. He cannot hinder you, but he will do all he can to do it. He will hinder you from having the blessing sooner. If you are fighting the demon powers, there is not the same liberty as if there were no demon powers fighting you. Nevertheless, it is a good thing to have them to fight. Don't be afraid of demon powers, don't be afraid of being in temptation, because the Scriptures are clear: if you are not worthy to be tempted, you are no good.

Now, supposing I came in this meeting this morning and I said, "Jesus, in Thy name I bind the powers of darkness." That is finished; Satan won't come there. But if I declare such and such a thing without guarding myself, I shall have to fight to get it.

Q: Should anyone keep the seventh day Sabbath? Is it binding on the Christian?

A: Yes, anyone that is living under the law will have to keep it, but anybody that is living under grace keeps the Sabbath every day.

I do thank God for one thing that is very blessed to me, and that is I do not know the difference between Sunday and Monday. I simply see that every day is holy. But I do thank God that we have a Sabbath, because it gives people rest, and it gives us a better chance to get together for worship. So I thank God for the Christian Sabbath, and I reverence it.

Q: Are we not a stumbling block when we buy or sell on the Sabbath Day?

A: You eat, you walk, you do all kinds of things on the Sabbath that are natural. You will always be natural, but you have to have supernatural controlling power so that you do the things that please Him. And blessed is the man who is not condemned in that which he allows. So you may see; another person may not see. You have no right to judge another man who does not see.

Q: Is it as necessary to urge people to seek the baptism of the Holy Ghost as it is for salvation?

A: No, because the baptism of the Holy Ghost cannot come to anybody until they are saved, and a person could go to heaven without the baptism of the Holy Ghost. The thief did. You must understand, the most important thing today is getting people saved. But do not forget that after you are saved, you must seek that you get *"the promise of the Father"* (Acts 1:4).

Q: Is it possible we will ever be lost after having a real born-again experience?

A: Believe that Jesus said, *"My sheep...follow me"* (John 10:27), and if you follow Him, you will be right to the end.

Q: When the Lord gives an interpretation, does He give it to the interpreter while the tongues are being given or when the interpretation is given?

A: The interpretation is not known to the interpreter at the time the tongues are given. The interpreter speaks as the Spirit gives him unction. He does not know what he is going to say nor what he is saying. He speaks as the Spirit gives him liberty.

Interpretation is like tongues. You do not know what you are saying when you speak in tongues. You don't know what you are saying when you give interpretation. But you know what you have said.

Amending this answer, I want to say a very important thing. There are some people who are so full of the Holy Ghost that they feel inwardly moved and sometimes their whole bodies move. When you are full of the Holy Ghost, you may be moved in your body, and the gifts are manifested; and then the other subsides. Everybody who is filled with the Holy Ghost, we are glad for them to have great joy and many things, but we want you to excel to the edifying of the church.

THE RICHES OF HIS GLORY
Bible Study #14 – July 27, 1927

ay the Lord of Hosts so surround us with revelation and blessing till our bodies get to the place they can scarcely contain the joys of the Lord. Why not so rich a place of divine order that forever we shall know we are only the Lord's? What a blessed state of grace to be brought into, where we know that the body, the soul, the spirit are preserved blameless till the coming of the Lord! Jude takes us one step higher and says, "That you might be preserved faultless till the coming of the Lord." (See Jude 24.)

What a blessed state of grace!

When our hearts are moved to believe God, God is greatly desirous for us to have more of His presence.

We have only one purpose in view in these meetings, and that is to strengthen the people, to build you up in the most holy faith, to present you for every good work, that you should be faultless in Him, quickened by the might of the Spirit, that you might be prepared for everything that God has for you in the future. Our human nature may be brought to a place where it is so superabundantly attended to by God that in the body, we will know nothing but the Lord of Hosts.

To this end, I bring you to the banquet which cannot be exhausted, a supply beyond all human thought, an abundance beyond all human extravagances. No matter how you come into great faith and believing in God, God says, "Much more abundantly, much more." So I trust you will be moved to believe for more.

Are you ready? "What for?" That you might, by the power of God, be brought into His coffers with a new plan of righteousness, that you might be able as never before to leave the things behind you and press on toward the prize of the high calling. (See Jude 24.)

Are you ready? "What for?" That you might be so in God's plan that you may know that the good hand of God is upon you, that He has chosen you that you might be a firstfruits unto God.

Are you ready? "What for?" That the Lord shall have His choice, that His will and purpose shall be yours, that the "Amen" of His character may sweep through your very nature, and that you may know as you have never known before that this is the day of the visitation between you and Him.

The Lord has been speaking to me about this meeting, and I believe we are going to take just the Scripture that will be pleasing to Him: the third chapter of Ephesians.

I do thank God for this stupendous, glorious exit of human into divine. I do praise God for these studies, which are showing us the fullness of the pleasure of God.

It is the God of all grace who is bending over us with the fullness of recognition. He sees us; He knows us; He is acquainted with us. He is bending over us that His infinite pleasure—His glorious, exhaustless pleasure—may move us today. What can please Him more than to see His sons and daughters clothed, in their right mind, listening to His voice, their eyes and ears awake, coming into the treasury of the Most High?

For this cause I Paul, the prisoner of Jesus Christ for you Gentiles, if ye have heard of the dispensation of the grace of God which is given me to you-ward: how that by revelation he made known unto me the mystery...which in other ages was not made known unto the sons of men, as it is now revealed unto his holy apostles and prophets by the Spirit; that the Gentiles should be fellowheirs, and of the same body, and partakers of his promise in Christ by the gospel.
(Ephesians 3:1–3, 5–6)

Oh! That we might be so clothed upon by the ministry of His grace, so understand the mystery of His wonderful initiative, that we may comprehend today more than ever before why the Gentiles have been brought into the glories of His treasury to feed on the finest of the wheat, to drink at the riches of His pleasure, to be filled with the God of love that has no measure.

Without doubt, the greatest mystery of all time, from the commencement of creation to now, is Christ made manifest in human flesh. What can there be greater than eternal life working mightily through eternal death? What can there be greater than the nature—that which was formed with the vestige and appearance of Adam—being changed by a new nature, which has to be the fullness of the expression of the Father in heaven?

> *Without doubt, the greatest mystery of all time is Christ made manifest in human flesh.*

"As we have borne the image of the earthly, we shall also bear the image of the heavenly" (1 Corinthians 15:49). Everybody recognizes the Adam race, but may God today let us understand fullness, divine reflection, the very expression of the Father, in the glorious position that we may be so changed—the living manifestation of the

power of God so changing our vestige—till terrestrial will pass away, celestial will come, the brightness of His glory will press through all our humanity, till heaven has its exhibition which it never before could have, till all the saints are gathered and the very expression of the Master's face and the very glory of the Father be in us.

Interpretation of Tongues:

> *It is the life from heaven that changes that which could not be changed. Only the very expression of the nature of the God of all grace moving in our human faculties makes us know that we are begotten from above, changed by His power, transformed by His love, till we are not, for God has taken us.*

> *Be still, for the grace that has come upon thee is to so transform thy fashion and so beautify thy comeliness till right within thee there shall be the expression of the glory of God in the old creation, making the new creation just longing to depart.*

Oh, that the breath of heaven would move us today till we would feel, whatever happened, we must move on to get ready for exit!

The fullness of the expression of the Holy Ghost order today is giving us a glimpse into what has been provided by the Father.

We know that in the old Israel, from Abraham right down, God had a special position. I am speaking now not of the mixed company but of those of whom Jesus said, "Is not this a daughter of Abraham?" (See Luke 13:16.) Paul speaks about it, knowing that he belonged to that royal aristocracy of Abraham's seed.

But the Gentiles had no right to it. The Master said to the Syrophenician woman, "Shall I take the bread of the children and give it to dogs?" (See Mark 7:27.)

Did Jesus mean that the Gentiles were dogs? No, He did not mean that, but He meant that the whole race of the Gentiles knew that they were far below the standard and the order of those people that belonged to the royal stock of Israel. The Samaritans all felt it.

"But isn't it possible for dogs to have some crumbs?" was the woman's question. (See Mark 7:28.)

God has something better than crumbs. God has turned to the Gentiles and He has made us of the same body, the same heirs. He has put no difference between them and us, but He has joined us up in that blessed order of coming into the promise through the blood of Christ.

Thank God! He met the need of all nations, of all ranks, of all conditions. And God so manifests His power that He has brought us into oneness, and we know we are sharing in the glory. We are sharing in the inner expression. We are sharing that beautiful position where we know that we belong to aristocracy of the church of God.

I want to bring you into very blessed privileges in this order, for I want especially to deal with the knowledge of the inner working of that joint fellowship in this holy order with Christ, *"as it is now revealed unto his holy apostles and prophets by the Spirit"* (Ephesians 3:5).

I want you to see that this revelation was given by the power of the Spirit, and I want you to keep in mind that revelations are within the very body where Christ is manifested in the body. When Christ becomes the very personality of the fullness of the Father's will, then the Spirit—the effectual working of the power of God—has such glorious liberty in the body to unfold the mystery and the glories of the kingdom, for it is given to the Holy Ghost to reveal them as He reveals them all in Christ.

It is wonderful to know that I am in the body at all. It is wonderful to know that the apostles and prophets and all those men who have passed down the years—holding aloft the torch, going on from victory to victory—all will be in the body. But how wonderful if we may be in the body so that we might be chosen out of the body to be the bride! It will be according as you are yielded to the "*effectual working of his power*" (Ephesians 3:7).

The "*effectual working of his power*" means to say that it is always Godward. The Holy Ghost has no alternative; He is here to fulfill the great commission of the Executive of heaven. Therefore, He is in the body for one express purpose: to make us understand the fullness of the glories that are contained in that which is in us, which is Christ in us, not only the hope of the glory, but all the powers of the manifestation of the glory of the Christ to be revealed in us.

It is for us to know the mysteries which have been laid up for us; it is for us to know the glories which shall be revealed in Christ; it is for us to know all the fullness of the expression of His Godhead within us. It is for us to know that in this purposing of Christ's being in us, we have to be loosed from everything else, and He has to be manifesting and declaring to us, and we have to be subservient that He may reign, rule, have perfect authority, till in the body we are reigning over principalities and powers and every evil thing in the world.

The greatest mystery that has ever been known in the world or ever will be known is not only the body as a mystical presence, but it is to know the gospel which has within it a creative power which brings light, liberty, immortality, and life. It is not only that, but it is that after the seed—which is the life of the Son of God—has been put within you, Christ may be so formed in you that every revelation God has designed is for you, because of His divine power in the body.

After the revelation came, after God began speaking to Paul, he felt so unworthy of this that he said, "I feel the least of all saints" (see Ephesians 3:8). There is nothing but revelation will take you to humbleness; if ever it goes the other way, it is because you have never yet under any circumstances been brought to a death likeness with Christ.

All lifts, all summits, all glories, all revelation is in the death, when we are so dead to selfishness and self-desire, when we absolutely have been brought to the place of worthlessness, helplessness; then, in that place, the power of the Holy Ghost works mightily through us.

"*Less than the least of all saints*" (Ephesians 3:8). What a blessed state of grace! He did not assert himself in any way. It did not matter where he saw the saint; he said, "I am less worthy than that." Oh, what a submission! How the principle of Christ was working through him!

Jesus knew that He was cooperating, perfectly united; that there was not a thing between Him and His Father, so in perfect order; yet He made Himself of no reputation. He submitted Himself to the Father, and just in the submission of going down, down, down, even to the death of the cross, God said to Him, "Oh, My Son! You are worthy of ten thousand thrones. You are worthy of all I have, and I will give You a name above every name." (See Philippians 2:9.)

There is not a name like the name of Jesus. All through eternity, that name will swing through the great anthems when they bring all the singers and all the angels, and there will be one song above all, "*Unto him that loved us*" (Revelation 1:5).

May that make you the least of all saints, make you feel, "How can I submit myself to God that He shall have royal preeminence, that I will not refer to myself but that He shall be glorified?"

Isn't He lovely? And it pleased the Father to give Him the place. Nothing but humility will do it. Always be careful when you begin bouncing about, thinking you are somebody. More grace, more death. More life, more submission. More revelation, baseness.

Why? That the excellency of the power, of the light, of the glory may be exhibited. Not I, but another.

And thus it behooves Christ to fulfill all righteousness in our human bodies, that we may come to a place where we cease to be, for God's Son has to be royal; He has to be all in all.

> *All in all! All in all!*
> *Strength in time of weariness,*
> *A light where shadows fall;*
> *All in all! All in all!*
> *Jesus is my all in all.*

Christ wants to be glorified right in your mortal bodies, that there shall be a manifestation of this very revelation of Christ in you, the hope, the evidence of eternal glory.

For what purpose is the church formed together? That they should be in the great mystery.

Abraham, Isaac, Jacob, the twelve patriarchs laid wonderful store upon the promise of God, and there was no hope for us Gentiles at all. But they missed the opportunity. They might have gone on to have been the greatest miracle workers, the most profound teachers of the truth. They might have been everywhere, all over the world, bringing such glorious revivals, because they were entrusted to it. But they failed God.

A very few of the apostles—when there was no open door for the gospel, when their bodies were just filled with luminous light and the power of God pressing them right on—they felt sure that that inward power had not to be exploded at nothing, so God moved upon them to turn to the Gentiles. Then a special revelation was given to Paul that God had joined up all the Gentiles.

My daughter often speaks of the ebony that will be around the throne because of the Africans that will be there. The Chinese will look very lovely around the throne, too, and the Japanese. All nations, peoples, kindred, and tongues are to be in the great mystical body, all nationalities, all colors. What a blending of beauty in the glory when all races shall be filled with the glory, every one in their own nationality, and yet the express image of the Father! What a sight!

It is coming. It is already working in the body, and the body is feeling now that we are members in particular. In order that there shall be no schism in the body, the Holy Ghost must have a royal place, effectually working through your mind, through your will, through every member of your body—till every part of you, the Word of God says—till your whole body is sanctified for the purpose that He shall have preeminence. God in, mightily through, in all ways making manifestation in the human flesh. Christ in you!

You have got the vision of the body. Now I want you to get the vision of your personality in the body. There is no greater language than this about the Lord: that "all fullness dwells in Him" (see Colossians 1:19). Christ is to be a manifestation in humanity, with all fullness.

Do not be afraid of claiming your right. It is not a measure that you have come to. Remember, John saw Him, and he said that he had a measure which could not be measured. And He is coming to us with this measure that cannot be measured with human calculation.

Paul goes on to say this remarkable thing, that we may be able to have some revelation of the mightiness in its comprehension:

> *Unto me, who am less than the least of all saints, is this grace given, that I should preach among the Gentiles the unsearchable riches of Christ; and to make all men see what is the fellowship of the mystery, which from the beginning of the world hath been hid in God, who created all things by Jesus Christ....* (Ephesians 3:8–9)

"To the intent..." (Ephesians 3:10). God would have us to understand that those mighty words are to a certain intent. What is the intent?

> *To the intent that now unto the principalities and powers in heavenly places might be known by the church the manifold wisdom of God."* (Ephesians 3:10)

The church is rising in all her vision and destroying the powers of darkness, ruling among the powers of wickedness, transforming darkness to light by the power of the new creation in us, to the intent that we might know the power that is working in us by the power of the resurrection of the life of Christ.

So we are enriched with all enrichment, we are endued with all beatitudes, we are covered with all the graces, and now we are coming into all the mysteries, that the gifts of the Spirit may be so manifested in us that we might be a constancy of firstfruit.

People are always asking me what I belong to; it makes a lot of difference. They either have plenty of room for your company or not. It all depends where you belong. So I always say, and they do not seem to understand it, "I will give you my credentials; they are right here. I put them down so I would always have them ready. T.S.E.W.S.A."

"Oh! We never knew there were a people that had such credentials. What are they?"

"The Sect Everywhere Spoken Against."

Glory to God! To the intent that this sect everywhere spoken against might be visionized by an institute of glorious authority. Christ in us is mightier than death, mightier than sin, triumphing over principalities and powers.

Christ in us is mightier than death, mightier than sin, triumphing over principalities and powers.

Some people keep saying to me, "Do you believe in eternal security?"

Surely I do.

Do you believe if you are saved once you will be saved forever?

He'll never forget to keep me!
He'll never forget to keep me!
My Father has many dear children,
But He'll never forget to keep me.

There can be within you a mighty moving of this intent purpose, of this habitual, divine activity of Christ being manifested in you, which was the revelation of Paul.

The second revelation of Paul, which never from the foundation of the world had been revealed, is that the Son of God—the very embodiment of the nature of the Most High, the very incarnation of His presence and power—could fill a human vessel to its utmost capacity, till the very nature of Him shall sweep through by the power of God in the body.

You cannot enter into this without being enlarged, abounding, superabundant. Everything in God is enlargement. God never wants a child of His in the world to be measured. You cannot measure your place. You might measure your land, you might measure your corn, but you cannot measure the purposes of the Spirit life. They are boundless. They are infinite. The riches of God are infinite, boundless. There is no such thing as measuring them. If ever you measure God, you will be thin and little and dwarfed. You cannot measure. You have an exhaustless place.

God's Son is in you, with all the power of development, till you shall be so enriched by this grace divine, till you live in the world knowing that God is transforming you from grace to grace, from victory to victory. The Spirit in you has no other ultimate than from glory unto glory.

Paul was so enlarged in the Spirit in this third chapter of Ephesians that his language failed to go on. And then, when he failed to go on in his language, he bowed his knees unto the Father. Oh, this is supreme! This is beyond all that could be! When language failed, when prophecy had no more room, it seems that he came to a place that he got down on his knees. Then, we hear, by the power of the Spirit, language beyond all ever Paul could say.

> *For this cause I bow my knees unto the Father of our Lord Jesus Christ, of whom the whole family in heaven and earth is named.* (Ephesians 3:14–15)

He realized that he was joining earth and heaven together. They are one, thank God! There is nothing between us and heaven. Gravity may hold us, but all in heaven and in earth are joined under one blood—no division, no separation. *"Absent from the body…to be present with the Lord"* (2 Corinthians 5:8).

God has here something for us in the language of the Holy Ghost which He wants to enlarge our hearts and take a breath of heaven. Let your whole soul waft out unto God, dare breathe heaven, dare be awakened to all God's mind. Listen to the language of the Holy Ghost. Paul is praying in the Spirit:

That he would grant you, according to the riches of his glory, to be strengthened with might by his Spirit in the inner man; that Christ may dwell in your hearts by faith; that ye, being rooted and grounded in love, may be able to comprehend with all saints what is the breadth, and length, and depth, and height; and to know the love of Christ, which passeth knowledge, that ye might be filled with all the fulness of God. Now unto him that is able to do exceeding abundantly above all that we ask or think, according to the power that worketh in us, unto him be glory in the church by Christ Jesus throughout all ages, world without end. Amen.

(Ephesians 3:16–21)

This is the Gentile's inhabitation. This is the Gentile's position. This is the body that is being joined up, this mystical body which has come into a fullness beyond all expectations.

You cannot expect the fullness that He has waiting for you. If you cannot think it, then I am sure you cannot expect it.

The Holy Ghost takes these things and brings them before us this morning and says, "To the intent that this wonderful divine appointment shall be ours."

How may I get nearer God? How may I be in the place of helplessness in my own place and dependent on God? I see a tide rising. *"Blessed are the poor in spirit: for theirs is the kingdom of heaven"* (Matthew 5:3). God is making us very poor, but we are rich in it because our hands are stretched out towards God in this holy day of His visitation to our hearts.

Believe that He is in you. Believe that He is almightiness. Believe that He is all fullness. Then let yourself go till He is on the throne. Let everything submit itself to the throne and the

King. Yield yourself unto Him in so sublime position that He is in perfect order over everything. Let God have His perfect way through you.

If you will let go, God will take hold and keep you up.

Oh, to seek only the will of God, to be only in the purpose of God, to seek only that God shall be glorified, not I! What a word we get over and over in our hearts: "Not I, but Christ."

How did it come? It came when he was less than the least of all saints. The effectual working of the power when he was less than the least of all saints buoyed him on till God was manifest in that mortal flesh, for surely Paul reached fidelity of access into all the fullness of that mighty God in extravagances.

I believe God wants to send you away filled with the Spirit. Oh, beloved, are you ready? What to do? To say, "Father, have Your way. Do not let my human will spoil Your divine plan, Father. So take charge of me today that I will be wholly, entirely on the altar for Thy service." And I am sure He will meet us in this.

WORKERS TOGETHER WITH GOD
Bible Study #15 – July 28, 1927

Interpretation of Tongues:

God has come to visit us and He has revealed Himself unto us, but He wants you to be so ready that nothing that He says will miss. He wants to build you on the foundation truth.

Are you ready this morning? "What for?" Because God has something better than yesterday. Higher ground, holier thoughts, more concentrated, clearer ministry. God wants us every day to be in a rising tide. It is a changing of faith. It is an attitude of the spirit. It is where God rises higher and higher.

God wants us to come into the place where we will never look back. God has no room for the man that looks back, thinks back, or turns back.

The Holy Ghost wants to get you ready for stretching yourself out to God and believing that He is a rewarder of them that diligently seek Him. You need not use vain repetition. Ask and believe.

> *God wants us to come into the place where we will never look back.*

People come with their needs; they ask; they go away still with their needs because they do not faithfully wait to receive what God has promised them. If they ask, they will get it.

Many people are missing the highest order. I went to a person who was full of the Spirit, but was all the time saying, "Glory! Glory! Glory!"

I said, "You are full of the Holy Ghost, but the Spirit cannot speak because you continually speak." He kept still then, and the Spirit began speaking through him. We are altogether in the way of God. Do more believing and less begging.

I want so to change your operation in God till you will know that God is operating through you for this time and forevermore. May the Spirit awake us to deep things today.

Are you ready? "What for?" That you may move and be moved by the mighty power of God that cannot be moved, and so chastened and built up till you are in the place, it doesn't matter where the wind blows or difficulty comes, you are fixed in God.

Are you ready? "What for?" To come into the plan of the Most High God, believing what the Scripture says, and holding fast that which is good, believing so that no man shall take your crown.

THE WORD CHANGES THE BELIEVER

God can so change us by His Word that we are altogether different day by day. David knew this. He said, "*Thy word hath quickened me*" (Psalm 119:50). "He sent his word and healed me." (See Psalm 107:20.) How beautiful that God can make His Word abound! "*Thy word have I hid in my heart, that I might not sin against thee*" (Psalm 119:11).

It is absolutely infidelity and unbelief to pray about anything in the Word of God. The Word of God has not to be prayed about; the Word of God has to be received. If you will receive the Word of God, you will always be in a big place. If you pray about the Word of God, the devil will be behind the whole thing. Never pray about anything which is "thus saith the Lord." It has to be yours to build you on a new foundation of truth.

I want to turn your attention now to the sixth chapter of 2 Corinthians. This is a summit position for us, although there are many ground lines to be examined to see if we are rising to the summit of these glorious experiences. This is also groundwork for deep heart searching. This is divine revelation of the spiritual character to us. The writer must have been immersed in this holy place.

If you turn to the first verse of Romans 12, you will see that the speaker is operated by an operation. He has been mightily under the operation on more than a surgical table. He has been cut to the very depths till he has reached a place absolutely on the altar of full surrender. And out of the depths of it, when he has got there, now he is giving his whole life, as it were, in a nutshell.

I beseech you, therefore, brethren, by the mercies of God, that ye present your bodies a living sacrifice, holy, acceptable unto God, which is your reasonable service.

(Romans 12:1)

Here in this sixth chapter of 2 Corinthians, we have, again, a beautiful word which ought to bring us to a very great place of hearing by the hearing of faith: "*We then, as workers together with him…*" (2 Corinthians 6:1).

It is a collective thought. It is preaching to the whole church in Christ Jesus. Paul has the Corinthians in his mind because the Corinthian church was the first church amongst the Gentiles, and he was the apostle to the Gentiles.

Receive Not God's Grace in Vain

"*We then, as workers together with him, beseech you also that ye receive not the grace of God in vain*" (2 Corinthians 6:1). This is one of the mightiest words there is in the Scripture. People are getting blessed all the time, having revelation, and they go from one point to another but do not establish themselves in that thing which God has brought to them.

If you do not let your heart be examined when the Lord comes with blessing or correction, if you do not make it a stepping stone, if you do not make it a rising place, then you are receiving the grace of God in vain. People could be built far greater in the Lord and be more wonderfully established if they would move out sometimes and think over the graces of the Lord.

Grace is to be multiplied on conditions. How? In the first chapter of 2 Timothy, we have these words: "*the unfeigned faith that is in thee*" (2 Timothy 1:5). Everyone in this place, the whole church of God, has the same like precious faith within him. And if you allow this like precious faith to be foremost, utmost on everything, you will find that grace and peace are multiplied.

Just the same, the Lord comes to us with His mercy, and if we do not see that the God of grace and mercy is opening to us the door of mercy and utterances, we are receiving it in vain.

I thank God for every meeting. I thank God for every blessing. I thank God every time a person says to me, "God bless you, brother!" I say, "Thank you, brother. The Lord bless you!" I see it is a very great place to have people desirous that we shall be blessed.

If we want strength in building in our spiritual character, we should never forget the blessings. When you are in prayer, remember how near you are to the Lord. It is a time that God wants you to change strength there, and He wants you to remember He is with you.

When you open the sacred pages and the light comes right through and you say, "Oh, isn't that wonderful!" thank God, for it is the grace of God that has opened your understanding.

When you come to a meeting like this, the revelation comes forth, and you feel this is what you wanted, receive it as the grace of the Lord. God has brought you to a place where He might make you a greater blessing.

CONSTANT SALVATION

> *For he saith, I have heard thee in a time accepted, and in the day of salvation have I succoured thee: behold, now is the accepted time; behold, now is the day of salvation.*
>
> (2 Corinthians 6:2)

Two processes of salvation: He succored you when the Spirit was moving you and when the adversary was against you, when your neighbors and friends wished it not to be and when everybody rose up in accusation against you. When you know there were fightings without and fightings within, He succored you. He coveted you till you came into salvation. And then He keeps you in the plan of His salvation.

This is the day of salvation. Being saved does not mean to say that you were not saved, but that you are being continually changed in the process of regeneration, being made like unto God, being brought into the operation of the Spirit's power, being made like unto Him.

This is the day of salvation. He has succored thee in a time when Satan would destroy thee, and He is with thee now.

This is the day of salvation. If we remain stationary, God has nothing for us. Everybody must see that they must be in progress. Yesterday will not do for today. I must thank God for yesterday. Tomorrow is what I am today.

Today: inspiration, divine intuition, where God is ravishing the heart, breaking forth all shorelines, getting my heart only responsive to His cry, where I live and move honoring and glorifying God in the Spirit. This is the day of visitation of the Lord. This is the great day of salvation, being moved on, into, for God.

Interpretation of Tongues:

> It is the Lord. Let Him do what seemeth Him well. It may be death, but He has life in the midst of death.
>
> We will praise and magnify the Lord, for He is worthy to be praised!

He has succored us, and now He is building us. Now He is changing us. Now we are in the operation of the Holy Ghost. You must every day make higher ground. You must deny yourself to get on with God. You must refuse everything that is not pure and holy and separate. God wants you pure in heart. He wants your intense desire after holiness. *"Seek ye first the kingdom of God, and his righteousness; and all these things shall be added unto you"* (Matthew 6:33).

In Perfect Harmony

> Giving no offence in any thing, that the ministry be not blamed.   (2 Corinthians 6:3)

That is lovely! Oh! The church can be built God will break down opposing things.

If you people in Angelus Temple are in a place where you would rather see one person saved here than two people saved at Bethel Temple, then you are altogether wrong and you need to be saved. If there is anybody here from Bethel Temple, if you would rather see one person saved in your temple than two people saved in Angelus Temple, then you are still out of order of the Spirit of the line of God, and you are strangers to real holy life with God.

If your ministry is not to be blamed, how will it not be blamed? You have to live in love. See to it there is never anything comes out of your lips or by your acts that will interfere with the work of the Lord, but rather live in the place where you are helping everybody, lifting everybody, and causing everybody to come into perfect harmony. For remember, there is always a blessing where there is harmony. "One accord" is the keynote of the victory that is going to come to us all the time.

There are thousands and thousands of different churches, but they are all one in the Spirit, just in the measure as they receive the life of Christ. If there is any division, it is always outside the Spirit. The spiritual life in the believer never has known dissension or break, because where the Spirit has perfect liberty, then they all agree and there is no schism in the body.

"*The letter killeth, but the spirit giveth life*" (2 Corinthians 3:6). When there is division, it is only because they take the letter instead of the Spirit. If we are in the Spirit, then we shall have life; if we are in the Spirit, we shall love everybody. If we are in the Spirit, there will be no division. There will be perfect harmony. God wants to show us that we must so live in the Spirit that the ministry is not blamed.

If we are in the Spirit, there will be no division. There will be perfect harmony.

It is a wonderful ministry God has given to us because it is a life ministry. Pentecostal positions are spiritual positions. We recognize the Holy Ghost, but we recognize first the Spirit quickening us, saving us from every rudiment of evil power, transforming our human nature till it is in divine order. Then, in that divine order, we see that the Lord of Hosts can be very beautifully arranging the life till we live in the Spirit and are not fulfilling the lusts of flesh.

Interpretation of Tongues:

> Let not thy goodness be evil spoken of, but so live in the spiritual life with Christ that He is being glorified over thy body, thy soul, and thy spirit, till thy very life becomes emblematic and God reigns over thee in love and peace.

I like that because I see that when the Holy Ghost has perfect charge, He lifts and lightens and unveils the truth in a new way till we grip it.

Oh! What it would be if every one of us would go away this morning with this word in our hearts: "Let not your goodness be evil spoken of." I know we all want to be good. It is not a wrong thing to desire that our goodness shall be appreciated. But we must watch ourselves because it is an evil day (although it is the day of salvation), and we must understand these days that the Lord wants to chasten and bring a people right into a full-tide position.

I believe that it is possible for God to sweep a company right into the glory before the rapture just as well as at the rapture. It is possible for you to be taken if others are left. May God grant unto us a very keen inward discerning of our hearts' purity. We want to go. It is far better for us to go. But it is far better for the church that we stay.

If you comprehend the truth of this word, which Paul realized was true—"it is far better for me to go" (see 1 Corinthians

9:15)—you will never take a pill nor use a plaster. You would never do anything to save you from going if you believed it was better to go. There is a definite, inward motion of the power of God for the human life to so change it till we would not lift a finger, believing it was far better to go.

Then, there is another side to it. Believing that God has us for the proclamation of the gospel, for the building of the church, we would say, "Lord, for the purpose of being a blessing further for Thy sake, and for the sake of the church, just keep us full of life to stay."

We would not be full of disease, but we would be full of life.

So the Lord grant unto us this morning a living faith to believe.

In Affliction for the Church

But in all things approving ourselves as the ministers of God,
in much patience, in afflictions, in necessities, in distresses.
(2 Corinthians 6:4)

Now, these afflictions are not the afflictions of the disease class. Paul is very definite on these lines. He suffered afflictions with the people; Jesus suffered afflictions with the people. There can be many afflictions within our human frame on the line of feeling; the association of our spiritual acquaintance is not ripening in the life of others.

You have to so live in the Spirit that when you see the church not rising into its glory, you have affliction for the church. You are sorry and deeply distressed because the church is not capturing the vision, and there is affliction in your sorrow.

God would have us so spiritual that we could have perfect discernment of the spirit of the people. If I can in a moment discern the spirit, whether it is quickening, whether the whole church is receiving it, whether my heart is moved by this power, then I can see the declination of positions, I can see the waning of positions, and I can see faith waning, and that will cause affliction and trouble to my life.

May God give us to realize that we are so joined to the church that we may labor to bring the church up. Paul said he travailed as in birth for people to be formed again. (See Galatians 4:19.) It was not to be saved again. But they had missed apprehension. They had missed fellowship of divine order, so he labored again that they might be brought into this deep fellowship in the Spirit.

God help us to see that we can travail for the church. Blessed is the person who can weep between the door and the altar. Blessed are the people of God that can take Angelus Temple on their hearts and weep behind, crying through till the church is formed again, till she rises in glory, till the power of heaven is over her, till the spiritual acquaintance rises higher and higher, till the song lifts them to the heights.

This is the order of the church of God. The ministry should not blamed, but rather seek a higher height, a glorious truth, a blessed fidelity, higher and higher.

"Possess Your Soul in Peace"

"In much patience…" (2 Corinthians 6:4). There is a word which needs to be in these days. I know I am speaking to people who have churches and who have a lot to do in churches. Remember this: *You never lose so much as when you lose your peace.* If the people see that you have lost your groundwork of peace, they know you have got outside of the position of victory. You have to possess your soul in peace.

Strange things will happen in the church, things will look as though they were all contrary, and you will feel that the enemy is busy. At that time, possess your soul in peace. Let the people know that you have acquaintance with One who, when He was reviled, reviled not again.

Let your patience be so possessed that you can suffer anything for the church or for your friends or for your neighbors, or anyone. Remember this: we build character in others as our character is built. Just as we are pure in our thought, tender and gracious to other people, and possess our souls in patience, then the people have great desire for our fellowship in the Holy Ghost.

Now Jesus was emblematic of that line. They saw Him undisturbed. I love to think about Him. He helps me so much because He is the very essence of help.

GIVE NOT OFFENSE NOR CAUSE DISTRESS

"In necessities and distresses" (see 2 Corinthians 6:4). This means spiritual distresses because of acquaintance with the church. It is the church we are dealing with here. Paul is in a place where he is breathing forth by divine appointment to the church.

The purpose of these meetings is to gather the church together in fidelity lines, because if five people could save Sodom and Gomorrah, five holy people in a church can hold the power of the Spirit till Light shall reign. *We do not want to seek to save ourselves, but lose ourselves that we may save the church.* You cannot help distresses coming. They will come, and offenses will come, but woe unto those that cause offenses. See that you do not cause offense. See that you live in a higher tide. See that your tongue cannot move.

I wonder if you have ever seen the picture in the twenty-sixth chapter of Matthew, "*Lord, is it I?*" (Matthew 26:22). Every one of them was so conscious of his human weaknesses that not a single one of them had a place where he could say that it would not be he.

"One of you shall betray me" (Matthew 26:21), Jesus said.

John was leaning on the breast of the Lord, and Peter beckoned to him and said, "Please get to know who it will be" (see John 13:24). He knew if anybody could get to know, it would be John.

How long do you think Jesus had known? He had known at least for three years. He had been with them in the room, He had been feeding them, He had been walking up and down with them, and He had never told any of them it was Judas.

> *The church that follows Jesus should be so sober, sober to a sensitiveness that they would not speak against another, whether it was true or not.*

The church that follows Jesus should be so sober, sober to a sensitiveness that they would not speak against another, whether it was true or not.

Jesus is the great personality. I have in every way to listen and also to be provoked by His holy inward generosity and purity, and also His acquaintance with love.

What would it have done? If He had told them, everyone would have been bitter against Judas. So He saved all His disciples from being bitter against Judas for three years.

What love! Can't you see that holy, divine Savior? Every one of us today would throw ourselves at His feet. If we had a crown worth millions, we would say, "You are worthy." O God, give us such a holy, intense, divine acquaintance that we would rather die than grieve Thee! Oh, for an inward savor that shall make us say, "A thousand deaths rather than sinning once." O Jesus, we worship Thee! Thou art worthy!

Interpretation of Tongues:

> *Into the very depths have I gone to succor thee. And in the very depths I called thee My own, and I delivered thee when thou wast oppressed and in oppression, and I brought thee out when thou wert sure to sink below the waves, and I lifted thee and brought thee into the banqueting house.*

It is the mercy of the Lord. It is the love of the Lord. It is the grace of the Lord. It is the Spirit of the Lord. It is the will of the Lord.

Be ready. Be alert for God. Live in the Holy Ghost. Oh, I can understand, "I would that ye all spake in tongues, but rather that ye prophesy except we have interpretation." I pray God that we may learn the lesson how to keep ourselves so that the Spirit shall blend and the harmony shall be beautiful. There is not a person in the place but is feeling the breath of the Almighty breathing over us. This is one of those moments when the Spirit is coming to us and saying, "Don't forget— this is the receiving of the grace of God." You are not to go away and forget. You are to go away and be what God intends you to be.

APPREHENDED IN SWEDEN

> *In stripes, in imprisonments, in tumults, in labours, in watchings, in fastings...*   (2 Corinthians 6:5)

How those first apostles did suffer. And how we together with them do suffer.

Sweden is a most remarkable place in many ways. When I was in Sweden, the power of God was upon me, and it was there that I was apprehended for preaching these wonderful truths, talking about the deep things of God, seeing people healed on every line.

The Lutheran churches, yes, and the doctors rose up like an army against me and had special meetings with the king to try to get me out of the country. And, at last, they succeeded; it was in Sweden that I was escorted out with two detectives and two policemen, because of the mighty powers of God moving amongst the people in Stockholm. But beloved, it was very lovely!

One of the nurses in the king's household came, and she was healed of a leg trouble—I forget whether a broken thigh or a dislocated joint. She went to the king, and she said, "I have been so wonderfully healed by this man. You know I am walking all right now."

"Yes," he said, "I know everything about him. I know all about him. Tell him to go. I do not want him turned out. If he goes out, he can come back; but if he is turned out, he cannot come back."

I thank God I was not turned out; I was escorted out.

They went to see the policemen to see if I could have a big meeting in the park on the Whitsen Tide. Monday, the policemen joined together, and they said, "There is only one reason that we could refuse him, and it is on this line: if that man puts his hands upon the sick in the great park, it would take thirty more policemen to guard the situation. But if he will promise us that he will not lay his hands upon the people, then we will allow you to have the park."

They came and asked me, and I said, "Promise them I know God is not subject to my laying hands upon the people. When the presence of the Lord is there to heal, it does not require hands. Faith is the great operation position. When we believe God, all things are easy."

So they built places where I could speak to thousands of people.

I prayed, "Lord, You know You have never been yet in any place fixed. You have the mind of all things. Show me how it can be done today without the people having hands laid upon them. Show me."

To the people, I said, "All of you that would like the power of God going through you today, healing everything, put your hands up."

There was a great crowd of hands; thousands of hands went up.

"Lord, show me."

And He told me as clearly as anything to pick a person out that stood upon a rock—it was a very rocky place. So I told them all to put their hands down but this person. To her, I said, "Tell all the people what are your troubles."

She began to relate her troubles. From her head to her feet, she was so in pain that she felt if she did not sit down or lie down, she would never be able to go on.

"Lift your hands high," I said. Then, "In the name of Jesus, I rebuke from your head to your feet the evil one, and I believe He has loosed you."

Oh, how she danced and how she jumped and how she shouted!

That was the first time that God revealed to me it could be done. We had hundreds healed without touching them, and hundreds saved without touching. Our God is a God of mighty power. Oh, how wonderful, how glorious, and how fascinating it is that we can come into a royal place! This is a royal place. We have a great God. We have a wonderful Jesus. I believe in the Holy Ghost.

IN PRISON IN SWITZERLAND

"*In imprisonments…*" (2 Corinthians 6:5). In Switzerland, I have been put into prison twice for this wonderful work. But, praise God, I was brought out all right!

The officers said to me, "We find no fault. We are so pleased. We have found no fault because you are such a great blessing to us in Switzerland."

And in the middle of the night, they said, "You can go."

I said, "No, I will only go on one condition. That is that every officer there is in the place gets down on his knees and I pray with all of you."

Glory to God!

A HIGH TIDE

Are you ready? "What for?" To *believe* the Scriptures. That is necessary. The Scripture is our foundation to build upon properly. Christ is the cornerstone. We are all in the building.

Oh! If I could let you see that wonderful city coming down out of heaven, millions, trillions beyond countless numbers, a city coming down out of heaven to be married, millions, trillions of people making the city.

Get ready for that. Claim your rights in God's order this morning. Do not give way. If you hear any spiritual breathing from anyone, believe that is your order. If you see Christ, believe He was your firstfruit. If you see Paul by the Holy Ghost penetrating your divine position, believe it is yours.

Have faith in God. Believe the Scripture is for you. If you want a high tide rising in the power of God, say, "Give me, Lord, that which I shall be, short in nothing." Have a real faith. Believe that love covers you, His life flows through you, His quickening Spirit lifts you.

PRAYER

O God, take these people into Thy great pavilion. Lead them, direct them, preserve them, strengthen them, uphold them by Thy mighty power. Let the peace that passeth understanding, the joy of the Lord, the comfort of the Holy Ghost be with them. Amen.

QUESTIONS AND ANSWERS

Q: In Ephesians 6:12, does "wrestling" mean wrestling in prayer? "For we wrestle not against flesh and blood, but against principalities," et cetera.

A: According to 2 Corinthians 10:5, we are able to smite the enemy and bring every thought into perfect obedience to the law of Christ: *"Casting down imaginations, and every high thing that exalteth itself against the knowledge of God, and bringing into captivity every thought to the obedience of Christ."*

Now, is that through prayer, or how? It is quite clear to me that faith inspires you to pray, but faith will command you to command. And if you are in the place of real faith, when these things come up against you, you will say, "Get thee behind me" (see Matthew 16:23), no matter what it is.

Prayer is without accomplishment unless it is accompanied by faith. Jude says we can pray in the Holy Ghost. Be sure you are filled with the Spirit; that you do not pray but another prays. Be sure you are filled with the life of Christ till faith rises, claims, destroys, and brings down

> *Be sure you are filled with the life of Christ till faith rises, claims, destroys, and brings down imagination and everything that opposes Christ.*

imagination and everything that opposes Christ. Faith and prayer, an act, a command.

Q: Which is the right way to baptize: in the name of Jesus, or the Father, Son, and Holy Ghost?

A: Always do that which causes no contention and no split. Water baptism in the name of Jesus causes more trouble than anything else, and you should never have trouble in the church; you should be at peace. The Lord said it was to be in the name of the Father, Son, and Holy Ghost, and when we keep in the right order, as He said, then there is no schism in the body.

When you go on your own line and strike out a new cord, you cause dissension and trouble. This thing has caused more trouble than anything because it has not been satisfied to go there. It has gone further and said that Jesus is the Father, Jesus is the Son, and Jesus is the Holy Ghost. If you do not keep on the right line—keeping the words where Jesus was—you will be tippled over in awful distress and darkness. Keep on the high line.

Q: What should be our attitude toward the coming of the Lord? Should we be enjoying His personal presence now, disregarding the time of His coming? Or, should we wait and anticipate His coming?

A: Do what Peter did. He hastened to the coming, and he left everything behind him to catch the gleam of it. You have to keep your mind upon it, looking unto and hastening it. It is a joy to the church; it is *"that blessed hope"* (Titus 2:13). It is that glorious appearing. And it will save you from any amount of things, for he that looks for that purifieth himself.

Q: Does a person have to go to school in order to save souls?

A: I think you will save more souls out of the school. What you have got to do is to understand that soul-saving work is never made in schools. Soul-saving work is the regenerative of the spirit, of the life, to make you eaten up with the zeal of the Lord. Soul saving is the best thing. It is the sure place, it is the right place, and I hope we are doing it when He comes.

Q: Is the Spirit of God within the individual that is born again? I have always thought so from the eighth chapter of Romans.

A: If you will rightly consider the truth and keep it before you, it will save you from any amount of error. The epistles are for people who are baptized in the Holy Ghost, baptized believers.

When you say, "Except you have the Spirit of Christ, you are none of His" (see Romans 8:9), You will find that is a perfect word right in the epistles. The new birth has within it the Spirit of Jesus, and it has the word also, "My word is spirit and life" (see John 6:63). It is not the Holy Spirit; it is the Spirit of Jesus.

The Holy Spirit is that which comes after, and is with you all the time. He was with you in revelation of conviction, but when you were filled, He came inside. And after He comes inside, it is so much different from being outside.

Q: Did Jesus think it not robbery to be equal with God? What did He mean by saying that?

A: It meant He was equal in power, equal in authority, equal in the glory. He was perfectly one, and what His Father was, He was, perfectly joined. Yet in order for perfect obedience, that all the people should learn obedience, He left the glory, left everything behind, to save us. He had as much right to stop and say, "Father, You go," but He was willing to go and left the glory, although He had the right to stop.

Q: If a contract were entered into by two people and broken by one party, should that be collected by law by the other party?

A: Yes, if you lived in the law. But if you lived in the Spirit, then you would not go to law with your brother. It depends upon whether you live in law or live in grace. If you live in grace, you will never go into law.

I thank God that I was in business for twenty-five years and might have picked up a lot of money, but it is still left there because I would not go to law. I do not believe in it.

But I am not a law to you people. I tell you what law is, and I tell you what grace is.

Q: What is the seal put upon God's people?

A: The seal is the Holy Spirit. It is different from anything else. It is upon you, and the devil knows it. All the evil powers of the earth know it. You are sealed with that Holy Spirit of promise till the day of redemption. You are also baptized in the same Spirit, and that is in the epistles. But don't forget that you get a great deal in your salvation, in the new birth. Press on and get sealed with the Spirit.

All they which are in Christ will be caught up at His coming. The twenty-second chapter of Luke distinctly says that Jesus would not sit down again to break bread till the kingdom had come. Now the kingdom is in every believer, and He will not sit down till every believer is there. The kingdom is in the believer, and the kingdom will come and millions of people, I am sure, will be there who never received the Holy Ghost. But they had the life of the Christ inside. When He comes who is our life—it is not the Holy Ghost who is the life; Christ is the life—when He comes who is our life, then shall we go to the Life.

Q: Is it every Christian's privilege to have his eyes so preserved that he need never wear glasses?

A: One thing will take place with every person here. There are any number of people who have been praying ever since they were ten years old, and if praying and the life within them could have altered the situation, it would have been altered. But I see they are here today with gray hair, and white hair, meaning that the natural man decays, and you cannot do what you like with it. But the supernatural man may so abound in the natural man that it never decays. It can be replaced by divine life.

There comes a time in life, at fifty or so, when all eyes, without exception, begin to be dim. But why? What kind of dimness? If we were living in the time of Moses, we should not require glasses, and we should have as good eyesight as he had. How do you know? Because those tables of stone that he carried were written on so that he could see or anybody else could see without glasses.

It doesn't mean to say that your eyes are any worse than were Moses'. It means to say that the natural man has had a change. I believe and affirm that the supernatural power can be so ministered to us that even our eyesight can be preserved right through. But I say this: any person is a fool that professes to have faith and then gets a big printed Bible so that he will not need glasses; it presents a false position before the people. What he has got to see is that if he will carry a Bible about in his hand which, as the whole of the Bible in very short space, his eyesight may require either some help, or he may not be able to read correctly.

I have been preaching faith to our people for thirty years. When my daughter came back from Africa and saw her mother and myself with glasses, she was amazed. When our people saw us put glasses on the first time, they were very much troubled. They were no more troubled than we were. But I found it was far better to be honest with the people and acknowledge my place than get a Bible that was right big print and deceive the people and say that my eyesight was all right. I like to be true.

My eyesight gave way at about fifty-three, and somehow God is doing something. I am now sixty-eight, and I do not want any kind of glasses different, and I am satisfied. God is restoring me.

When I was seeking this way of divine healing, I was stumbled because all the people that had such testimony of divine healing were wearing glasses. I said, "I cannot go on with this thing. I am stumbled every time I see the people preaching divine healing wearing glasses." And I got such a bitterness in my spirit that God had to settle me on that line—and I believe yet that I have not fully paid the price.

My eyes will be restored, but until then, I will not deceive anybody. I will use glasses till I can perfectly see.

A woman came up to me one day and I noticed she had no teeth.

"Why," I said, "your mouth is very uneven. Your gums have dropped in some places, and the old gums are very uneven."

"Yes," she said, "I am trusting the Lord for a new set of teeth."

"That is very good," I said. "How long have you been trusting Him for them?"

"Three years."

"Look here," I said, "I would be like Gideon: I would put the fleece out, and I would tell the Lord that I would trust Him to send me teeth in ten days or money to buy a set in ten days, and whichever came first I would believe it was He."

In eight days, fifty dollars came to her from a person whom she had never been acquainted with in any way, and it bought her a beautiful set of teeth—and she looked well in them.

A person is prayed for eyesight, and as soon as he is prayed for, he believes, and God stimulates his faith, but his eyesight is about the same. "What shall I do?" he asks. "Shall I go away without my glasses?"

"Can you see perfectly?" I ask. "Do you require any help?"

"Yes. If I should go as I go now, I would stumble."

"Put your glasses on," I say. "For when your faith is perfected, you will not require any glasses, and when God perfects your faith, your glasses will drop off. But as long as you have need, use them."

You can take that for what you like, but I believe in common sense.

SECOND CORINTHIANS 3
Bible Study #16 – July 19, 1927

All thoughts of holiness are God's. All manner of loving-kindness and tender mercies are His. All weaknesses are made for us that we might be in that place of absolute helplessness, for when we are weak, then we are strong. All divine acquaintance with Him today will put us in the place where we may be the broken, empty vessels, ready for Christ's use.

Whom have I in heaven beside Thee?
And there is none on earth but Thee.

Oh! That is a wonderful place, where all your springs are in Him, all your desires are after Him, and you long only for Him.

Get ready that you may be touched by His inward earnestness this morning, that you may see the power of possibility in an impossible place, till you may see that God can change you, till you will change other things, till you may see today that your song will keep on the wing.

Are you ready? "What for?" *That God shall be all in all and you will lose your identity in the perfection of His glorified purity.* You will be lost to everything else except Him.

Are you ready? "What for?" That you may come to the banquet house with a great faith, nothing stopping you, pressing into, laying hold of, believing all things, and you will have a time of great refreshing as you come expressing yourself to God.

We must not stop this holy pursuit. We must remember that whatever shall happen in these days is happening for our future benefit. If it deals with the flesh, with the carnal senses at all, and with the human spirit, it is that God has to have a right-of-way till we will live in the Spirit.

In the third chapter of 2 Corinthians, we have a very blessed word. If you get this truth into your heart, you will not be moved anymore by anything. This is just the difference between the human and the divine. If human is there, prominent, then divine vision will be dimmed. *When the divine has the full control, then all earthly cares and anxieties pass away. If we live in the Spirit, we are over all human and animal nature. If we reach the climax that God's Son said we had to come into, we shall always be in the place of peace.*

If ye abide in me, and my words abide in you, ye shall ask what ye will, and it shall be done unto you. (John 15:7)

Jesus was a manifestation of power to dethrone every evil thing, and He dealt always with the flesh. It was necessary for Him to say to Peter, "*Get thee behind me, Satan…for thou savourest not the things that be of God, but those that be of man*" (Matthew 16:23). Everything that interferes with your plan of putting to death the old man is surely the old man that is comforting you.

> *Everything that interferes with your plan of putting to death the old man is surely the old man that is comforting you.*

There is a test of faith if we have entered into it, ceased from out own works, ceased from our own struggling, ceased from making our own plans. It is a rest in faith, a place where you can smile in the face of any eruption. No matter what came, you would be in the place of real rest. It is in the position of this word in the third chapter of 2 Corinthians.

Epistles of Christ

Do we begin again to commend ourselves? or need we, as some others, epistles of commendation to you, or letters of commendation from you? Ye are our epistle written in our hearts, known and read of all men: forasmuch as ye are manifestly declared to be the epistle of Christ ministered by us, written not with ink, but with the Spirit of the living God; not in tables of stone, but in fleshly tables of the heart.
(2 Corinthians 3:1–3)

Here we have a very remarkable word which the Spirit wants to enlarge on us. It is true that we must be an epistle of Christ. The epistle of Christ is a living power in the mortal flesh, quickening, dividing asunder everything which is not of the Spirit, till you realize that now you live in a new order. It is the Spirit that has manifested Himself in your mortal body. The Word has become life; it has quickened you all through, and you are not in any way subject to anything around you. You are above everything. You reign above everything.

You are evidently sent forth this morning by the Word of God as an epistle of Christ, meaning to say that all human ideals, plans, and wishes for the future are past. For you, to live is Christ. For you, to live is to be His epistle, emblematic, divinely sustained by another power greater than you. So you do not seek your own anymore. You are living in a place where God is on the throne, superintending your human life, God changing everything and making you understand this wonderful truth.

I believe it would be good to read just a little word in the next chapter:

> *For God, who commanded the light to shine out of darkness, hath shined in out hearts, to give the light of the knowledge of the glory of God in the face of Jesus Christ. But we have this treasure in earthen vessels, that the excellency of the power may be of God, and not of us.* (2 Corinthians 4:6–7)

The excellency of the power of the life of Christ is in the mortal body, subduing it in every way till the Spirit is full of life and vitality in the body, that Christ, that God, and the Holy Ghost may be illuminating the whole body. The body is there just as the temple, that all the glory should roll back to God. Not seeking your own, not seeking your place, but all your body giving place to the glorifying of the Christ. Set free, loosed, created by, and made likened unto Him in this glorious order.

Live Not under the Law

If you go at any time into law, under any circumstances, you miss the divine order of the Spirit. You have not to go back to law. You are in a new order. Law can only deal out one thing, and I will read what it deals in Hebrews 7:16: "*Who is made, not after the law of a carnal commandment, but after the power of an endless life.*"

You never deal with law but you find it is a carnal commandment, always dealing with carnal things. It is always, "Thou shall not."

There is no law to the Spirit. There never has been. You cannot find a law to Truth. The law has never had a place in a human body that has been filled with the power and the unction of the Holy Ghost. Law is done away; law is past. Life is begun; the new creation is formed, living after the new order. Christ has become the very principle of your human life, and you no more touch law. You are above the law.

How many people are missing the greatest plan of the earth because they are continually trying to do something? My wife and I many years ago were strongly convinced on Sabbath Day holiness lines. We got so far that we thought it was wrong to have the milkman call, and it was a very fearful thing to ride in anything on a Sunday. We were so tightened up by the law that we were bound hand and foot.

There are thousands of people like that today. There are people that take up the new order of what they call the Seventh-day Adventists. But I want to tell you, you are touching miry clay when you touch anything on eating, drinking, or anything pertaining to the law. God would have you in a new order.

It is the law of the Spirit. It is a law of life; it is not a law of death and bondage.

As sure as you are in law, you are in judgment and you judge everybody. Law is always judgment, and no one is right but those people who are keeping the law. They are full of judgment.

We have passed from death, from judgment, from criticism, from harshness, from hardness of heart.

> *Ye are our epistle...known and read of all men....And such trust have we through Christ to God-ward: not that we are sufficient of ourselves to think any thing as of ourselves; but our sufficiency is of God.*
>
> (2 Corinthians 3:2, 4–5)

Every person that begins thinking anything about himself is touching human weakness, just as if you in any way try to please anybody, you are down. And you are very low down if you begin to worship anybody. No one must be worshipped.

When the glory appeared on the mount, as soon as it appeared and the disciples saw the whiteness, the brilliancy, the glory, the expression of the Master, and the very robes He wore becoming white and glistening, they began at once to think what they could do. Law will do it. What can we do? And they began *doing*, and they wanted to make three tabernacles, one for Moses, one for Elias, and one for Jesus. And then the cloud came. No person in the world has to be worshipped but the Lord. When the cloud lifted, there was no one seen but Jesus; if you turn to anybody but Jesus, you will be law, you will be nature, you will be human.

It has always been so; people are always planning out things to do. What can I do? That is the reason why, in the fourth chapter of Hebrews, we read that the man that begins to do is a debtor to what he does. But the man that believes God, it is counted to him for righteousness—not doing but believing.

So God wants you to see that you have to cease from your doing; get away from it. Believe there is a spiritual vitality which shall bring into your very nature a new creation, which must be in the sons of God with power.

Interpretation of Tongues:

It is the Light that lighteth everyone that cometh into the world. It is the purity of the Son of God which is to bring us into a place where we will behold light in His light; it is the revelation from the Most High God. For in the old days, men spoke as the prophets, but now, in the last days, God speaks to us by His Son.

His Son is in evidence, not the prophets but the Son. But if the prophets speak, as it will be, concerning the Son, then you will find the prophet position will be Amen to the Word of God.

Who also hath made us able ministers of the new testament; not of the letter, but of the spirit: for the letter killeth, but the spirit giveth life. (2 Corinthians 3:6)

In this new order, Jesus has one great plan for us: to fill us with the Holy Ghost, so that He should have a perfect focus in our human life, making all the displays of the brilliancy centered around the Son. And as we come into the light of this revelation by the Son, by the quickening of the Spirit, we will find our whole bodies regenerated with a new touch of divine favor, and we will think about spiritual things, and we will talk about spiritual things, and we will not touch anything that pertaineth to the flesh.

Interpretation of Tongues:

It is the light that dawneth just in the early morning and sets thy soul aglow with fervent heat of the light of the revelation of the Son, for whom He loveth He correcteth and changeth, and bringeth him to a desired heaven.

I love the dawning of the morning, breaking upon my soul with refreshing and keeping you in perfect order.

THE SPIRIT OR THE LETTER?

"*The letter killeth, but the spirit giveth life.*" Think about this very sincerely. Many people go along very well for a time.

We have no trouble with the people that are getting baptized or seeking for the baptism or just at the time when the Holy Ghost has touched them. All those three positions are lovely.

When are we troubled?

When the people cease to pursue, and they turn aside and spoil all that has been before. What's up? They were all right in the pursuit. They would have been all right continuing in the pursuit. There is not a place in the Scripture that you are ever allowed to drop the weapons which are spiritual attainment. You must see that you must denounce the powers of evil, the powers of darkness, the powers that would bring you into bondage. Denounce them all. You have been created now, filled now, sustained in power. You go right on with God. Never turn again to the things round about you; set your heart just upon Him as Jesus set His heart upon the cross.

There are three things which are wonderful: there is a good, there is a better, and there is a best.

After you have come into the fullness of the refreshing of God, you can get the letter instead of the life of the Word, and the letter will turn you to yourself, but the Spirit will turn you to Christ.

I say it without flinching: the people that have turned to water baptism in Jesus' name have turned away from a higher order of God. The people who have made a Trinity of Jesus have turned away from the "best," and they have "good." That's all they have got.

But there is a best. What is it? Not the Spirit but the letter killeth. If they had gone on with God, the Spirit would have kept them in life. People turn away from the Spirit and take the letter, and when they get in the letter, they are full of condemnation. As you live in the Spirit, there will be no condemnation in you. There is something wrong when you are the only one that is right just as the church rises into the glory of the Lord and the vision of the Lord. Will the church be full of the love of the Lord then?

The Holy Ghost wants you to sweep through darkness. The Holy Ghost wants to fill you with truth. The Holy Ghost wants to stimulate you in liberty. The Holy Ghost wants you to rise higher and higher.

What does the devil do? Try to get you to believe that you have some special revelation—some special revelation that is part truth. The devil never gives whole truth; he always gives part truth. What did the devil say? *"If thou be the Son of God...."* (See Matthew 4:3, 6; 27:40; Luke 4:3, 9.) The devil knew that Jesus was the Son of God.

I hear there is a place even in Los Angeles where they spend all their time in tongues. How ridiculous! How foolish! What's up? Letter. Turning away from the real truth of the Word of God.

God will shake this thing through you. If you turn away from the Word of God and won't have the Word, you will be judged by the Word of God, and you will be brought into leanness.

Spiritual power will not have human attainment. The man that is living in the Spirit will not turn aside to please anybody. The man that is filled with the Spirit it is going on with God all the time, and he will cease from his own works.

I am here to save you from ruts. I am here to stir your holy fidelity to know *there is a place in the Holy Ghost that can keep you so that you do not get hard in the law, in judgment, in criticism, in hardness of heart.* Get to a place where the Spirit has such a place with you that you will love to go God's way.

> *Get to a place where the Spirit has such a place with you that you will love to go God's way.*

The judgment of God will begin at the house of God.

You have the best when you have the Spirit, and the Spirit brings life and revelation. Don't turn to the law. Don't turn to the natural. See to it that in the spiritual, you are free from the law. The law of the Spirit is life to keep you out of death, to keep you out of judgment, to keep you out of bondage.

When Moses knew that he was bringing the tables of stone with the commandments down to the Israelite people, his heart was so full of joy, his whole body was so full, his whole countenance was so full that the people could not look upon him because of the glory that was expressed in his face. What was it? He was bringing liberty to the people, and it was law.

> But if the ministration of death, written and engraven in stones, was glorious, so that the children of Israel could not stedfastly behold the face of Moses for the glory of his countenance; which glory was to be done away: How shall not the ministration of the Spirit be rather glorious?
>
> (2 Corinthians 3:7–8)

If the law, which had with it life and revelation and blessing for Israel, could bring that wonderful exhibition of beauty and glory, what is it, then, if we are freed from the law and have the Spirit living, moving in us, without harshness, without "Thou shalt not"—the Spirit of the Lord—breathing through us and making us free from the law of sin and death?

Let us see to it that we get there.

For a moment, I want to speak to you about the body. There are people in this place who want to be loosed from their afflictions in their minds, in their bodies, loosed in every way.

You will never get loosed in the flesh. You will never get loosed in the letter. You will only get loosed as the Spirit of the Lord breathes upon the Word, and you receive it as the life from the Lord, for the Word of the Lord is life. You receive the Word of the Lord just as it is and believe it, and you will find it quickens your whole body.

Any number of people are missing it because they are full of examination. You have to take the Word of God as the life of the Spirit, and you have to allow it to breathe through you, quickening your whole body, for the Spirit quickeneth, but the flesh profiteth nothing.

The Word may be quick and powerful, or it may be death-like. *God wants us to be through with death.* You are to be through with death and enter into death and keep in death till death is swallowed up with perfect victory of the perfect resurrection of the life of the Spirit that moves in you, quickening your mortal body.

The moment you turn from the spiritual health of this revelation of Christ, that moment you have ceased to go forward.

A man came to my meeting, and he was wonderfully blessed. He was a Wesleyan minister. He groaned, he travailed, he paid the price. Every time the Spirit came in, he went down and down and down into that death, and God quickened him by the Spirit.

So forcefully, so powerfully did the Spirit of the Lord breathe upon him that he became like a flame of fire. He was in Vancouver. Every place became too small. Every place became enlarged. Money flowed in—thousands of dollars. Oh, the glory! Vancouver, looking at this young man, felt the glory, the expression of God flowing through his face, so beautiful.

But he turned aside to baptizing in the name of Jesus. His glory departed. He lost everything he had, and then he was shoved into a small theater. He lost everything.

What is it? Going back to letter, missing the summit, that glory that was upon him.

He wept and wept and wept, and said, "How can I get back?"

"Repent, brother," I said. "Repent."

Some people are all the time covering the thing up when they know they are wrong. They won't repent. If you have gone off the line and gone the wrong way because people have said to go that way, and left the first principles of the Christ of God, why not repent and get right? And I heard that he had repented.

(A voice from the balcony): "Yes he has, Brother Wigglesworth, and he has gotten the victory, too. Praise God!"

Oh, that is the man! God will restore you everything. When we repent, God restores.

Interpretation of Tongues:

> It is of the depths, and where thou cannot trace and wonders come, and in the mystery of the wonderment, where two ways meet and thy heart cries; and even thy nakedness appears in such a way that thou dost not know. Then in thy lowliness, thou turneth again to the habitation of the Spirit, and the Lord turns thy captivity and heals thy lands, and restores again to thee the vineyard and opens the heavens upon thee for blessing.

Oh! I see young men come into this work, I see people come into this work, and I know it is like opening the greatest door. Oh, what can happen! I see men passing through colleges! I see men clothed upon with abilities! Oh, how God can move them!

I never went to school, my mother and father never could read and write, and I never went to school but my wife taught me to read, but I come to you just because the Holy Ghost has got my life. I come to you to help you. What can happen to a man that has been at the feet of Gamaliel and touched all the fullness of the fragrance of knowledge? What could God do if you let Him? Will you let Him?

Thou didst begin well. What hath hindered thee? Was it the Lord that came in the way? No, the Lord never stops your progress. It was some human thing. There was something that glittered, but it was not pure gold. There was something that shook thy confidence, but it was never God.

So I pray for you this morning, you mighty of the Lord, you children of the Most High God, you people whom the Lord is looking upon with great favor, that you wil believe that as the Holy Ghost moved upon Paul, moved upon the apostles, He can bring you forth as tried as gold and purified.

Will you believe? May the blessing of God, the Father, the Son, the Holy Ghost, fill you so that all the powers of hell shall not be able to prevail against you.

I had no thought of what has been going on this morning, but I do praise God. There has risen in my heart such love for this brother, and I have wept alone, very sorry, troubled, wondering what would be the outcome of it. I got three men to pray with me that we should bind the powers, that he should be loosed. He does not know anything about it. My daughter and I have gone before the Lord for him.

Oh, I do hope that the future shall be so mighty! Let us pray that God shall send him to Vancouver with this new thrill of holy life pressing through, till Vancouver will feel the warmth of heaven!

Prayer

O God, we pray Thee, bless this dear soul. He has been heartbroken so long. He has been in great stress and trial for so long. O God, let the Holy Spirit rest upon him and move him for Vancouver, and let no power in the world interfere with his progress, in Jesus' name.

Now it is the glory side I am coming to. I want you to notice that there is an exceeding glory, and it is only in the knowledge of the Lord Jesus.

"*But if the ministration of death…was glorious…which glory was to be done away…?*" (2 Corinthians 3:7–9). Was it ever thought possible that law could be done away? Yes, by something which is far more glorious.

There were three things in the old dispensation far different from three things in the new dispensation. Look at the old.

"*What doth the* Lord *require of thee, but to do justly…?*" (Micah 6:8). That is a thing that law was continually confronting them with. There was everybody, out of order, and so the God of almightiness drew them to the place that the first thing necessary for them to know was how to do justly.

"*What doth the* Lord *require of thee, but…to love mercy…?*" (Micah 6:8). In the law, they had no mercy, and God brought this right into the midst of the law—a thing that they did not know how to do.

"*What doth the* Lord *require of thee, but…to walk humbly with thy God…?*" (Micah 6:8). The person that keeps the law never walks humbly but is always filled with self-righteousness.

But now let the Spirit speak to us in the last days. What is it the Lord thy God desires of thee?

"*Thou shalt love the Lord thy God with all thy heart*" (Mark 12:30). Isn't that a new spiritual vision? That isn't the law; that is a boundless position. Law could never do it.

"*Thou shalt love the Lord thy God…with all thy soul*" (Mark 12:30).

"*Thou shalt love the Lord thy God…with all thy strength*" (Mark 12:30). No reserve.

"Thou shalt love the Lord thy God…with all thy mind" (Mark 12:30)—with all of your pure mind serving the Lord.

The law had to be done away with because, though it was glorious, it had to be exceeding in glory by a pure heart, with all strength for God.

Just fancy your knowing you are so created after the fashion of God that you want all the strength out of your food for God, all the strength. Just think of you who have wonderful capabilities and wonderful minds, that your minds have to be all for God.

Glorious, more glorious! It is exceeding glory. Your own has to be done away. Nothing will put law away, only perfect love. There is no law to love. Love never had a law. It never had a sacrifice; if ever you talk about sacrifice, it means to say you do not know what it is to love.

For the joy that was set before Him, Jesus endured the cross. (See Hebrews 12:2.) "The cross is nothing to Me. Death itself is nothing to Me. All that they do to Me is nothing. Oh, the joy I shall have of saving all the people of Los Angeles!"

Oh, this depth of the grace of the loftiness, of the holiness, the sweetness!

> *Oh, this is like heaven to me.*
> *This is like heaven to me.*
> *I've crossed over Jordan*
> *To Canaan's fair land,*
> *And this is like heaven to me.*

If you are in this love, you will be swallowed up with holy desire. You will have no desire, only the Lord. Your mind will be filled with divine reflection. Your whole heart will be taken up with the things that pertain to the kingdom of God, you will live in the secret place of the Most High, and you will abide there.

Remember, it is abiding where He covers you with His feathers. It is a place of inner, inner, inner, inner, where you have moved outer and outer, altogether, and where the Lord now has the treasures.

> *There is a glory where you forget your poverties, where you forget your weaknesses, where you forget your human nature history, and you go on to divine opportunity.*

There is an exceeding glory. There is a glory where you forget your poverties, where you forget your weaknesses, where you forget your human nature history, and you go on to divine opportunity.

For if the ministration of condemnation be glory, much more doth the ministration of righteousness exceed in glory.
(2 Corinthians 3:9)

You see, it is a ministry of condemnation, the law; the Spirit is a ministry of righteousness. The difference is this: instead of preaching to the people, "Thou shalt not" anymore, you preach now that there is a superabundant position in the Holy One in the life of the Son, in the reflection by the Holy Ghost, into the entirety of your whole heart, where He has come in and transformed the whole situation till every judged thing is past, life flows through, and you preach righteousness.

You will never get free by keeping the law, but if you believe in the blood, that will put you to death; you will have life divine, and you can sweep through the thing that binds you, because righteousness will abound where the law is of the Spirit.

The Jews will never have this light revealed to them until one thing happens. What is happening now? I have talked with rabbis; I have good times with them. I visit the synagogues and see good things there, and I have good times with these people.

When I was in Jerusalem on the platform with a number of Jewish rabbis, I had a chance. I had been preaching every place round about there. I had preached in the prison. I tell you, it was lovely to preach at the foot of Mount Carmel. It was very lovely for me to wake up and look across the Lake of Galilee and see that place where the demons came into the pigs and ran down the hill.

I had a good time there, but it was most glorious of all, that last address for half an hour on a Jerusalem platform in front of all these judges, addressing these people from all over the country, as the power of God fell upon me, with tears running down my face, telling about the Nazarene, the King of Kings, the Lord of Glory, moving them to the Spirit instead of the law.

It was glorious. They came around me afterward, and several of these Jews and one of the rabbis would ride with me in the train, and then when we got to Alexandra, and they would go with me to have some food.

"There is something about your preaching which is different from the rabbi," they said.

"Well, what is it?" I asked.

"Oh, you moved us! There was a warmth about it!"

"Yes, brother. It wasn't law. The glory position is that it is warm. You feel it. It is regenerative. It is quickening. It moves your human nature. It makes you know that this is life divine."

They listened round the table, and these Jews said, "Oh, but it is so different!"

252 · *Smith Wigglesworth on the Power of Scripture*

"Yes," I said, "and the day is coming when your veil will be taken from your eyes, and you will see this Messiah."

After dinner, they said, "We have to leave. Oh, we do not feel we want to leave you!"

Ah, brethren, the Jews someday will be grafted in again. The day of the Jews is coming. But, oh, I don't want us Gentiles to miss the opportunity!

God wants us now so filled with the Spirit that we do not lose the glory by judging and harshness. We forget these things, and we press on to the prize of the mark of our high calling in Christ Jesus (see Philippians 3:13–14), and we see that we have received the life of the Spirit, which has quickened us, for *"where the Spirit of the Lord is, there is liberty"* (2 Corinthians 3:17).

Liberty? What kind of liberty?

Liberty from glory to glory. Liberty of loosing you till the very affection of the nature of the Son of God begins to be, till you are absorbed in this glory.

> *What is man, that thou art mindful of him? and the son of man, that thou visitest him? For thou hast made him a little lower than the angels, and hast clothed him with glory and honour.*
> (Psalm 8:4–5)

It is the Spirit that quickens; it is the Word that brings life. We want you to eat of the hidden manna. We do not want you to eat the sour grapes that turn the edge of your teeth. (See Jeremiah 31:29–30; Ezekiel 18:2.) We want you to eat and be satisfied. Eat of that which is spiritual, quickening, and divine.

Gifts of Healing

The Holy Ghost people have a ministry. All the people that have received the Holy Ghost might be so filled with the Holy

Ghost that, without having the gift, the Holy Ghost within them brings forth healing power.

That is the reason why we say to you people, "Never be afraid of coming near me when I am praying for the sick." I love to have people help me. Why? Because I know there are people in this place who have a very dim conception of what they have got. I believe the power of the Holy Ghost which you have received has power so to bring you into concentration that you dare believe for God to heal apart from knowing you have a gift.

Now I deal with the gifts—*gifts* of healing, not gift of healing. There is a difference, and we must give it the proper name.

Gifts of healing can deal with every case of sickness, every disease that there is; it is so full, beyond human expression, but you come into the fullness of it as the light reveals to you.

There is something about a divine healing meeting, which may be different in some respects to others. I have people continually coming to me and saying, "When you are preaching, I see a halo about you. When you are preaching, I have seen angels standing round about you."

I am confronted from time to time about these things, and I am thankful for people to have vision. I do not have that kind of vision, but I have the express glory, the glory of the Lord, covering me, the intense inner working of His power, till every time I have stood before you, I have known I have not had to choose language. The language has been chosen, the thoughts have been chosen, and I have been speaking in prophecy more than in any other way. So I know we have been in these days in the School of the Holy Ghost in a great way.

The only vision I have had in a divine healing meeting is this: so often, I have put hands upon the people, and I have seen two hands go before my hands many, many times.

The person that has the gifts of healing does not look. You will notice on the platform, after I have got through, many things are manifested, but it doesn't move me. I am not moved by anything I see. I have never seen anything yet that is like what I have to see.

The divine gift of healing is so profound in the person that has it that there is no such thing as doubt, and could not be, and whatever happens would not change the man's opinion or thought or act. He expects the very thing that God intends him to have as he lays hands upon the seeker.

Wherever I go, the manifestation of divine healing is greater by ever so much in every way after I get away than when I am there. Why? God's plan for me. God has great grace over me. Wonderful things have been established and told as they happened when I was there, but were hid from me. God has a reason why He hides things from me.

When I lay hands upon people, I tell you that thing will take place. I believe it to be so, and I never turn my ear or my eyes from the fact. It has to be.

Divine healing—the gift of it—is more than audacity. It is more than an unction. Those are two big things. It is a rigid fact of a divine nature within the human man, pressing forward the very nature and act of the Lord if He were there. We are in this place for the glorifying of the Father, and the Father will be glorified in the Son as we are not afraid of acting in this day.

People sometimes come to me very troubled. They will say, "I had the gift of healing once, but something has happened and I do not have it now."

You never had it. "*The gifts and calling of God are without repentance*" (Romans 11:29), and they remain under every circumstance, only this: if you fall from grace and use a gift wrongly, it will work against you. If you use tongues out of the will of God, interpretation will condemn you. If you have been used and the gift has been exercised and you have fallen from your high place, it will work against you.

The gift of the Holy Ghost, when He has breathed in you, will make you alive so that it is wonderful; it seems almost then as though you had never been born. The jealousy God has over us, the interest He has in us, the purpose He has for us, the grandeur of His glory, are so marvelous that God has called us into this place to receive gifts.

Now I want to tell you how to receive a gift. The difference between the speaking in tongues by the gift and speaking in tongues by the Spirit is this: everybody that is baptized speaks as the Spirit gives utterance. But this is not the gift. The gift is a special manifestation in the life that they know, and they could talk in tongues as long as they would. But the man or woman should never speak longer than the Spirit gives unction, should never go beyond. Like the person giving prophecy, he will never go beyond the spiritual unction.

The trouble is this: after we have been blessed with tongues, there is the natural thing. Everything that is not the rising tide of the Spirit is law or letter. What is law or letter? Law is that you have dropped into human order. Letter is that you are depending upon the Word without the power. These two things will work against you instead of working for you. The letter and the law bring harshness; the Spirit brings joy and felicity. One is perfect harmony; the other genders strife. One is higher tide; the other is earthly. The one gets into the bliss of the presence of heaven; the other never rises from earthly associations.

Claim your right. Claim your position. The man will never get a gift under any circumstances who asks for it twice. I am not moved by what you think about it. I believe this is sovereignty from God's altar. You never get a gift if you ask for it twice. But God will have mercy upon you if you stop asking and believe.

> *You never get a gift if you ask for it twice. But God will have mercy upon you if you stop asking and believe.*

There is not a higher order that God has set on foot today over the person that believes than, *"Ask, and ye shall receive"* (John 16:24). If you dare ask for any gift, if you really believe that it is a necessity gift, if you dare ask and will not move from it, but begin to act in it, you will find the gift is there.

If you want to be in the will of God, you will have to be stubborn. "What do you mean?" Unchangeable. Do you believe that if you got a gift you would feel it? Nothing like it. If you ask for a gift, do not expect to have a feeling with it. There is something better. There is a fact with it, and the fact will bring the feeling after the manifestation. People want feeling for gifts. There is no such thing. You will make the biggest mistake if you dare to pray on any line till you feel like doing anything. As sure as can be, you have lost your faith. You have to believe that after you receive, you have the power, and you begin to act in the power.

The next morning after I received the gift of tongues, I went out of the house with a box of tools on my back, going down the street to do some work. The power of God lit me up, and I broke out in tongues, loud. My! They were loud. The street was filled with people, and there were some gardeners trimming some hedges and cutting the grass. They stuck their heads over like swan necks.

"'Whatever is up? Why, it is the plumber."

I said, "Lord, I am not responsible for this, and I won't go from this place till I have the interpretation."

God knows I wouldn't move from that place. And out came the interpretation. This was the interpretation:

Over the hills and far away,
Before the brink of day,
The Lord thy God will send thee forth
And prosper thee all thy way.

This is the point: the gift was there. I did not pray for it. I did not say, "Lord, give me the interpretation." I said, "If You don't give it to me, I won't move." And that meant to say that I was determined to have the gift.

It has been surprising, but at every place where I am, the Spirit of the Lord moves upon me.

I want to say something about the gift of interpretation, because it is so sublime, it is so divine, it is such a union with the Christ. It is a pleasing place with the Christ. It is not the Holy Ghost that is using it so much, but it is the Christ who is to be glorified in that act, for the Trinity moves absolutely collectively in the body.

As soon as that had taken place, wherever I went, when anybody spoke in tongues, I did not say, "Lord, give me the interpretation." That would have been wrong. I lived in a fact. Now, what is a fact? A fact is that which produces. Fact produces. Fact has it. Faith is a fact. Faith moves fear and faction. Faith is audacity. Faith is a personality. Faith is the living Christ manifested in the believer.

Now, what is interpretation? Interpretation is that which moves and brings forth without thought. If you are on the line of interpretation, and if you get words before you are to them, that is not interpretation. The person who interprets does not have the words. The gift breathes forth, the person speaks on and never stops till he is through, and he says things that he does not know what he is saying till the words are out. He does not form them; he does not arrange for them. Interpretation is a divine flood, just as tongues is a divine flood. So it requires faith continually to produce this thing.

Now, I come back to the gift of healing. Gift of healing is a fact. It is a production. It is a faith. It is an unwavering trust. It is a confidence. It is a reliability. It knows it will be.

A divine gift has apprehension. It is also full of prophetic utterances. There is no such thing as an end to the divine vocabulary.

What is faith? Is it an earnest? More. Is it a present? More. It is relationship. Are there better things than relationship? Yes. What are they? Sonship is relationship. But heirship is closer still, and faith is "God manifested in flesh."

"What was Jesus?" you ask.

Jesus was the manifested glory in human incarnation.

"Anything else?"

Yes. Jesus was the fullness of the express image of the Father. (See Hebrews 1:3.)

"Who are the chosen ones?" They that ask and believe and see it done by God. He will make you chosen if you believe it.

Let us repent of everything that is hindering us. Let us give place to God. Let us lose ourselves in Him. Let us have no self-righteousness, but let us have brokenness, humbleness, submittedness. Oh, may there be today such brokenheartedness in us today! May we be dead indeed and alive indeed with refreshings of the presence of the Most High God!

Some of you have been saying, "Oh, I wish I could know how to get a gift." Some of you have felt the striving of the Holy Ghost pressing you through. Oh, beloved, rise to the occasion this day. Believe God. Ask God for gifts, and it may come to pass in your life. But do not ask without you know it is the desire of your heart. God grant to us gifts and graces!

Preparation for the Second Coming of the Lord, Part One

Bible Study #21 – August 11, 1927

I am conscious today that God has a design for us greater than our thoughts or even our language, and so I am not frightened of beginning on the line of the spiritual exaggeration. I shall say I dare believe that God will help me say things to you that shall inspire you to dare to believe God.

Up to this present time, the Lord's word is for us: "Hitherto ye have asked nothing." (See John 16:24.) Surely you people that have been asking great things from God for a long time would be amazed, if you entered into it with clear knowledge that it is the Master, it is Jesus, who has such knowledge of the mightiness of the power of the Father and of the joint union with Him that nothing is impossible for you to ask. Surely it is He only who could say, "Hitherto you have asked nothing."

So God means me to press you another step forward. Begin to believe on extravagant asking, believing that God is pleased when you ask large things.

If you will only dispose of yourself in a short time—for it is nothing but yourself that will hinder you—dispose of your human mind, dispose of your human measure, dispose of

> *Begin to believe on extravagant asking, believing that God is pleased when you ask large things.*

261

your strength and dispose of all you have—it is a big word for me to say—and let inspiration take whole charge of you, bring you out of yourself into the power of God, it may be today that God shall so transform you into another man as you have never been before.

Interpretation of Tongues:

> *Only the divine mind has divine thought to meet human order, for, knowing us from the beginning and understanding us as a Father and pitying us as children, He begins with the blade and the ear and the full corn in the ear so that we might know that He won't take us out of our death but He will transform us moment by moment till we can come into full stature of the mind and thought and prayer and act.*

Hallelujah! God is on the throne.

Now, beloved in the Lord, I come to you this morning to inspire you to dare believe that this day is for you as a beginning of days. You have never passed this way before. So I bring you to another day of passing over any heights, passing through mists or darkness; dare believe that the cloud is upon thee, shall break with an exceeding reward of blessing.

Don't be afraid of clouds. They are all earthly. Never be afraid of an earthly thing. You belong to a higher order, a divine order, a spiritual order. Then believe that God wants you to seat high this morning.

Interpretation of Tongues:

> *Fear not to enter in, for the Lord thy God has thee now in preparation. He is proving thee and He is chastising thee, but His hand is not heavy upon thee as thou mayest think, for He is gentle and entreating to bring thee into the desired place of thy heart's affections.*

Be still and know that I am God. It is I and I alone that openeth to thee the good treasure. Oh, to be still that my mind be so surfeited with the cares of this life that I might be able to enter into the joy and the bliss God has called me to, for I have not passed this way hitherto.

So God is going to speak to us about entering into something we have not entered into before.

The thoughts of this morning's message are primary to the message of the coming of the Lord. There must be a preparing place and an understanding line because of the purposes God is arranging for us. I know He is even at the door. Spiritual perception makes us know of His near return. But we must be so built on the line of truth that when He comes, we are ready.

In the few days to come, I am going to declare unto you the revelation of Christ to me of the readiness, and what it is—the knowledge of it, the power of it, the purpose of it—till every vestige of our human being is so filled with it, it would be impossible for us to be out of it. We shall be in the midst of it.

I have a message this morning leading up to the knowledge of His coming. It is in Peter's second epistle, the third chapter.

Knowing this first, that there shall come in the last days scoffers, walking after their own lusts, and saying, Where is the promise of his coming? for since the fathers fell asleep, all things continue as they were from the beginning of the creation. For this they willingly are ignorant of, that by the word of God the heavens were of old, and the earth standing out of the water and in the water: whereby the world that then was, being overflowed with water, perished: but the heavens and the earth, which are now, by the same word are kept in store, reserved unto fire against the day of

judgment and perdition of ungodly men. But, beloved, be not ignorant of this one thing, that one day is with the Lord as a thousand years, and a thousand years as one day. The Lord is not slack concerning his promise, as some men count slackness; but is longsuffering to us-ward, not willing that any should perish, but that all should come to repentance. But the day of the Lord will come as a thief in the night; in the which the heavens shall pass away with a great noise, and the elements shall melt with fervent heat, the earth also and the works that are therein shall be burned up. Seeing then that all these things shall be dissolved, what manner of persons ought ye to be in all holy conversation and godliness, looking for and hasting unto the coming of the day of God, wherein the heavens being on fire shall be dissolved, and the elements shall melt with fervent heat? Nevertheless we, according to his promise, look for new heavens and a new earth, wherein dwelleth righteousness. Wherefore, beloved, seeing that ye look for such things, be diligent that ye may be found of him in peace, without spot, and blameless. And account that the longsuffering of our Lord is salvation.
(2 Peter 3:3–15)

I may deal with many things on the line of spiritual awakening, for this is what is needed this day. This day is a needy day of spiritual awakening, not so much as a knowledge of salvation but a knowledge of waking in salvation.

The seed of the Lord Jesus Christ is mightily in you, which is a seed of purifying, a seed of truth and knowledge, a seed of life-giving, a seed of transforming, a seed of building another person in the body till the body that bears the seed only lives to contain the body which the seed has made, until that comes forth with glorious light and power till the whole body has yielded itself to another, a fullness, a manifestation of the perfect formation of the Christ in you. This is the great hope of the future day.

I want to speak to you very exactly. All the people that are pressing into and getting ready for this glorious attained place where they shall not be found naked, where they shall be blameless, where they shall be immovable, where they shall be purified by the power of the Word of God, have within them a consciousness of the very presence of God within, changing their very nature and preparing them for a greater thing, and causing them to be ready for translation.

You will find that this thing is not now already in the world in perfection. There are millions and millions of real believers in Christ who are losing this great upward look, and in the measure they lose this upward look, they lose perfect purification. There is only perfect purification in this upward look.

When we see the day dawning, as the manifestation of the sons of God appear, just as these things come to us in light and revelation, we will find that it makes us know that everything is on the decay. Millions of people who are Christians believe this world is being purified. All the saints of God that get the real vision of this wonderful transformation of the body are seeing every day that the world is getting worse and worse and worse and ripening for judgment. And God is bringing us to a place where we that are spiritual are having a clear vision which we must at any cost put off the works of darkness. We must be getting ourselves ready for the glorious day.

These are last days. What will be the strongest confirmation for me to bring to you of the last days?

There are in the world two classes of believers. There are believers that are disobedient—or, I ought to say, there are children that are saved by the power of God who are disobedient.

And there are children that are just the same saved by the power of God who all the time are longing to be more obedient.

In this great fact, Satan has a great part to play. It is on this factor in these last years that some of us have been brought to great grief at the first opening of the door with brazen fact to carnality forces. And we heard the word come rushing through all over—"new theology"—that damnable, devilish, evil power that lived in some of these disobedient children, which in these last days opened the door to the next thing.

As soon as this was noised abroad everywhere, "new theology,"' everybody began to say, "What is new theology?" Why, new theology is exactly on the same plane as being changed from monkeys to men. What does it mean? I want to make a clean sweep of that thing this morning. There is not a man that can think on those lines [but that it leads to] atheism. Every person that touches a thing like that is an atheist behind all he has to say.

New theology was born in infidelity. It is atheism, and it opened the door for Russellism, which is full of false prophecy. Take the book of Russellism and go into the prophecy. What was the prophecy? In 1924, the prophecy that the Lord had to come. Russellism is false prophecy. Russellism is exactly the perfect plan of what will make the man of sin come forth. Russellism is preparing the door for the man of sin, and they are receiving openheartedly.

They declared that He would come in 1914. I went to see a dear beloved brother of mine who was so deluded by this false prophecy that he was utterly deceived by it. I said, "You will be deceived as sure as you live."

They said, "We are so sure it is true that if we are deceived, we will give up all Russellism and have nothing to do with it."

But what does false prophecy do? *False prophecy always makes a way out.* The moment it did not come to pass, they said they were mistaken in dates. What is the devil? If it had been a true prophecy, Jesus would have come. And the Word of God says if any prophecy does not come true, that prophet has to prophesy no more.

But those people were deluded by the spirit of this world and the devil, which is the spirit of this world, and instantly allowed themselves to be gripped again, when the same prophet came forth, saying that He was going to come in 1925.

In order to cover that, what did they do? They placarded in every nation, almost, in big cities, "Millions alive that will never die." And they have been going at that now since 1925, and they are dying all the time, and their prophecy is still a cursed, evil prophecy. Still they go on.

The spirit of this age is to get you to believe a lie. If you believe a lie, you cannot believe the truth. When once you are seasoned with a lie against the Word of God, He sends you strong delusion that you shall believe a lie. Who does? God does. God is gracious over His Word. His Word is from everlasting; His Word is true.

> *The spirit of this age is to get you to believe a lie. If you believe a lie, you cannot believe the truth.*

When we see those things which are coming to pass, what do we know? We know the time is at hand. The fig tree is budding for these false prophecies and these positions.

Now, you see, they never stop at that; they go on to say Christ never has risen. Of course, if ever you believe a lie, if ever you turn the Word of God to some other place, you cannot believe the truth after that.

Then, the last days opened the door for the false demon power that is in the world rampant everywhere, putting up the most marvelous buildings—Christian Science, which is devilish, hellish, and deceivable. I am preaching to you this morning that you shall deliver yourself from this present-day evil thing. How shall you do it? You can do it only on one line. Let the seed in. Let in the seed of truth, the seed of righteousness, this power of God.

The seed of Christ is an inward incorruptible. The new birth, the new life, is a quickening power, incorruptible, dealing with corruptible, carnal things—evil, sensuous, devilish. And when it comes to the Word of God, the seed of the Word of God is the life of the Word, and you are living the life of the Word of God and are tremendously transformed all the time by the Word of the Lord.

This is the last days. You go out in the world, and there is no difficulty. What are you going to do now? Is this a fact? Is this true? Aren't people today almost afraid of sending their sons to the colleges because they come out more devils than they went in? Isn't atheism right in the seat of almost all these colleges? Then what have you to do? How shall you possess your soul in peace? How shall you preserve your children? How shall you help them? You say they have to go because you want them to come out with certain letters to their names. You want them to progress in knowledge, but how shall you save your children?

Nothing but the Word can save them.

I wish all the young men in this place would read these words in the first epistle of John: "*Young men, because ye are strong…ye have overcome the wicked one*" (1 John 2:14). By what? By the Word.

They are mighty words we read in this Scripture. What does it say? The Word is holding these things, even the fires that are going to burn the world. The Word is holding them back. What is the Word? The Word is the mighty power of the revelation to us of the Son of God. And the Son of God is holding all these powers today in the world, ready for the greatest conflagration that ever could be, when the heavens shall be burnt up, when the earth shall melt with fervent heat.

The Word of God is keeping these things reserved, all ready. What manner of men ought we to be in all manner of conversation in purifying ourselves. Remember this: in heaven, the glory, the revelation, the power, the presence—that which makes all heaven so full of beauty—is that time has no count. It is so lovely! A thousand years are as a day and a day as a thousand years.

Interpretation of Tongues:

> All the springs are in thee; all the revelations are in the midst of thee. It is He, the mighty God! It is He, the King of kings! It is He, the Son of the living God, who is in the very innermost being of thy human nature, making thee know that before these things shall come to pass, thou shalt be preserved in the midst of the flame. Whatever happens, God shall cover thee with His mighty covering; and that which is in thee is incorruptible and undefiled and fadeth not away, which is reserved in the glory.

God says to us, "In patience possess thy soul." (See Luke 21:19.) How beautiful! Oh! How the enrichment of the presence of the power of the Most High is bursting forth upon our—what shall I say?—our human frame. Something greater than the human frame. *Knowest thou not that that which is born in thee is greater than anything formed around thee?* Knowest thou not that He who has been begotten in thee is the very God of power to preserve thee, and to bring forth light and truth and cause the vision to be made clearer?

You notice this: there is an elect of God. I know that God has in this place people who, if you would examine yourself, you would be amazed to find that you are elect of God.

People are tremendously afraid of this position because they have heard so much on this line: "Oh, you know you are the elect of God! You are sure to be all right." There have been in England's great churches, which were laid out upon these things. I thank God that they are all withered. You will find, if you go to England, those strong people that used to hold all these things are almost withered out. Why? Because they went on to say whatever you did, if you were elect, you were right. That is wrong.

The elect of God are those that are pressing forward. The elect of God cannot hold still. They are always on the wing. Every person that has a knowledge of the elect of God realizes it is important that he press forward. He cannot endure sin or darknesses or shady things. The elect is so in earnest to be elect for God that he burns every bridge behind him.

"*That day shall not come, except there come a falling away first*" (2 Thessalonians 2:3).

Knowing this, that first, God shall bring into His treasury the realities of the truth and put them side by side—the false and the true, those that can be shaken in mind and those that cannot be shaken. God wants us to be so built upon the foundation of truth that, it doesn't matter what comes, we cannot be shaken in our mind.

When I was in Sydney, they said, "Whatever you do, you must see this place that they built for the man, the new man coming."

Theosophy has a new man. Nothing but theosophy could have a new man. The foundation of the theosophy has always been corruptible. From the beginning, it has been corruptible. In the formation of theosophy, it was joined up to Bradlaw, one of the greatest atheists of the day. So you can only expect theosophy to be atheism. It sprung out of atheism.

The "Man of Sin," as he comes forth, will do many things. There will be many false Christs, and they will be manifestations of the forthcoming of the Man of Sin, but they will all come to an end. There will be the Man of Sin made manifest.

These people are determined to have a man. They know someone has to come. We know who He is that is coming. They begin to make a man. So they find a man in India, they polish him up as much as they can, and they make him up as well in appearance; but you know we are told by the Lord that there is soft clothing that goes onto wolves' backs.

We find they are going to bring this man forth in great style. When I went around the amphitheatre in Sydney, which was made for this man to come, I saw as clearly as anything it was the preparation for the Man of Sin. But they do not believe that.

What will make you to know it is the Man of Sin? This: every religious sect and creed there are in the world all join to it. Romanism you see joined up with it. Buddhism joined with it. There is not a religion known but what will be joined to it.

Why, that is exactly what the devil will have. He will have all the false religions joining right up; and the Man of Sin, when he comes, will be received with great applause.

Who will be saved? Who will know the day? Who knows now the Man of Sin? Why, we feel when we touch him, when he opens his mouth, when he writes through the paper, when we see his actions—we know who he is.

What has the Man of Sin always said? Why, exactly what Russellism says. What? No hell. The devil has always said that. What does Christian Science say? No hell; no devil. They are ready for him. The devil has always said no hell, no evil. And these people are preparing, and they do not know it, for the Man of Sin.

We have to see that these days have to come before the Lord can come. There has to be a falling away. There has to be a manifestation in this day so clear, of such undeniable fact, that when they begin to build temples for the Man of Sin to come (but they don't know it), you know the day is at hand.

A person said to me, "You see, the Christian Scientists must be light—look at the beautiful buildings. Look at all the people following them."

Yes, everybody can belong to it. You can go to any brother you like, you can go to any theater you like, you can go to any race course you like, you can be mixed up with the rest of the people in your life—and you can still be a Christian Scientist. You can have the devil right and left and anywhere, and yet still belong to Christian Science.

When the Man of Sin is come, he will be hailed on all sides. When he is manifested, who will miss him? Why, the reverent, the holy, the separated. How will they miss him? Because they will not be here to greet him!

But there will be things that will happen prior to his coming that we shall know. You can tell I am like one this morning that is moving with a liquid, holy, indispensable, real fire in my bosom. I know that it is burning and the body is not consumed; it is real fire from heaven that is making my utterances come to you to know that He is coming. He is on the way. God is going to help me tell you why you will know. You that have the breath of the Spirit, there is something now moving as I speak. As I speak, this breath of mighty, quickening, moving, changing, desirable power is making you know, and it is this alone that is making you know that you will be ready.

No matter who misses it, you will be ready. It is this I want to press upon you this morning, that *you will be ready*. And you won't question your position. You will *know*. Ah! Thank God, ye are not of the night. Ye are of the day. It shall not overtake you as a thief. Ye are the children of day. You are not the night. You are not drunken. Yes, you are. There is so much intoxication from this holy incarnation that makes you feel all the time you have to have Him hold you up. Praise the Lord! Holy intoxication, inspired revelation, invocation, incessantly inwardly moving your very nature, so that you know as sure as anything that you do not belong to those who are putting off the day. You are hastening unto the day, you are longing for the day.

You say, "What a great day!" Why do you say it? Because the creature—is this body the creature? No, this is the temple that holds the creature—the creature inside the temple longeth, travaileth, groaneth to be delivered, and will be delivered. It is the living creature. It is the new creature. It is the new creation. It is the new nature. It is the new life.

What manner of men ought we to be? I am going to read it:

The Lord is not slack concerning his promise, as some men count slackness; but is longsuffering to us-ward, not willing that any should perish, but that all should come to repentance.
(2 Peter 3:9)

I want you to notice this: this is not the wicked repentant. The epistles are always speaking to the saints of God. When I speak to you saints of God, you will find that my language will make you see that there is not within you one thing that has to be covered. I say it without fear of contradiction, because it is my whole life, inspired by the truth. You know that these meetings will purify you.

It is on this line that every time you hear people speak upon this—I do not mean as a theory. This is not a theory. There is a difference between a man standing before you on theory. He has chapter and verse, line upon line, precept upon precept, and he works it out upon the scriptural basis. It is wonderful; it is good; it is inspiring.

But I am not there this morning. Mine is another touch. Mine is the spiritual nature showing to you that the world is ripening for judgment. Mine is a spiritual acquaintance bringing you to a place of separation, holiness unto God, that you may purify yourself and be clean, ready for the great day.

This is the day of purifying. This is the day of holiness. This is the day of separation. This is the day of waking. O God, let us wake today! Let the inner spirit wake into consciousness that God is calling us. The Lord is upon us. We see that the day is upon us. We look at the left side, we look at the right side, we see everywhere new theories. New things will not stand the light of the truth. When you see these things, you know that there must be a great falling away before *the* day. And it is coming. It is upon us.

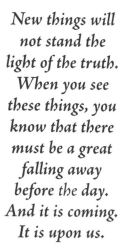

New things will not stand the light of the truth. When you see these things, you know that there must be a great falling away before the day. And it is coming. It is upon us.

Paul said he travailed in birth. Jesus did the same. John did the same. So, brothers and sisters, may God bless you and make you see that *this is a day of travailing for the church of God, that she might be formed so that she is ready for putting on the glorious raiment of heaven forever and forever.*

> *Seeing then that all these things shall be dissolved, what manner of persons ought ye to be in all holy conversation and godliness, looking for and hasting unto the coming of the day of God, wherein the heavens being on fire shall be dissolved, and the elements shall melt with fervent heat? Nevertheless we, according to his promise, look for new heavens and a new earth, wherein dwelleth righteousness. Wherefore, beloved, seeing that ye look for such things, be diligent that ye may be found of him in peace, without spot, and blameless.*
>
> (2 Peter 3:11–14)

Without spot! Without spot! Without spot and blameless!

Do you believe it? Who can do it? *The blood can do it!* The blood, the blood. Oh, the blood! The blood of the Lamb! The blood of Jesus can do it. *Spotless, clean, preserved for God.*

Give the devil the biggest chase of his life and say these words: *"The blood of Jesus Christ* [God's] *Son cleanseth us from all unrighteousness"* (1 John 1:7).

If ever you hear a row like that in any Christian Science meeting about the blood of Jesus, go, and I will tell you that they are being converted. If you ever hear tell of Russellism getting excited over the blood of Jesus, I can tell you, God has dealt with them. If ever you hear about this new man in theosophy getting excited about the blood of Jesus, you can tell them from Wigglesworth that there is a new order in the world. But they have no room for the blood. And yet we see the blood is preparing us for this great day.

In the amphitheatre in Sydney, when I spoke about the blood and when I spoke about this infernal thing, the whole place was upset. You be careful when anybody comes to you with a sugarcoated pill or with a slimy tongue. They are always of the devil. The Spirit of the Lord will always deal with truth. These people never deal with truth. They always cover up the truth: "Oh, you know, we are all sons of God. We all belong to God." That is what people said when Jesus was here, and He said, "You are mistaken. You belong to the devil." And if Jesus dared say things like that, I dare.

QUESTIONS AND ANSWERS

Q: Is it true if we believe a lie we cannot believe the truth?

A: That is not what I said. If you once believe the Word of God to be a lie, then you cannot believe the truth of the Word of God. The Word of God comes to you like life and revelation, but Satan in his spurious condition comes, as he has done with many, and moved them from truth to believe in some theory of truth. They have gotten a theory of something else which is not truth, and they have denied the truth to take hold of the theory. It is all theory when people have left the truth. The people that live in truth never have a theory; it is always fact.

Q: Because I have laid aside my Christian Science books, the people are now using what they call "malicious magnetism" against me. I know Jesus is stronger than they.

A: This is a very important thing. There are many people so under delusion and devil oppressed on these lines that they join together to damage the character of others because they do not go their way. That is the devil if nothing else is. The greatest fact about Christian Science's false position is that they are led captive by the father of liars. He has been a liar from the beginning. They have stepped out of truth and been taken in charge by this monster devil till they cannot believe the truth.

Yet Jesus said, "I am the light of the world; any man that walketh in Me shall not be in darkness. I am the light to every man that cometh into the world." (See John 8:12.)

If you will go back to the time when you knew the light of the truth was burning through you, you will find that there you turned from that to take something else which was not light. Keep in the light, and there is no power of Satan. If a hundred people came and stood around you and said to you, "We will join together to bind you that you shall be crippled," or your mind be affected, or anything, if you know you have the Light, you can smile and say, "You can do nothing to me."

Never be afraid of anything. There are two things in the world: one is fear, the other faith. One belongs to the devil; the other to God. If you believe in God, there is no fear. If you sway toward any delusion of Satan, you will be brought into fear. Fear always brings bondage. There is a place of perfect love in Christ where you are always casting out all fear, and where you are living in the place of freedom.

Be sure that you never allow anything to make you afraid. God is for you; who can be against you? (See Romans 8:31.)

The secret of many people going into Christian Science is a barren church that had not the Holy Ghost. Christian Science exists because the churches have a barren place because they haven't the Holy Ghost. There would be no room for Christian Science if the churches were filled with the Holy Ghost. But because the churches had nothing, then the needy people went to the devil, and he persuaded them they had something, and they are coming out knowing they have got nothing, only a wilderness experience.

Let us save ourselves from all this trouble by letting the Holy Ghost fill our hearts.

> *Will you be baptized in this faith,*
> *Baptized in the Holy Ghost?*
> *To be free indeed 'tis the power you need,*
> *Baptized in the Holy Ghost.*

Don't depend on any past tense, any past momentum, but let the unction be upon you; let the presence and the power be upon you. Are you thirsty? Longing? Desiring? Then God will pour out of His treasures all you need. God wants to satisfy us with His great, abounding, holy love, imparting love upon love and faith upon faith.

The secret of all decline is refusal of the Holy Ghost. If you have fallen short, it is because you refused the Holy Ghost. Let the Holy Ghost be light in you to lighten the light which is in you, and no darkness shall befall you. You will be kept in the middle of the road.

Hasten unto the coming of the Lord. Set your house in order. Be at peace. Live at peace. Forgive and learn how to forgive. Never bear malice. Don't hold anybody any grudge. Forgive everybody. It does not matter whether they forgive you or not, you forgive them. Live in forgiveness. Live in repentance. Live wholeheartedly. *Set your house in order, for God's Son is coming to take that which is in the house.*

BAPTISM OF THE HOLY SPIRIT
Bible Study #22 – August 12, 1927

What it means for people to have faith! What it will mean when we all have faith! We know that as soon as faith is in perfect operation, we shall be in the perfect place where God is manifested right before our eyes. *"The pure in heart...shall see God"* (Matthew 5:8), and all the steps of purity are a divine appointment of more faith. More purity, more faith.

When Jesus knew that Mary, Martha, and all round about had lost confidence and faith, then He turned to the Father—unity fellowship. And He said, "Father, I know that Thou hearest Me always." (See John 11:41–42.)

And death had to give up Lazarus, and everything had to come to pass as He said.

Fellowship, purity, unity is a living cooperation of a changing from faith to faith. May the Lord grant unto you this thought today: how may I more and more abandon myself from any earthly human fellowship? I will say fellowship till we are absolutely so bound to God that God has the right-of-way to the throne of our hearts; till there, the seat of affection is blessedly purified; till there is no room for anything, only the Son of God, who is the Author and the Finisher of faith. And then it will be Christ manifested in the flesh, destroying everything outside.

—⁂—

When the Spirit of the Lord is upon us, we impart not words but life.

—⁂—

When the Spirit of the Lord is upon us, we impart not words but life. Words are only that you may understand what the Word is, but the Word is really life-giving. So when we are covered with the Spirit, we are imparting life. Every time we get up, when we are filled with the Holy Spirit, we impart life. If you are ready to receive it, it is amazing how it will quicken your mortal body every time you touch this life. It is divine life. It is the life of the Son of God.

I want to lay down a foundation today on why Jesus emphasized the baptism of the Holy Spirit, how to receive the baptism, and the cause of the baptism, because Jesus expressed all these things to His disciples. I want to dwell on this to get you to a real foundation for the baptism truth so that you will never wait before God without a clear understanding of what the baptism is for, what you are waiting for, et cetera.

To begin with, we find a remarkable word in Matthew:

> *I indeed baptize you with water unto repentance: but he that cometh after me is mightier than I, whose shoes I am not worthy to bear: he shall baptize you with the Holy Ghost, and with fire.* (Matthew 3:11)

The expression of a man who was so filled with the Spirit of God that his very voice became an active process of a divine flame that moved the whole of creation of that day. From east to west and north to south, he spoke by the power of the Holy Ghost till people gathered at Jordan in multitudes, drawn by this voice of one crying in the Spirit. What a remarkable word he gave!

Most of us have seen water baptism in action so often that we know what it means. But if I could only get you to see that

that form of baptism covering you is the very great desire of God, that you should be so immersed and covered and flooded with the light and revelation of the Holy Ghost, the third Person of the Trinity, that it shall be filling your whole body. And not only filling but overcovering you till you walk in the presence of the power of God.

Interpretation of Tongues:

> *God's life for your life, His light for your darkness, His revelation for your closed brain. He brings forth a new order in divine power till thou shalt be changed into another man, till the very nature of thee shall be burning with a burning in thee of divine purifying, till thou art like one who has come from the presence of the glory to exhibit truths that God has revealed to thee. In thy lot, in thy day, the power of another covering girding thee with the power of truth.*

O Jesus, let it come to pass that we never do anything in our own strength, but that all we do shall be done to the glory of the Lord!

We cannot stop there. That was the first breath of revelation of what should take place for individuals—yes, and communities—yes, and the world.

Turn now to John, chapter seven:

> *In the last day, that great day of the feast, Jesus stood and cried, saying, If any man thirst, let him come unto me, and drink. He that believeth on me, as the scripture hath said, out of his belly shall flow rivers of living water. (But this spake he of the Spirit, which they that believe on him should receive: for the Holy Ghost was not yet given; because that Jesus was not yet glorified.)* (John 7:37–39)

Jesus saw all the people, and He had not only a great heart of scrutinizing, inwardly to be able to unfold, but also He saw things at a glance. He took the situation all in. In a moment, He knew when the people were about to famish and die by the wayside and supplied all their need.

We must not forget that He was filled with the Holy Ghost. He was lovely because He was full of divine inflow of the life of God.

Look how He deals with this thing. He saw the people that had been at Jerusalem at the feast, and they were coming back dissatisfied. My Lord could not have anybody dissatisfied. My Lord could never be satisfied when anybody was dissatisfied.

It is not in the canon of history of the spiritual fellowship between heaven and earth that you shall be famished, naked, full of discoid, full of evil, full of disorder, full of sensuality, full of carnalities.

That is what was taking place at the feast, and they came away hungrier than they were. Jesus saw them like that, and He said, "*He, every one that thirsteth, come ye to the waters*" (Isaiah 55:1). "*If any man thirst, let him come unto me, and drink*" (John 8:37).

Oh! The Master could give. The Master had it to give! Beloved, He is here to give this morning, and I am sure He will give.

Interpretation of Tongues:

> God first, last, Alpha, Omega, beginning, and end. He is at the root of all things this morning. He will disturb that which needs to be disturbed. He will unfold that which needs to be unfolded. He will turn to death that which needs to be broken and put to death. He will put a spring within thee and lift thee to life. God will deal with thee in mercy but

*in severity, because all divine love is a sword and divides
asunder soul and spirit, joint and marrow, and deals with
the inward desires of the heart.*

Yes, all the heavy hand of God is full of mercy. All the two-edged sword is full of dividing. All His quickening Spirit puts everything that needs to be dead, dead, that He might transform thee by the resurrection of His life.

And this is the order of the Spirit. Can't you see how He says, "Come, thirsty; come, needy; I will give you a drink that shall create a thirst in you that shall prepare you for the coming of the Holy Ghost, that shall make that spring that I give you a river of living water"?

Which have you got? Have you the spring or the river? The spring is good because it has the same kind of water as the river. But the plentifulness is the river, and the Holy Ghost is the river. That is the reason why Jesus was portraying, forecasting, sending out these wonderful words, that He might prepare the people for all the fullness that had to come on.

I want you to go away from these meetings just infused. Make up your mind that you won't be ordinary. You have an extraordinary God, with revelation. Be determined that you won't go away as you came, but you will go away endued, imbued, with the living touch of the flame of the Master's torch.

There are not ordinary meetings—God would not have a meeting to be ordinary. I refuse to be an ordinary man. You say, "Why do you?" Because I have an extraordinary God that makes extraordinary people. And it is between believing God's plan and not.

When we speak this way, we are at the root of the matter that can bring forth anything. Because Abram believed God, every person is blessed today through faithful Abraham. He was an extraordinary man on faith. He believed God in the face of everything.

You would like to be extraordinary, wouldn't you? If you are prayed for this morning, though you see not change at all, if you believe it is done, you may become extraordinary on that line. You people who have been longing for the baptism of the Holy Ghost and every day you have been waiting and tarrying, if you have got to a place of believing, you have got to a place where you have become extraordinary.

Interpretation of Tongues:

> The peace that comes from above is always full of purity and life-giving, and it never brings destruction to anyone. And the wisdom is on the same line. And all purification on every line never disturbs you. It is only that which is earthly which disturbs you. You cannot be disturbed by a heavenly breath. God is with us on a heavenly breath, and in that action, you cannot be disturbed. If you are disturbed from this day, know it is an earthly thing that is disturbing you.

Now I want to open out the fourteenth chapter of John— it is the Master's word. It is the Master's desire.

He has just said to them, in the twelfth verse, "Greater things than these shall ye do." (See John 14:12.) Why was His perspective so full? Because He had admiration before Him. Jesus had great admiration before Him when He saw the disciples. He knew He had the material that would bring out that which would prove to the world a real satisfaction—to heaven and to the world. Those glorified, exercised, wonderfully modified, and then glorified positions of these fishermen were surely ideal places.

What were they? Unlearned, in one place (not that I am going to build on an unlearned position). Ignorant men in another place (not that I am going to build on that). But, look: they were unlearned, but God taught them. It is far better to have the learning of the Spirit than anything else. They were ignorant; He enlarged them. They were beside themselves because they had been touched with the divine life. If the Most High God touches you, you will be beside yourself. As long as you hold your own, the natural and the spiritual will be mixed. But if ever you jump over the traces by the power of the new creation, you will find He has got hold of you.

Divine wisdom will never make you foolish. Divine wisdom will give you a sound mind. Divine wisdom will give you a touch of divine nature. Divine life is full of divine appointment and equipment, and you cannot be filled with the power of God without a manifestation. I would to God today that we understood that to be filled with the Holy Ghost is to be filled with manifestation, the glory of the Lord being in the midst of us, manifesting His divine power.

Jesus knew that these people He had before Him were going to do greater things than He had done. How could they do it? None of us is able. None of us is capable. But our incapability has to be clothed with His divine ability, and our helplessness has to be filled with His power of helpfulness. This is why He knew.

And He knew He was going away, and that if He went away, it was expedient, it was necessary, it was important that another came in His place and took up the same thing in them, as He had been telling them: "I in you and you in Me." (See John 17:21.) There was a plan of divine order. So the Holy Ghost was to come.

I want you to see what has to take place when He does come:

And I will pray the Father, and he shall give you another Comforter, that he may abide with you for ever; even the

Spirit of truth; whom the world cannot receive, because it seeth him not, neither knoweth him: but ye know him; for he dwelleth with you, and shall be in you. I will not leave you comfortless: I will come to you. (John 14:16–18)

I don't know a word that could be so fitting at this time as this word, *"Comforter."* I want to take you with me into the coming of the Holy Ghost.

Jesus ascended. When He ascended, He prayed the Father that He would send the Comforter. A needy moment, a needy hour, a necessity. Why? Because the disciples would want comforting.

How could they be comforted? By taking the word of Christ and revealing it unto them. What could help them so much as a word by the Spirit? For the Spirit is breath, life, person, power—the breath of Himself to us, the nature of Him.

How beautiful that the Spirit, when He came, should be the Spirit of Truth! Oh, if we would only read that into our hearts!

Some people have said, when the Holy Ghost came, "Could it be an evil power, or could an evil power possess us when we were waiting for the Holy Ghost?" Why, brother, when you receive the Holy Ghost, you receive the Spirit of Truth, the Spirit of Revelation, the Spirit that taketh the words of Jesus and makes them life to you. In the needy moment, He is the Comforter.

What will the Holy Ghost do? The Holy Ghost is prophetic. *"Be of good cheer"* (John 16:33). Live in peace. *"Take my yoke upon you and learn of me"* (Matthew 11:29). You say, that is what Jesus said. It is what the Holy Ghost is taking and revealing to us and speaking to us. The Holy Ghost is the spokesman in these days. The Holy Ghost came to be the spokesman, and He spoke the Word. He is still taking the Word and speaking it. The Holy Ghost takes the words of

Jesus, and He is so full of truth that He never puts anything to it. He gives you the unadulterated word of truth, of life.

The Holy Ghost came to be the spokesman, and He spoke the Word. He is still taking the Word and speaking it.

"He takes of mine and reveals it unto you." (See John 16:14–15.) What is His? *"I am the light of the world"* (John 8:12; 9:5). He came not to condemn the world, but that the world through Him should be saved. (See John 3:17.) The Holy Ghost takes these words and gives them to you. Here are words of the Master: *"Come unto me, all ye that labour and are heavy laden, and I will…"* (Matthew 11:28). Who is speaking? The Holy Ghost—in the last days, the Spirit of Truth bringing forth the Word of life: *"I will give you rest"* (Matthew 11:28). Rest? Oh, there is no rest like it! It can come when you are in the most tried moment.

When my dear wife was lying dead, the doctors could do nothing. They said to me, "She is done. We cannot help you." My heart was so moved, and I said, "O God, I can't spare her!"

I went up to her and I said, "Oh, come back! Come back and speak to me. Come back, come back!"

And the Spirit of the Lord moved, and she came back and smiled again. Then the Holy Ghost said to me, "She is Mine. Her work is done. She is Mine."

Oh, the comforting word! No one else could have done it, but the Comforter came from that moment my dear wife passed away.

Ah, beloved, it is true to me—the Comforter has a word for us this day. He is the Comforter. There is only one Comforter, and He has been with the Father from the beginning. He never comes but to give light. The Holy Ghost, when He comes into you, is to come to unveil the King, to insure you of His presence.

The person who says "I am ready for anything" will never get it.

"What are you seeking, my brother?"

"Oh, I am ready for anything."

"You will never get anything."

"Oh! Well, tell me how to get it."

"One thing have I desired…that will I seek after" (Psalm 27:4). When the Lord reveals unto you that you must be filled with the Holy Ghost, seek only that one thing, and God will give you that one thing. It is necessary for you to seek one thing first.

I went to two young men in a meeting one day and said to them, "Young men, what about it?"

They had just passed through their degrees, and beautiful young men they were.

"Oh!" they said. "We don't believe in it the same as you do. We don't believe in receiving the Holy Ghost as those people do."

There was a crowd of people tarrying at the front.

"You are dressed up as you would like to have it," I said. "You are dressed like preachers. And, seeing you are dressed like preachers, it is a pity for you to have the dress with the Presence."

"Well, we don't believe it that way," they said.

"But look," I said, "the apostles believed it in that way. Wouldn't you like to be an apostle? Wouldn't you like to go on the same line as they? They believed it that way."

Never you forget, the baptism will always be as it was in the beginning. It has not changed. And if you want a real baptism, expect it just the same as they had it at the beginning.

"What had they at the beginning?" you ask.

Well, they knew they had the same as they had at the beginning, for they heard them speak in tongues, and that is the only way they did know, because they heard them saying the same things in the Spirit as they said at the beginning. It has never been changed; it has always been the same, right down. As it was in the beginning, so shall it be for ever and ever.

When these two young men realized that Peter and John and the rest of them had it, they walked up. They were beautifully dressed. In about half an hour's time, they looked strange. They had been rolling somehow; I had not caused them to do it. But they had been so lost and so controlled by the power of God that they were just rolling all over, and their clothes were changed, but their faces were wonderful.

What was up? They got it just as they got it at the beginning.

They had been ordained by men—I do not say anything against that, I think it is very good—but there is an ordination that is better, and it is the ordination with the King. This is the only ordination that is going to fit you people for the future. The king is already on His throne, but He wants crowning, and when the Holy Ghost comes, He crowns the King inside.

The person that has passed through that ordination goes forth with fresh feet—the preparation of the gospel; goes with a fresh voice—speaks as the Spirit gives utterance; and goes with a fresh mind—the mind being illuminated by the power of God. He goes forth with a fresh vision and sees all things new.

When He comes, He shall reveal things unto you. Has He revealed them yet? He is going to do it. Only expect Him to do. The best thing for you is to expect Him to do it now.

Put up with any disorder you like when you are coming through into the baptism. You can have the biggest time on earth if I am there. You can scream as much as you like. Some people are frightened.

A woman came to me in Switzerland after I had helped her and asked to speak to me further.

"Now that I feel I am healed," she said, "and that terrible carnal passion which has bound and fettered me is done, I feel that I have a new mind. I believe I would like to receive the Holy Ghost, but when I hear these people screaming, I feel like running away."

After that, we were at another meeting in Switzerland, where a great hotel was joined to the building. At the close of one of the morning services, the power of God *fell*—that is all I can call it—the power of God fell. This poor, timid creature, who couldn't bear to hear anybody scream, screamed so loud that all the waiters out in this big hotel came out with their aprons on and their trays to see what was up. Nothing especially was "up." Something had come "down" and had so altered the situation that this woman could stand anything after that.

When God begins dealing with you on the baptism, He begins on this line: He starts with the things which are the most difficult. He starts with your human nature. He starts with your fear. He gets the fear away, gets the human nature out of place; and just as you dissolve, just as the power of the Spirit brings a dissolving to your human nature, in the same act, the Holy Ghost flows into the place where you are being dissolved, and you are quickened just where you come into death. And as you die—naturally, humanly, carnally, selfishly—of every evil thing, the new life, the Holy Ghost floods the whole case till it becomes a transformed case.

No man can tame the tongue, but when the Holy Ghost begins, He tames the whole body, till the tongue—moved by the power of the Spirit—till it says things exactly as the Lord would be delighted for them to be said.

The Holy Ghost is the Comforter. The Holy Ghost takes the necessary word at the right time and gives you. After the Holy Ghost takes charge of you, He is the Comforter to bring thought and language to your life, and it is amazing.

After the Holy Ghost takes charge of you, He is the Comforter to bring thought and language to your life, and it is amazing.

If we get to the place where we take no thought for ourselves, then God takes thought for us. But as long as we are taking thought for ourselves, we are somewhat hindered in this divine order with God. Taking no thought for yourself, no desire for your human self, not seeking anything for your human order, but that God shall be glorified in your body and spirit, and that He shall be the chief worker on every line—this is divine appointment; this is holy order.

There is a holy order. There are sects today which use this name. But the only holy order is where God has got so through with your nature that the Trinity comes in with perfect blending. Where the nature could not help itself, then God turned the captivity of the wheels of nature and poured in His divine power till the nature itself became an existence of divine property.

Another of the necessity positions of the Holy Ghost today we find in John 14:26:

> *But the Comforter, which is the Holy Ghost, whom the Father will send in my name, he shall teach you all things, and bring all things to your remembrance, whatsoever I have said unto you.*

First, He will "take of Mine and reveal it." (See John 16:15.) Everything that has been revealed to you is taken. Then, you come to the place where you need another touch. What is it? In the necessity of your ministry, He will bring to memory everything that you need in your ministry. That is an important thing for you preachers. God will give us His Word, and if there is anything special we need, He will bring that to our remembrance. The Holy Ghost is here this morning to bring the Word to us in remembrance.

I throw this word out to you as a help for future thought. In 1 John 2:20, we read, "*Ye have an unction from the Holy One.*" God grant we may not forget it! Ye have received power. (See Acts 1:8.) Oh, God grant that we may not forget it!

What do I mean by that? Many people, instead of standing on the rock word of faith to believe that they have got it, say, "Oh, if I could only feel that I have got it!"

Brother, your feeling robs you of your greatest place of unction. Your feelings are a place, very often, of discouragement. You have to get away from the sense of all human feeling or desire. Earthly desires are not God's desires. All thoughts of holiness, all thoughts of purity, all thoughts of power are from above. Human thoughts are like the clouds, which are always of the earth. God's thoughts are not our thoughts. (See Isaiah 55:8.)

Interpretation of Tongues:

It is the shadows that flee away. It is your feelings that have to be moved from you this day. It is the divine unction of a new creation, moving in thy human nature, which has to change all, even thy environment, and make thee so that from thy heart, even thy mind and thy tongue and everything, shall be in a place of magnifying the Lord. Remember, it is from above in thine heart to change all thy life till thou shalt be as He has promised, sons of God with power.

Remember, "Ye have an unction" (1 John 2:20).

Some things are of necessity. Here is a woman dying. Here is a man who has lost all power of his faculties. Here is a person apparently in death. Here they are; I see the great need. I drop down on my knees and cry. I miss it all.

God does not want me to cry; God does not want me to labor; God does not want me to anguish and be filled with anxiety and an anguished spirit.

What does He want me to do?

Believe only. After you have received, believe only. Come to the authority of it. Dare to believe. "I will do it!"

So the baptism of the Holy Ghost says to me, *"Ye have an unction."* The unction has come, the unction abideth, and the unction is with us. But what about you if you have not lived in the place that unction can be increased? Ah! Then the Spirit is grieved. Then you are not moved. You are like one dead. You feel that all the joy is gone.

What is up? There is something between you and the Holy One, not clean, not pure, not desirous of only Him, but something else has come in the way. Then the Spirit is grieved, and you have lost unction.

Is the Unctioner there? Yes. When He comes in, He comes to abide. He will either be grieved, full of groaning and travail, or He will be there to lift thee above the powers of darkness, transform thee by His power, and take thee to a place where all is filled with equipment.

Many people lose all future positions of attainment because they fail to understand this:

> But the anointing which ye have received of him abideth in you, and ye need not that any man teach you: but as the same anointing teacheth you of all things, and is truth, and is no lie, and even as it hath taught you, ye shall abide in him.
>
> (1 John 2:27)

What anointing? *"How God anointed Jesus of Nazareth with the Holy Ghost and with power: who went about doing good"* (Acts 10:38).

The same anointing is with thee, and thou requirest not that any man shall teach thee, but the same anointing is with thee and shall teach thee all things.

O lovely Jesus! Blessed Incarnation of holy display! Thank God for Trinity displayed in our hearts today! Thank God for this glorious open way! Thank God for darkness that is turning into day! Thank God for life all along the way! Praise God for hope that we may all be changed today! Hallelujah!

> *Peace, peace, sweet peace,*
> *Coming down from the Father above,*
> *Peace, peace, wonderful peace,*
> *Sweet peace, the gift of God's love.*

The very position and presence that will bring everybody into a fullness.

QUESTIONS AND ANSWERS

Q: After being baptized in water, if one goes back in sin and then repents, is it necessary to be baptized again?

A: There has to come into your life a real knowledge that after you have had hands laid upon you, you have not to expect hands to be laid upon you again. After you have received the baptism, you are not to expect to be baptized again, neither in water nor anywhere else. The Word of God is very clear: as you go on to perfection, you are leaving the first principles, you are leaving them behind, because God says, "Come on!" Don't repeat anything that is passed on. Believe it is finished.

Q: Can anyone receive the baptism of the Holy Ghost in his own room?

A: Yes. I believe after hands have been laid upon you to receive the Holy Ghost, you can go away believing that you will certainly receive, whether it is in your bed or anywhere. I laid my hands on a very remarkable man in London—we considered him one of the finest men we had. He went home and received the baptism of the Holy Ghost in his bed.

Remember that no person is a baptizer; Jesus is the only baptizer, and you never get away from His presence. He is with you in your bedrooms; He is with you in your counting rooms; He is with you everywhere. "*Lo, I am with you always*" (Matthew 28:20).

Remember that no person is a baptizer; Jesus is the only baptizer, and you never get away from His presence.

Q: Is it possible for a Christian to have the the baptism of the Holy Spirit and still retain afflictions in his body?

A: Paul says these light afflictions are working out for us a far exceeding and eternal weight of glory. If you try to save yourself through the afflictions, it means to say you are not ready for going. We have to come to a place—a higher standard than many people have looked into, but we are coming to it—that if you knew you could stop a day longer in the earth by lifting your finger, you would not do it. We are coming to a place of knowledge of the spiritual quickening of these divine orders of Christ; we are coming to a place that, if we knew there was a pill lying there, and we knew that pill would save us from death, we would refrain from taking it, knowing it was far better to go. If we ever wake up—and, thank God, we are waking—to the fact that it is better to go than to stay, we will never save ourselves.

Q: The Holy Ghost, through John, said, "We shall baptize you with the Holy Ghost and with fire." Is it necessary that I shall receive the baptism of fire, and can I receive the Holy Ghost till I receive the baptism of fire?

A: It is one and the selfsame thing; it is only one Holy Ghost, only one baptism, and only one reception. When He comes in, He comes to abide.

We can't always give all the figurative positions of the Holy Ghost, but the Holy Ghost fire is more than figurative. It is assimilation. The Holy Ghost is a great assimilation to the whole body. When He comes in, you will feel fire going through the body. You feel a burning of all inward corruption.

The baptism of the Holy Ghost is essential to bring into you a divine, holy fire which burns up all dross and quickens all purity, making you ablaze for perfect love to continue.

The baptism of the Holy Ghost and the baptism of fire are one and the same. The baptism is the divine Third Person of the Trinity.

Q: But on the day of Pentecost, the fire fell upon them as tongues of fire, and afterward, the Holy Ghost came. Will you explain that?

A: First, there was the rushing mighty wind. Why did the Holy Ghost have to come? Simply because when Jesus was here, He was local; He was a person, but He was a person of ideal perfection, the Father presenting all fullness in Him. And yet, when all fullness came, it was necessary for Jesus to receive the flow of breath to formulate the Word, and the Spirit breathed, and Jesus said the words, "*I speak not...but the Father that dwelleth in Me*" (John 14:10)—the Breath, which was making language.

The Holy Spirit could fill people in England, in America, in China, in Africa, in the islands of the sea, everywhere, all over the world. When He came, the Breath, the Power could fill the whole universe, because it was the breath of the mighty power of God personally.

Also, He was a flame. Tongues of fire. What could be more inspiring? Flames of fire, tongues of fire, burning up that which was inflammable within. And they saw it. It has been seen many times since then.

But in the wind they were not baptized. In the fire they were not baptized. When were they baptized? When the fire and the wind got inside and caused eruption.

Q: Is the baptism of the Holy Ghost a personality?

A: Yes, it is. It is not an "it," not an influence; but it is a presence, a power, a person—the Third Person of the Trinity. That is the reason why the Lord said, "When He comes."

Q: Can a person receive the baptism of the Holy Ghost before being sanctified?

A: Do you know what it is to be saved? Yes. As you go on with God, you are being saved, and the more you go on with God, the more confident you are that you are saved. It was an accomplished fact that you were saved, but you are being saved as you walk in the light to a greater depth of knowledge of salvation. You were sanctified, but you are being sanctified according to light, and you are not what you were yesterday.

Light! Light! Light! When you received the Holy Ghost, it is certain the Lord is pleased with where you got to, but it is not where you are going to. Every man is sanctified, but no man in this place has received sanctification who has not an increased sanctification. There is no man being saved today that has not to have an increased salvation, line upon line, truth upon truth, to know he is ripe for heaven, but he is going on to perfection. He is from glory to glory. The process is wonderful: being saved, being sanctified, being made ready every day!

Q: Is sanctification a definite work of grace?

A: Yes, and salvation also. And the next day you will find out, as light comes, you will be like Isaiah in the presence of God. You will find you need another cleaning. Light makes cleansing needed.

Q: I have been tarrying for the baptism of the Holy Spirit for a long time, have been told if I would say "Glory!" or "Hallelujah!" till I have lost myself, I would receive, but so far I have not received.

A: You have had a great deal of things in your mind as to what ought to bring it, and you are forgetting what will bring it, and that is Jesus. Jesus is the Baptizer. As soon as you are ready, He will fill you.

PREPARATION FOR THE
SECOND COMING OF THE LORD,
Part Two
Bible Study #23 – August 16, 1927

T he life of the Lord Jesus should be so upon us that we are being prepared and made ready for the rapture. The object of this meeting is that the very nature of the Son of God might be presented to us by the Word of Life, that we may know what is this life. Have we got it? If we have not, may we have it? What will be the evidence of it?

I want you to be so acquainted with the Word of Life that you will have no doubt that you are coming to a like precious faith, or that you are coming to the life divine, or that you have knowledge of a Greater than you working out this mighty power of redemption in your mortal bodies.

These are foundation lines. We shall have to have a foundation before we can begin. God can look over a million things and jump us in, but I believe that people ought to have the things already in without jumping in. The Spirit of the Lord is so mighty that just as He brought Philip and dropped him down in the desert and brought him back out of the desert, the same Spirit can come upon the whole church.

There is a "knowledge of know," and they that know can speak with confidence about what they do know. I want you to know so that when you go away from here, you will be able to talk about what you know, about what will happen when Jesus comes, and what will be the cause of the happening—for there has to be a cause for the happening.

Interpretation of Tongues:

> *Prepare thy heart, for the Lord is at the door and waiting now to open thy inner vision. For that which is created in thee is that which shall come out of thee to be clothed upon with that which is from above. It is not that body, but it is the body that shall be. (It is the spiritual body I am dealing with, not the natural body.)*

THE LIFE IN HIM, IN US

Let us turn now to the Word of God, the first chapter of John: *"In him was life; and the life was the light of men"* (John 1:4).

As we go into the Scripture, we shall find that this same light—this same spiritual acquaintance or knowledge, this same divine power and authority, the life which is eternal, which is divine and eternal, which is incorruptible, which cannot see corruption—this life was in the Son of God, and He came to be the light and the life of men.

God wants us to comprehend this life which was in the Son, which was to be in us, which was to be resurrection, which was to overcome death, which was to have all power in the mortal body, transforming it in every way, till it should be in you a manifestation of the invisible but spiritual, not known and well known, having nothing and possessing all things, in you but mightier than you, pulling down strongholds, triumphing graciously over everything.

Now let us come to the twelfth verse, which has another side to it. First is the manifestation of the Son. The next thought is in the twelfth: *"But as many as received him"* (John 1:12).

Don't get the idea of receiving the Son of Man in His natural order; if you do, you will miss it. As many as received His life—the revelation that was made manifest by Him, the fact that He was in the midst of them with a new order, greater than His natural, mighty in its production, with forceful language and acts divine, every move supernatural—*"to them gave he power to become the sons of God, even to them that believe on his name"* (John 1:12).

As they received Him, they had power to become acquainted with this inward knowledge of what He was presenting to them. Not His hair, not His head, not His feet, not His hands, not His legs, but the very life which was in Him had to come into every living one that understood Him, that received Him, with a power.

Now let us look at what power it had to have: *"Which were born, not of blood, nor of the will of the flesh, nor of the will of man, but of God"* (John 1:13).

Born of God. The first order was there. The first order is here. The first physique that was manifested. Adam is in the midst of us in all his manifestations.

But now they know they are confronted with a life, a power, which has to come to them, to be absolutely created of it, born of it, made of it. Just as He was, we have to be inwardly, knowing that we are now born of another nature, quickened by another power, living in a new revelation, having the same things that He had.

He came. They saw Him. In 1 John 1:1, we read,

That which was from the beginning, which we have heard, which we have seen with our eyes, which we have looked upon, and our hands have handled, of the Word of life.

This is not His hands; this is not His eyes. They have an inward looking, and they are seeing a new creation. They are seeing a Word with power. They are seeing the nature of God. They are seeing the manifestation of God in human flesh. This is exactly what we are when we are born of this.

> *For the life was manifested, and we have seen it, and bear witness, and show unto you that eternal life.*
>
> (1 John 1:2)

Now here is another order. Here is another stream. It is not a temporal thing. This is divine, with supernatural power. This is an eternal thing. This is something that cannot pass away. This is something that is to be given to us. This is something that is to be in us. This is the very nature of God. This is as eternal as God, this manifestation of the Son they are looking at—the Word, the power, the eternal source, eternal power.

Interpretation of Tongues:

> *It is the Lord. It is the Life from above. It is that which came by the Spirit. He left the throne, He came igniting humanity till they became a living, quickened spirit of divine order. It is eternal life.*

Again we read:

> *For the life was manifested, and we have seen it, and bear witness, and show unto you that eternal life, which was with the Father, and was manifested unto us.* (1 John 1:2)

Now they have it, and they begin manifesting it themselves. They begin writing about it, and they know as they write that they are writing *life*. The next verse gives it:

That which we have seen and heard declare we unto you, that ye also may have fellowship with us: and truly our fellowship is with the Father, and with his Son Jesus Christ.

(1 John 1:3)

Eternal life inward, now conversation heavenward, now fellowship with the Father, now divine acquaintance with God, till you know that this which was in Him is in us. This is why they wrote. This is why they knew. And they expressed it by their mouths and it became a quickened, powerful Spirit as they gave it, as it was when He gave it. I feel the same thing as I am breathing out this message.

I know there is a supernatural, quickening power coming through me by the Holy Spirit.

> *Eternal life inward, now conversation heavenward, now fellowship with the Father, now divine acquaintance with God, till you know that this which was in Him is in us.*

Interpretation of Tongues:

Not that which was first; no, God moved away the first that He might establish the second. The first was the natural man, but now the second is a spiritual man. In thee, through thee, by thee, coming into manifestation.

Awake! The vision, the life, the power is now revealed. Enter in that thou mightest not be naked when the King comes.

God wants to establish in our hearts the fact that we must be ready for the King. Now we are talking about the fact, which is greater than the possibility. Fact works possibilities. Possibilities are in the fact, but you must have the fact first before the possibilities.

Joy in This Life

To continue in this Scripture in 1 John, brought in to show the life manifested, let us consider the fourth verse: *"And these things write we unto you, that your joy may be full"* (1 John 1:4).

The Word of Life is to make your joy full. We must remember that what is absent in the world is joy. The world has never had joy. The world never will have joy. Joy is not in the five senses of the world. Feelings are there, happiness is there, but joy can only be produced where there is no alloy. Now, there is no alloy in heaven. Alloy means that there is a mixture. In the world, there is happiness, but it is a mixture. Very often, it comes up very close to sorrow. Very often, in the midst of the ballroom, there comes a place of happiness, and right underneath that, there is a very heavy heart and a strange mixture. So in those five senses that the world has, they have happiness.

But this that we have is this: it is joy without alloy, without a mixture. It is inwardly expressive. It rises higher and higher till, if it had its perfect order, we would drown everything with a shout of praise coming from this holy presence.

We want all the people to receive the Holy Ghost, because the Holy Ghost has a very blessed expression to the soul or the heart, and it is this: the Holy Ghost has an expression of the Lord in His glory, in His purity, in His power, and all His beatitudes. All these are coming forcefully through as the Holy Ghost is able to witness to you of Him. And every time the Son is made manifest in your hearts by the Holy Ghost, you get a real stream of glory on earth, joy in the Holy Ghost—not eating and drinking—something higher, something higher, something better, something more substantial. Joy in the Holy Ghost! And the Holy Ghost can bring this joy to us.

We move on now in still further foundation. This is the first foundation of the truths of the coming of the Lord. *The coming of the Lord is for the life of the Lord.* The coming of the Lord is not for my body. Our bodies will never be in heaven. They will never reach there. They are terrestrial things, and everything terrestrial will finish upon a terrestrial line.

What is going to be there?

The *life*—the life of the Son of God, the nature of the Son of God, the holiness of the Son of God, the purity, the life, the likeness, and all pertaining.

As we go on, we shall see that He is in this life, which is going to have a new body. This life will demand a new body; it is demanding it now. We cannot develop this in this moment, but I want to throw out some thought of it. This is a law of life. Now, you have a law in nature of life. But now you have to have a law of a spirit of life, which is to make free from everything of natural order. And this is the law of life, of the life of Christ which is in you, which I am taking you through or bringing you to, that you might be firmly fixed on the perfect knowledge that no matter what happened, you know you would go.

When I say "you," it is right to say you will go. You will go up, but you won't go in. You will be dissolved as you go. But the nature of the Son, the new life, will go in with the new body.

We turn again to the first chapter of John and read the fourteenth verse. They saw. They heard the Word. Now this is to be ours.

> *And the Word was made flesh* [they saw it], *and dwelt among us* [it was right in the midst of them and they couldn't help seeing the glory of it], *(and we beheld his glory, the glory as of the only begotten of the Father,) full of grace and truth.* (John 1:14)

Now you have to receive that—full of grace, full of truth, the glory of the Lord. You must remember that glory is not a halo round your head. Probably, in some pictures of the Lord Jesus or of saints, you would see a light patch painted just over the top, the idea being to exhibit glory. Glory never is that way. Glory is expressive, and glory is impressive before it is expressive. Glory is not an outside halo. Glory is an inward conception.

The more they were in the midst of glory, the more they were convinced of it and preserved it. It had two mighty powers with it. It not only had grace, which was the canopy of the mercy of the high order of God, all the time prevailing and covering and pressing Him, but also it had truth. He spoke so that every heart was filled with what He said.

And this is what we have to have. This is that which will be caught up, expressive. Can expressiveness be taken up? Yes, because it is the nature of the new birth. Will truth be taken up? Yes, for truth is the very embodiment of the Son. Just as this life permeates through your body, it would be impossible for any saint ever to be free to give anything but absolute truth. The saint has to become an embodiment of Truth, Life, Christ manifest. We have to be like Him, just as He was, filled with His glory, this divine order, speaking out of fullness, greater than anything we have ever had; mind and soul perceiving the things of God that we live, move, and act in this glory.

They saw it, and you have seen it this morning. The glory of the Lord, the presence of the Lord, the power of the Lord, the life of the Lord is being made manifest. I will tell you how you know it. As I speak, your hearts are burning; your very inward motions are crying out for more. Why? This is that which will be taken. It is not you He is after. It is that which has been created in you.

How did it come? It wasn't of flesh; it wasn't of blood; it wasn't through the mind of man. But it came by God. This new life came by God. You had the three things before, but now the fourth comes. What place did it take? The very thing that would bring you to death changes by beginning in life. The moment this change began in your life, it made you so different, so new, that you felt you had never called God "Father" before in your life. There was something new that said "Father" differently. You knew that now you were joined up to an eternal Fatherhood. You knew you were moved from earth and were joined up to heaven.

The greatest thing that I can talk about this morning is the rapture, and I touch it occasionally but cannot go into it yet. The greatest word there is in the world is rapture. The worst thing that ever man knows about in the world is death. Death makes you shudder. There is something about it; nobody wants it. But this new life frees you from death. You know there is no death in it. It is life.

This eternal life, this inward force, makes you know, as you think about rapture, that you are not here; you are off. That is why I want to get you into the thought, you are off, and I want you to live in a place of divine acquaintance with rapture.

You have to get to know how to possess your souls in patience.

Now come to the third chapter of John:

Jesus answered, Verily, verily, I say unto thee, Except a man be born of water and of the Spirit, he cannot enter into the kingdom of God. That which is born of the flesh is flesh; and that which is born of the Spirit is spirit. Marvel not that I said unto thee, Ye must be born again. The wind bloweth where it listeth, and thou hearest the sound thereof, but canst not tell whence it cometh, and whither it goeth: so

is every one that is born of the Spirit. Nicodemus answered and said unto him, How can these things be?
(John 3:5–9)

So we see that no natural man that ever lived can understand these things. This is a supernatural teaching, and when we come to the line of this truth, we are able to put supernatural things into place to discern natural things. But we must be supernatural first before we can deal with supernatural things.

> *Jesus was a supernatural evidence, and He was dealing with a supernatural production, and He was dealing with a man who was natural.*

Jesus was a supernatural evidence, and He was dealing with a supernatural production, and He was dealing with a man who was natural. This man that was natural could not comprehend how it could be possible for him who had been born say, forty-five or fifty years before, to be born again.

Jesus spoke to him as I am speaking to you now, that this birth, this new birth, is not flesh and blood. This new birth is the life of God. It is a spiritual life as real as God, as true as God, and as forming as God. God is a formation, and we are formed after His formation, for He made us in His very image. But He is a spiritual God, and He has quickened us and made us inward like Him, with a spiritual life; just as we have natural formation, so the new nature. The new power is forming continually a new man in us after the order of Him. The first Adam was formed, and we are in the vision of him. The last Adam, the new creation, is going to have a vision and expression like Him. As we have borne the image of the earthy, we are going to bear the image of the heavenly. It is already in, but the casket is not broken. The casket will be dissolved, and the heaven nature—the heaven body—will prove itself, and we shall be like Him.

I want you to follow the Word and rightly divide it, asking yourself these questions: Am I in the faith? Have I this that Nicodemus was seeking?

I was once exactly where Nicodemus was, and said, "How can these things be?" Then, there came by faith a regenerating power which made me know I was born of God. It came like the breath; I could not see it, but I felt it. It had a tremendous effect upon my human nature, and I found myself a new creation. I found I wanted to pray and to talk about the Lord. Oh! I shall never forget saying, "Father"!

If you catch this truth, it does not matter where you are— if you are in exile somewhere, on a farm where no one is near you, exiled from everybody, cannot get near anybody for comfort. If this life gets into you, you will know this: that when He comes, you will go. This is the life which I want you to know—the life in the body.

The new birth, the new creation, the quickening, the being made after Him—the begotten of God—is a very beautiful thought, if you put it in this perfect order: when you are born of God, God's nature comes in. I won't call it the germ of eternal life, but the seed of conception of God, because it says we are conceived by the Word, we are quickened by the power, we are made after His order. That which is from above has entered into that which is below, and you have become now a quickened spirit. You were dead, without aspiration, without desire. As soon as this comes in, aspiration, desire, prayer ascend, lifting higher and higher; and you have already moved towards heavenly things. This is a new creation, which cannot live on the earth; it always lives, soaring higher, higher, and higher, loftier and loftier, holier and holier. This is the most divine order you could have. This is the spiritual order. God, manifested in the flesh, quickening us by the Spirit, making us like unto Him. Hallelujah!

Now turn to the fifth chapter of John, the twenty-fourth verse:

> *Verily, verily, I say unto you, He that heareth my word, and believeth on him that sent me, hath everlasting life, and shall not come into condemnation; but is passed from death unto life.* (John 5:24)

"He that heareth." Then, the Word of Life can go into the ear? Yes, in through the ear, right into the heart. The Word, the life, the nature of the Son of God.

What does it do? "*He that heareth my word, and believeth on him that sent me, hath everlasting life.*" Who can value that?

There is a good deal of controversy about this, as to the length of time it is. What do you say it is? What does Jesus say it is? Everlasting life. Some people say it might be for ten, fifteen, or twenty years. What do you say it is? Everlasting life.

If you get there, there is no difficulty about being ready. But if you doubt the Word of God, how can you be ready? I am speaking to the wise, and a word to the wise is sufficient. It does not matter who brings a wrangling accusation against the Word; if they say anything about this everlasting life, ask them what they believe about it, for Jesus said this.

Supposing you say, "Well, I doubt it," then you will be done. Jesus says if you doubt it, it is damnation; if you believe it, it is everlasting life. It just depends upon what you are going to believe about it. Do you believe it is everlasting life? Are you going to let your opinions rob you and bring you into condemnation, or are you going to receive what the Word says?

What is the Word? The Word is truth. What is truth? Jesus is *the* Truth. Jesus said these words: "He that heareth My word, and believeth on him that sent me, hath everlasting life, and shall not come into condemnation; but is passed, passed, *passed, passed* from death unto life." (See John 5:24.)

> *Holy, holy, holy, Lord God of Hosts!*
> *Heaven and earth are praising Thee,*
> *O Lord, Most High!*

These meetings will go higher and higher. I want you to get a foundation position so that when you go out in the world of service, you will have a laid-down fact in your heart as to what is the coming of the Lord. As I go on, I shall be able to give you a clear distinction of its expression. In, out of, a living expression of a living personality. For Christ is now already manifested, or being manifested, in us. The sons of God are coming forth with power, and God will show us, as we go on with the Word of God, this living, glorious fact or hope or crown of rejoicing.

May God the Holy Ghost sanctify us and purify us with a perfect purification till we stand white in the presence of God. Let us do some repenting. Let us tell God we want to be holy. If you are sure you have this eternal life in you, I want you to consider it worth not looking back, keeping your eyes upon the plan, looking towards the Master. Believe that God is greater than your heart. Believe that God is greater than your thoughts. Believe that God is greater than the devil. Believe He will preserve you. Believe in His almightiness. And on the authority of God's faith in you, you will triumph till He comes:

> *Bring me higher up the mountain,*
> *Into fellowship with Thee!*
> *In Thy light, I see the fountain*
> *And the blood that cleanseth me.*

QUESTIONS AND ANSWERS

Q: You said there is no body in heaven. Is Jesus Christ sitting at the right hand of the Father in flesh or in Spirit?

A: We shall have bodies in heaven, but they will be spiritual, glorified bodies. I believe that Jesus is different from anyone else in the glory because of the marks. But I have Scripture to bear me out that there is no flesh and blood in heaven, but we will be different. We shall have our hands, but glorified hands, glorified bodies. Your own character, your own crown will be there.

How will the crown be made? The crown is this: the wood, the hay, the stubble will be burned, and the gold, the silver, and precious stones will be left. And everybody will know what kind of a crown of life they have had because the crown will be made up of your own gold and your own precious stones after it has got through the fire.

Everybody will know. We shall know as we are known; there will be no mistake about that. But it will be an expression of brightness, of glory. For instance, we shall be really transparent in so many ways, the glory will be so wonderful. Let us look at Jesus for a moment. When Jesus was with Peter and John in that holy mount, the very vesture, the very nature, everything that He had was turned to transparent glory till the very raiment was as white as snow and the whole of His body was transformed in that vision.

That very thing that was in the man will be exactly expressive. Moses was known, Elias was known, in their glorified bodies. Jesus will be known to everybody as the Son of God and as the Lamb slain. The marks will be there, the glorified body with the marks. It will be very wonderful. We shall be there.

What will have passed away from us is this: the marks of sin, the marks of deformity, the marks of corruption, the marks of transgression. We shall be there, whiter than snow, purified through and through. The Lamb of God will be known. He will be different; He will have a glorified body, for flesh and blood does not enter into the kingdom of God. It could not stand the glory. It would be withered up in His presence, so it has to be a changed body. God calls it, in 1 Corinthians 15, the "celestial body." (See verse 40.)

Q: Didn't Christ, after the resurrection, have a body of flesh and bones?

A: Yes, He did. When we get to heaven, what we shall be first most pleased about: He will be the same Lord, just the same, only a glorified body, and neither flesh not bones.

Q: What did Job mean when he said, "Though…worms destroy my body, yet in my flesh shall I see God" (Job 19:16)?

A: That is a different thing altogether. I believe that everybody will see God perfectly and in a very wonderful way. "The pure in heart…shall see God" (Matthew 5:8). I believe we shall see God and see Jesus in our flesh, but it will be the last time of the flesh. We shall know Him no more after the flesh, but we shall see Him in the spirit. You will never see Jesus anymore after that in the flesh.

Q: Will the celestial bodies and terrestrial bodies be gathered together?

A: Terrestrial bodies will never be in the presence of God. Terrestrial is always earthly. Celestial bodies in the glory will leave terrestrial bodies, and we shall all be together—the angels, archangels, God—and all will be there, perfect. The angels may never understand the fullness of our redemption, but they will all be there in perfect harmony. He will gather all into perfect harmony. It will be a wonderful place, heaven. But in order to fit us properly, He knows it will be necessary to have a new earth and a new heaven to fit the situation.

Q: If, in accordance with 1 John 5:14, we realize that the Father listens to us, and we ask according to His will and have what we ask for, then why is it more miracles are not wrought through those of us who profess to have faith in God?

A: There is a good deal of difference between professing to have faith in God and having faith in God. There is a good deal of difference between persuading yourself that you have confidence toward God and having confidence. There is a good deal of difference between faith and saying you have faith. As you go on, you should come into perfect line of the knowledge of the Word you are asking for. For what will give you confidence like the Life? You will have to give place to the Life. You won't have to have a mixture, a life of flesh and a life of the Spirit. You cannot get confidence that way. You have to come into line to know that He has to reign supremely, preeminently, over you, and He has to be there forthcoming as the Son of God with power. And in this place you will have confidence, and in this place you will ask and will know it is according to the will of God. Don't condemn the Word of God because you do not reach the standard of perfection. Let your minds be subject to the will of God. *Never rule the Scripture by your mind; let the Scripture rule your mind.*

> *Never rule the Scripture by your mind; let the Scripture rule your mind.*

Q: Is there a Scripture that the Christians of today without the baptism of the Holy Ghost go up in the rapture?

A: What is rapture but eternal life? Could you imagine that anything down here that has had eternal life in it would not be in the rapture? It is contrary to the mind of God, contrary to the teaching of God. It is impossible for anyone to have eternal life in them and not that life to go, for eternal life, the life within you, is the life and the nature of the Son, and when He comes, it is impossible for you to stop. "When He comes who is our life, then also we shall appear." (See Colossians 3:4.) What will make it? The life, the joint life.

Q: Shall we see the Father as a personality, or will Jesus be the expression of the Father?

A: One thing will be certain: when we get to glory, we shall be very much taken up with the Son, but we must not forget that the Son will not rob the Father of His glory, but He will take us all, and He will take Himself in the great day of all things, and He will present us all and Himself to the Father. So I know the Father will be in a glorious place in the glory, and I know the Son will be in a wonderful place, and I know the Holy Ghost, who has comforted us all—what a great joy it will be to see Him who has been the great Comforter and the great Leader and the great Speaker and the great Operator. My! Won't we give Him a great place in the glory?

Q: Is it possible after a person has been truly born again to get away from the Lord and to be lost?

A: The Scripture says, "They that believe on the Lord shall have everlasting life." (See John 3:36.) The Word of God will not change for anyone. The Word of God is like a two-edged sword, dividing asunder, and it is all the time putting away what man says and giving you what God says.

Q: Will we be happy in heaven without our loved ones who are not saved?

A: My wife has been in the glory now fourteen and a half years. What will she have to say to me when I get there? She will have to say many things, I know she will—that is, if she has time, because all the time will be taken up talking about Jesus. This thought I want to bring to you because it will make a wonderful change in your life: if my wife, in the glory, could have thought about her sons being in the war, it would not have been heaven. The earthly things are not known. People in the glory are taken up with the things of the glory.

A woman said to me, "If I thought my son, John, would not be in heaven, I do not want to go."

"My dear sister," I said, "when you are in heaven, your celestial body will be so incarnated with all the glories of heaven that family relations will be in the Spirit only and never in the flesh. There is nothing about the flesh in the glory. Everything in the glory will be spiritual."

Why, bless you, you have had plenty of trouble about the flesh. How many have wept and groaned and agonized because of the flesh! There is going to be no flesh there, there is going to be no lie there, there is going to be no death there, there is going to be no weakness there—nothing that disturbs the glory. So you will be all right there.

Q: You said if our eyes are open, we could see the Lord right among us. We know that He ascended in one body. How could that be, provided there were half a dozen meetings going on at the same time— how could He be right in the midst?

A: The Holy Ghost is here and—I want to say it reverently—Jesus is not. Don't misunderstand me. Has Jesus ever been here since He went to the glory? No. Is He coming to the earth the next time? No. He is coming in the heavens, and we meet Him.

But who is here? The Holy Ghost, and He makes Jesus as real to me just as if He were here. That is the position of the Holy Ghost—to reveal the Father and the Son—and He makes them just as real to us as if He were here. And the Holy Ghost fills the whole earth, and He could make a million assemblies see every spiritual thing possible. We do not want to see spirits; we want to see bodies filled with the Spirit of the living God.

For our comfort and consolation, He says, "*Lo, I am with you alway*" (Matthew 28:20), and He is with us; He is with us in power and in might. The Holy Ghost makes Him real to me. He is with me.

Q: "Verily, verily, I say unto you, He that heareth my word, and believeth on him that sent me, hath everlasting life" (John 5:24). Does that not hinge on that word "believeth"? That is a present, continuous tense. He believes now and he keeps right at it. And doesn't it hinge right on that keeping at it as to whether we gain the glory and keep the eternal life or not? First, John says if our heart condemn us not, then hath we confidence, then can we believe. If I do something that makes my heart condemn me, how can I keep on believing?

A: If eternal life in you depends upon your always thinking about nothing else but that thing, most of these people in this place would say, "Well, I am no good, then." But we must remember that the blood of Jesus is not a past-tense cleansing power, but is a "cleanseth" power. You have been asleep all night, you know very well you were neither trying to believe nor thinking to believe nor anything, but the blood of Jesus cleanseth you in the night, and He cleanseth you this morning. Your salvation does not consist of always your shouting, "I believe!"

The new birth is a new life. It is regenerative, it is holy, it is divine, it is faith, it is Christ. And He is with you always, moving you, changing you, thrilling you, causing you to live in the glory, without pressure, a believing position. "*I delight to do thy will*" (Psalm 40:8). My condition of salvation is not a pressure of binding me always to say if I do not continually believe, I shall be lost. Faith is a life. Life is a presence—a presence of changing from one state of glory to another.

My attitude of yieldedness to God continually keeps me in His favor. If I thought that my salvation depended upon that, I should know then that I have lost the knowledge that God was greater than my heart and greater than my life, for I am not kept by what I do; I am kept by the power of God.

Q: Doesn't the same thing depend on me in His keeping power as depends on me when I gained His favor?

A: What you are doing, you are putting your weakness in the place of God's almighty power. If you believe, you are kept from falling. After God gives faith, He does not take it away.

Q: I know a number of people who have truly belonged to God and the glory has been upon them, but today they are serving the devil just as faithfully as they ever served the Lord. They have lost eternal life, have they not?

A: You are not responsible for them. They have had the light. Light has come to the world and they refused light. They are in awful jeopardy and darkness and sorrow. If you do not allow God to be greater than your heart, you will be in trouble about them.

Q: I am not in trouble about them, but I cannot quite catch the thought that they are still saved.

A: I have not told you that they are still saved. I believe they have tasted, but they have never been converted. I tell you the reason why: "*My sheep…follow me*" (John 10:27), and they are not of the fold if they do not follow. Jesus said it.

If I find people that want me to believe that they belong to God, and they are following the devil, I will say, "Well, either the Word or you is a liar." I do not take it for granted that because a person says he has been saved that he is saved. He is only proving to me he is saved if he follows.

Don't you for a moment believe I am here standing for eternal security. I am trying to help you to see that God's eternal security can be so manifested in your mortal bodies that there could not be a doubt toward rapture or life or anything. That is what I want the Word of God to make you know: that it is eternal word, it is eternal life, it is eternal power.

I have never known a moment in my life that God has not made me long for more holiness. I have been saved for sixty years, and I have never lost the sense of that saving, peaceful place. "He that believeth hath the witness." (See Romans 8:15; Galatians 4:6.) I cannot change the Word of God because a few people tasted and then went

> *I have never known a moment in my life that God has not made me long for more holiness.*

away. I believe that when you have been really born of God, you are either in deep conviction or you are on the top. It could not be otherwise.

Q: Is it possible for a real, true believer to quench the Holy Spirit and not know it?

A: No. The very life manifest in your mortal bodies in a very marvelous way is the Holy Ghost quickening the Word. How is it possible for you to grieve the Holy Spirit and not know it? I feel somehow that I should go almost insane if I had to think I had done such a thing as that. If I could come on this platform and the Holy Spirit was not upon me, it would be awful. I dare not come to you people without the presence of the Spirit was upon me. How do I know? If I kneel down here a moment and just say three words, I know. If I open the Word, in a moment I know. If I shake hands with a person, I know.

There is something about the Holy Ghost that makes you divinely operable. The Holy Ghost is an operative position in human nature, manifesting the power of God through His mortal flesh, and every day you feel the power of the Holy Ghost remanifesting—reorganizing, as it were— higher and higher; the Holy Ghost taking the things of God and making you know all the time. If you miss that, it would be awful. I don't know what would become of me if I missed that. I do not think any of you could rest if you missed that.

Q: Will you please explain Ezekiel 18:24: "But when the righteous turneth away from his righteousness, and committeth iniquity, and doeth according to all the abominations that the wicked man doeth, shall he live?"?

A: We ought to see that our righteousness is greater than the righteousness of filthy rags. *We ought to see that our holiness is so purified that we are not holy for the sake of being holy, but we are holy because of an incarnation of God in us making us holy.*

It is necessary that we face the truth and get to know. If we do not, what awful awaiting would be for us! The books are not to be opened and the crown is not to be given until the end. But I know some crowns are being increased, and I know God is making a great preparation for the saints.

But I warn you today: see to it that your lives are holy. See to it that you do not give place to the devil. See to it that you buy opportunities. See to it that you know the Scripture says that your whole body is sanctified and made meet for God. See to it that no sin ever has anything to do with your life. Believe God that He can keep you from falling. Believe God that He can present you holy. Believe God that you can have a reward. I am going in for the reward. Because other people do not care for going in for the reward, it makes me the more earnest for it.

Preparation for the Second Coming of the Lord,
Part Three
Bible Study #24 – August 17, 1927

Y ou may be amazed when you step into the glory to find there the very Word, the very life, the very touch—that which has caused aspiration, inspiration. The Word is settled there. The Word createth right in our very nature this wonderful touch of divine inspiration, making us know that they that are in heaven and we that are on earth are of one Spirit, blended in one harmonious knowledge, created in a new order, being made like unto Him by the power of the Spirit of the Word of God, till we are full of hopefulness, filled with life, joyously expecting, gloriously waiting.

One word is sufficient for me continually: *"Therefore being justified by faith, we have...access by faith into this grace wherein we stand, and rejoice in hope of the glory of God"* (Romans 5:1–2). Salvation fills us with hope of the glory of God, with a great access into the grace.

Let us turn to the sixth chapter of John, the twenty-seventh verse. We are still on the grounding, or the foundation, of the construction of the saint of God in the new order of the Spirit. We are still building upon the foundation principles of the living Word of God for the purpose that we may not be like those that are drunk in the night or those that are asleep, but that we shall be awakened.

Being awakened does not mean particularly that you have been actually asleep. Sleeping doesn't mean actually asleep. It means dense to activity of spiritual relationship. Sleeping does not mean that you are fast asleep. Sleeping means to say that you have lost apprehension and you are dull of hearing and your eyes are heavy because they are not full of light that shall light you. So God is making us understand that we have to be alive and awake.

Here is the word, John 6:27: *"Labour not for the meat which perisheth."* Jesus has been feeding the sheep at the commencement of this chapter, and because they have been fed by His gracious hands, the crowd came around Him again. He saw that they were of the natural order, and He broke forth into this wonderful word: *"Labour not for the meat which perisheth."*

Interpretation of Tongues:

> *The Lord Jesus, seeing the needy missing the great ideal of His mission, turned their attention, "It is more needful that you get a drink of a spiritual awakening. It is more needful that you eat of the inner manna of Christ today, for God has sealed Him for that purpose and He has become Bread for you."*

The Master was dead in earnest when He said, *"Enter ye in at the strait gate: for wide is the gate...that leadeth to destruction"* (Matthew 7:13).

Strive to enter in at the straight gate. Get a live, inward inheritance in you. See that the Master has food for us, bread enough and to spare.

Interpretation of Tongues:

> *It is the living Word; it is the touch of His own spiritual nature that He wants to breathe into our human nature today.*

It is the nature of the Son; it is the breath of His life; it is the quickening of His power; it is the savor of life unto life. It is that which quickens you from death into life; it is that which wakens you out of all human into the glorious liberty of the sons of God. It is the Spirit that quickeneth.

Let me read the Word:

Labour not for the meat which perisheth, but for that meat which endureth unto everlasting life, which the Son of man shall give unto you: for him hath God the Father sealed.

(John 6:27)

Everlasting life is a gift. The Holy Ghost is a gift. But the gift of God is eternal life, and we have this life in His Son. And he that hath not the Son hath not life, but he that hath the Son is passed from death into life. (See 1 John 5:12.) This is the life that will be caught up. This is the life that will be changed in a moment. (See 1 Corinthians 15:51–52.) This is the life which will enter into the presence of God in a moment of time, because it is divine, because it has no bondage. It is not hindered by the flesh.

So God is pruning us, teaching us to observe that they who shall enter into this life have ceased from their own works. They that enter into this spiritual awakening have no more bondages. They have learned that no man that warreth after this entangleth himself with the affairs of this life. He has a new inspiration of divine power. It is the nature of the Son of God.

But it says, "Labor to enter in."

Yes, beloved, and it means labor, because your own nature will interfere with you. Your friends will often stand in the way. Your position will many a time almost bring you to a place; if you take that stand you will be doomed.

I understand it that Jesus could have no other interpretation; "He that seeketh to save his life shall lose it, but he that loseth his life for My sake shall find it" (see Matthew 16:25), and he shall find the life that never ceases. Human life has an end. Divine life has only a beginning.

This is the life that the Son of Man was sealed to give. He was specially sealed; He was specially anointed; He was specially separated—gave Himself over to God that He might become the fiistfruit of the first-begotten of a new creation that was going to be in the presence of God forever. A new creation, a new sonship, a new adoption, a new place, a new power.

Hallelujah! Are you in for it?

Peter had just entered into this divine position. He had just got this new life. He had just entered into the place where he knew that Jesus was the Son of God, and in the same glory that filled the whole mountainside with exceeding glory in that place, Moses and Elias spoke to Jesus of His decease at Jerusalem, and when He came down from the mountain, He began breaking the seal of His ministry, and He said, "*The Son of man shall be betrayed into the hands of men: and they shall kill him, and the third day he shall be raised again*" (Matthew 17:22–23).

Peter said, "It shall not be so, I'll see to that! You leave that business with me. Let anybody touch You, and I will stand in Your place; I will be with You." (See Matthew 16:22.)

And Jesus said, "*Get thee behind me, Satan*" (Matthew 16:23). "Anything that hinders Me from falling into the ground—if the seed falls not in the ground, it abideth alone; everything that interferes with My going to Calvary or to death or separation from the world or cleaning My life up or entering through the narrow gate—anything that interferes with that is Satan's power." "*Get thee behind me, Satan: for thou savourest not the things that be of God, but those that be of men"* (Matthew 16:23).

Labor to enter in. Seek to be worthy to enter in. Let God be honored by your leaving things that you know are taking your life, hindering your progress, blighting your prospects, and ruining your mind—for nothing will dull the mind's perceptions like touching earthly things, which are not clean.

When God began dealing with me on holy lines, I was working for thirteen saloons, among hundreds of other customers. Of course, God dealt with me on this line, and I squared the whole thing up in the presence of God. That was only one thing; there were a thousand things.

> *Let God be honored by your leaving things that you know are taking your life, hindering your progress, blighting your prospects, and ruining your mind.*

God would have us holy, pure, perfect right through. The inheritance is an incorruptible inheritance, and it is undefiled, and it fadeth not away. (See 1 Peter 1:4.) Those that are entering in are judging themselves, that they shall not be condemned with the world. Many people are fallen asleep. Why? Because they listened not to the correction of the Word of the Lord. Some have been sickly, and God dealt with them. They would not heed, then God put them to sleep.

Oh, that God the Holy Ghost shall have a choice with us today; that we shall judge ourselves that we be not condemned by the world! What is it to judge yourself? If the Lord speaks—if He says, "Let it go"—no matter if it is as dear as your right eye, you let it go. If it is as costly as your right foot, you let it go. It is far better to let it go. (See Mark 9:45, 47.)

Labor to enter in.

Interpretation of Tongues:

God's Word never speaks in vain. It always opens to you the avenues where you can enter in. God opens the door for you. He speaks to your heart. He is dealing with you. We are dealing with the coming of the Lord, but how shall we be prepared without all is burnt? For the wood, the hay, the stubble must be burned. The gold, the silver, and the precious stones will be preserved.

Be willing, beloved, for the Lord Himself to deal with you.

Let us pass on to another important word of Scripture:

> *Then Jesus said unto them, Verily, verily, I say unto you, Moses gave you not that bread from heaven; but my Father giveth you the true bread from heaven. For the bread of God is he which cometh down from heaven, and giveth life unto the world.* (John 6:32–33)

Bread! O beloved, I want God to give you a spiritual appetite that you will have a great inward devouring place; that you will eat the Word, you will savor it with joy, you will have it with grace. Also, it will be mingled with separation. As the Word comes to you—the Word of God, the bread of heaven, the very thing you need, the very nature of the life of the Son of God—as you eat, you shall be made in a new order after Him who hath created you for His plan and purpose.

"Then said they unto him, Lord, evermore give us this bread" (John 6:34). I want that same expression to be made in our hearts because He is helping us into this.

> *And Jesus said unto them, I am the bread of life: he that cometh to me shall never hunger; and he that believeth on me shall never thirst.* (John 6:35)

The process of the Word of God must kindle in us a separation. It must bring death to everything except the life of the Word of Christ in our hearts. I want to save you from judging, because in the measure that you have not come into the standard of the revelation of the principle of Christ of this eternal working in you, in that relation you will not come right through believing in the true principle of the Word of Life.

They that drink shall never thirst; they that eat shall never hunger. The two things are necessary. I shall never expect any person to go beyond his light. The Word of God is to give you light. The Spirit of the Lord and the Word of the Lord—one is Light, the other is Life. We must see that God wants us to have these two divine properties, Life and Light, so that we are in a perfect place by the Word of God to judge ourselves, because the Word of God shall stand true whatever our opinions be. The Scripture says very truly, "Supposing some did not believe? Shall that affect you? Will it change the Word?" (See Romans 3:3.) The Word of God will be the same whether people believe it or not.

God will in these meetings sift the believer. This is a sifting meeting. I want you to get away from the chaff. Chaff is judgment. Chaff is unbelief. Chaff is fear. Chaff is failing. It is the covering of the weak, and as long as it covers the weak, it hinders the weak coming forth for bread. So God has to deal with the chaff, to get it away so that you might be the pure bread, the pure life, the pure word, and that there shall be no strange thing in you, no misunderstanding.

God has to deal with His people, and if God deals with the house of God, then the world will soon be dealt with. The dealing first is with the house of God, and then, after that, with the world.

When the house of God is right, all the people will get right directly. The principle is this: all the world needs and longs to be right, and so we have to be salt and light to guide them, to lead them, to operate before them so that they see our good works and glorify our Lord.

I was preaching on these divine elements, and one person in the midst of the meeting said, "I won't believe! I won't believe! Never anything like that moves me. You cannot move me. Nothing can move me."

"I believe! I believe! I believe!" said I.

I went on dealing with the things of God. This man was a great preacher. He came to a place where the chaff had to be taken up, where God was dealing with him, where his life was opened out. He said again, "I won't believe!" It made no difference to me; I went on preaching. He was so aroused that he jumped up and went out, shouting as he closed the door, "I won't believe!"

Next morning, the pastor got a note saying, "Please come immediately," and the pastor went. As soon as he got to the door, a woman met him, tears in her eyes, weeping bitterly.

"Oh!" she said. "I am in great distress!"

She took him inside. When he got inside, the first thing that confronted him was the man that shouted out, "I won't believe!" He got a parchment, and he wrote, "Last night, I had a chance to believe. I refused to believe, and now I cannot believe, and I cannot speak."

Dumb, because he would not believe; is he the only one? No; Zacharias and Elizabeth were blameless, we read, but when he was in the Holy of Holies, when God spoke to him telling him that He was going to give him a son, his heart was unmoved, and his language was contrary to faith. So Gabriel said to him, "Thou shalt be dumb, and not able to speak, because thou wilt not believe." (See Luke 1:20.) And he came out of that place dumb.

It seems to me that if we will not judge ourselves, we shall be judged. I am giving you the Word. The Word should so be in you that, as I speak, the fire should burn, the life should be kindled, the very nature of Christ should transform you. You should be so moved in this meeting that you are ready for rapture, you are longing for rapture. You know that you have the life, and you know this life will be held till it gets loose.

You need the bread to feed the Life. The Word of God is the bread. There is no famine on now. God is giving us the Bread of Life. *"He that cometh to me shall never hunger; and he that believeth on me shall never thirst"* (John 6:35). A constant satisfaction, an inward joyful expression, a place of peace.

All that the Father giveth me shall come to me; and him that cometh to me I will in no wise cast out. For I came down from heaven, not to do mine own will, but the will of him that sent me. And this is the Father's will which hath sent me, that of all which he hath given me I should lose nothing, but should raise it up again at the last day.
(John 6:37–39)

Nothing—He should lose nothing! Do you believe that? Some people are still on the hedge. "After all, He may lose us." I would rather believe the Word of God!

I find people continually deceived because they look, and many people have lost all because they feel. There was one man in the Old Testament [Isaac] very terribly deceived; he felt for Esau, but he was deceived because it was Jacob. If you feel, you will be deceived.

God would not have us to feel; He would have us on one line only—believing. I would like you to understand that you did not come to Jesus; God gave you to Jesus. Where did He find you? He found you in the world, and He gave you to Jesus, and Jesus gave you eternal life. As He received everyone that He had given His life for and given His life to, He said He would lose nothing, but He would preserve them.

"Oh!" you say. "That all depends."

Yes, it does. It depends upon whether you believe God or not. But I find people always getting outside of the plan of God because they use their own judgment.

I am not going to believe that everybody that says they are believers believe, because they came up to Him and said, "We are the seed of Abraham; we have Abraham for our father." (See John 8:33.)

He said, "You are mistaken; you are the seed of the devil." (See John 8:44.)

> *He that believeth hath the witness, and we know that we are the sons of God because we do those things that please Him.*

He that believeth hath the witness, and we know that we are the sons of God because we do those things that please Him. And we know we are the sons of God because we love to keep His commandments; His commandments are not grievous. And we know we are the sons of God because we overcome the world.

That is what the son of God has to do—overcome the world. And this life we receive of Him is eternal and everlasting and cannot see corruption, but God is feeding us this morning with that wonderful Word of promise that we might know that we have the inheritance in the Spirit, and that we may know that we are going on to the place of "ready, Lord, ready!"

Are you ready to go? I am here getting you ready to go, because you have to go. It is impossible for the life of God or the law of the life of the Spirit to be in you without it is doing its work. The law of the life of the Spirit will be putting to death all the natural life and quickening you continually with spiritual life till you will have to go.

When I see white hair and wrinkled faces, I say, "You have to go. It does not matter what you say; you cannot stay. You have to go. You begin blossoming and, in a short time, you will bloom and be off."

That is a natural plan, but I am talking about a supernatural plan. We know that as we have borne the image of the earthly, we are going to bear the image of the heavenly. Mortality will be swallowed up in life. The very nature of the Son of God is in us, making life, immortality, and power. The power of the Word of the living Christ!

The gospel of the grace of God hath power to bring immortality and life. What is the gospel? The Word, the Bread of the Son of God. Feed upon it. Feed upon it in your heart. It is immortality. It is life, by the Word of quickening, by the Word of Truth.

You look good, you are an inspiration, but you know there are many marks and blemishes. You know, as you pass through the weary days of toil and battling with sin on every line, there is a light in you, a life in you, that is going to pass off, and you are going to be like Him. It will be the same face, but the marks, the scars, and the spots will have gone. What will do it? The Bread! Ever more give us this Bread! The Bread of the Son of God!

Verily, verily, I say unto you, He that believeth on me hath everlasting life. I am that bread of life. (John 6:47–48)

"*Everlasting life*" means bread. Men cannot live by bread alone, but by the Word of the living God.

When I read this in the Revelation, my heart was moved: "*And his name is called The Word of God*" (Revelation 19:13).

His name, the very name, is the Word of God, who giveth His life for the world. And of His life, of His Spirit, of His grace, of His faith, have we received. What does it mean? On you tried ones, grace inpoured, grace from heaven, grace enriched, grace abundantly, grace poured, His grace for thy weakness, that thou mightest be sustained in the trial, in the fire, passing through it, coming out more like the Lord.

This inspires me. Why? Because time finishes. All the beautiful buildings in the world, the mountains, the heavens, and all, shall pass away. The heavens shall be rolled up as a scroll, and all things shall melt with fervent heat. (See 2 Peter 3:10–12; Revelation 6:14.) But one thing cannot be burned, one thing cannot be changed, one thing can stand the fire, can stand the water, can stand persecution, can stand anything. What is it? The same that went into the fire and remained untouched when the men on the outside were slain by it. They were in the fire, but it burned them not, and the king was amazed when he saw them walking.

"Oh!" he said. "Did we not cast three men into the fire?"

"True, O king."

"Behold, I see a fourth, and his likeness is like the Son of God." (See Daniel 3:25.)

No consuming. There is a life of the Son of God that cannot be burned, cannot see corruption, that passes through fire, passes through clouds, passes through legions of demons that will clear out of the way, passes through everything. Oh, that life! What is it? The life of the Son of God. He came to give life—resurrection life!

Have you got it? Is it yours? Are you afraid you will lose it? Do you believe He will lose you?

"What makes you say it?" you ask.

Because sometimes I hear doubters. So I am going to read a wonderful word for the doubters.

> *My sheep hear my voice, and I know them, and they follow me: and I give unto them eternal life; and they shall never perish, neither shall any man pluck them out of my hand. My Father, which gave them me, is greater than all; and no man is able to pluck them out of my Father's hand.*
>
> (John 10:27–29)

Oh, that Life! Full of deity, full of prospectiveness, full of assurance, full of victory, full of a shout. There is the shout of a King in the midst of you this morning. Will you be ready? How can you help it? Is it possible not to be ready? Why, bless you, it is not your life; it is His life. You did not seek Him; it was He who sought you. You cannot keep yourself; it is He who keeps you. You did not make the offering; it was God that made the offering. So it is all of grace. But what a wonderful grace!

Interpretation of Tongues:

> *The trumpet shall blow, and all shall be brought forth, for God shall bring them with Him; and those which are awake shall not interfere with those which are asleep, but all with one breath shall rise. What will rise? The life will rise to meet the Life that has preserved it, and we shall be ever with the Lord.*

What is going? The life. He giveth everlasting life, and they shall never perish.

Oh, where is your faith? Is your faith inspired? Are you quickened? Is there within you a truth which is saying, "I feel it; I know it. It moves me; I have it!"

Yes, and you will be there—as sure as you are here, you will be there.

This we are entering into is going to continue forever. Let us feed on this Bread. Let us live in this holy atmosphere. This is divine nature that God is making us know, which will last forever.

Keep us, Lord, in a place of buying up opportunities, burning up bridges, paying the prices, denying ourselves, that we might be worthy of being Thine own forever!

Questions and Answers

Q: Is there distinction in the Word between the life that brings forth the rapture and eternal life where some go down into the grave?

> *Those asleep in Jesus have the same life, but they are not asleep in the grave. The spirit never sleeps; the soul never sleeps.*

A: No. Those asleep in Jesus have the same life, but they are not asleep in the grave. They fall asleep to rest, but it is not a sleep—not a rest—of the spirit. The spirit never sleeps; the soul never sleeps. The bridegroom said, "*I sleep, but my heart waketh*" (Song of Solomon 5:2). Remember that the moment the body is put to rest, the spirit requires no rest. It is always young. It will know nothing about time.

When you come to a divine healing meeting ready to receive, life flows through us who are speaking to you. But when you come inactive, dormant, with lack of faith, then the very life of us seems to be crushed some way. As we get people in the meeting where they receive the Word of Life, the preacher can preach forever—no darkness, all light; no weariness, all power. I could go on for hours, because the Spirit giveth life.

Whichever way the body goes, it will be the same. If it goes to the grave, what will happen? The body—all that is earthly—will pass away. It will come to dust. Supposing it goes up? The Word of God says it will be dissolved. The same thing, dissolved either way it goes. Why? Because flesh and blood are not going there, but the life of the Son of God. God will pick up a new body, resembling the old in every way—likeness, character, everything—the spirit will enter into a celestial body, whether it goes up or down—only we want you all to go up.

Q: Our Lord Jesus claimed equality with the Father, yet in another Scripture, He said, "My Father is greater than I" (John 14:28). Please explain.

A: In the sovereignty of grace, we each esteem others better than ourselves when we are really in grace and in love. He gave reverence to the Father and honored Him. He said, *"I and my Father are one"* (John 10:30), but He said also, *"My Father is greater than I"* (John 14:28).

I esteem others better than myself.

Q: I heard Revelation 3:5 brought up to prove that a name could be blotted out of the Book of Life. Will you please explain?

A: I am dealing with people that are receiving everlasting life that are not going to be lost. I am persuaded better things than that of you. I never shall believe that any human man is greater than my God. I believe that God is greater than all and that God can preserve us all. But I do believe that there are any number of people that have tried to make people believe they were the seed of God when they have not been really born again. The life of the new birth is ever after God. It has no time for decline; it has no time for the world; it is always hungry for God. Except you get this fundamental truth deep down in your heart, you fail, because you have to go on to holiness, inseparableness. "*Holiness becometh thine house, O* LORD" (Psalm 93:5). How can you be anything but holy and long to be holy?

Q: Is it possible for a person to be holy and yet lack divine wisdom?

A: I cannot see what you mean, because if you read 1 Corinthians 1:30, you find that Jesus is made unto you wisdom, righteousness, sanctification, and redemption, and He is made it to everyone. But there is this about it: you are holy today according to light. Tomorrow, revelation of a further light will show you many things that you were not holy in yesterday. Revelation takes you to holiness, but you are perfect just as you live in the light.

Q: Is it necessary that there be travail in prayer on someone's part for every soul to be born into the kingdom?

A: You are not told anywhere that it is the travail of prayer that saves; it is faith that saves. If you get away from a lot of travailing and do a lot of believing, you will see things change all the time.

THE BREAD OF LIFE
Bible Study #25 – August 18, 1927

T he Lord has revealed to me a new order concerning the Word of God. This is called the Book of Life; it is called the Spirit of Life. It is called the Son of Life. The Word of Life, the Testament of the new covenant, which has been shed in blood. There it is—the Bible. I hold it before you, and it is no more than any other printed page without the Spirit of revelation. It is a dead letter. It is lifeless; it has no power to give regeneration. It has no power to cause new creation. It has no power to cause the new birth apart from the Spirit. It is only print. But as the Spirit of the Lord is upon us, is in us, we breathe the very nature of the life of the new creation, and it becomes a quickened word. It becomes a life-giving source. It becomes the breath of the Almighty. It becomes to us a new order in the Spirit.

Interpretation of Tongues:

> *We shall not die, but we shall live to declare the works of the Lord. We have passed from death unto life. We are a new creation in the Spirit. We are born of a new nature, we are quickened by a new power, we belong to a new association. Our citizenship is in heaven, from whence we look for our nature, our life, our all in all.*

That is beautiful! The Spirit moving, the Spirit giving, the Spirit speaking, the Spirit making life! Can't you hear the Master say, "My Word is spirit and life"? Only by the Spirit can we understand that which is spiritual. We cannot understand it. We have to be spiritual to understand it. No man can understand the Word of God without his being quickened by the new nature. The Word of God is for the new nature. The Word of God is for the new life, to quicken mortal flesh in this order.

I read to you this morning some words from the sixth chapter of John:

> *Verily, verily I say unto you, He that believeth on me hath everlasting life. I am that bread of life. Your fathers did eat manna in the wilderness, and are dead. This is the bread which cometh down from heaven, that a man may eat thereof, and not die.* (John 6:47–50)

My! I hope you have got it, for I tell you, it has changed me already. It is all new. The Word of God never is stale. It is all life. May we be so spiritually minded that it becomes life and truth to us. *"I am the living bread"* (John 6:51).

Living bread! Oh, can't you feel it? Can't you eat it? Your gums will never be sore and your teeth will never ache eating this bread. The more you eat, the more you will have life. And it won't wear your body out, either. It will quicken your mortal body. This is the living bread. Feed on it. Believe it. Digest it. Let it have a real, new quickening in your body.

I could sit here and listen to anybody read these verses all day, and I could eat it all day. Living bread! Eternal bread! Eternal life! Oh, the brightening of the countenance! The joy of the new nature! The hope that thrills us! The bliss that awaits us! Oh, the glory forever which will never decay!

Oh! For that eternal day where all are holy, all are good, all are washed in Jesus' blood! But guilty sinners unrenewed come not there. There is no sickness there. This is no death there. They have never had a funeral in that land since He went. They have never known what it was to ring the death toll nor have the drum muffled. Never once has anyone died up there. No death there. No sickness. No sorrow.

Will you go there? Are you getting ready for it?

Remember this: you are created by the power of God for one purpose particularly. God has no thought in creation but to bring forth, through mortality, a natural order that you might be quickened in the Spirit, received into glory, and worship God in a way that the angels never could. But in order that this could be, He has brought us through the flesh, quickened us by the Spirit, that we may know the love, the grace, the power, and all the perfect will of God.

He is a wonderful God—His intelligence, His superabundance in all revelation, His power to keep everything in perfect order. The sun in all its glory, which is shining so majestically on the earth today, is the mighty power of our glorious God, who can make a new heaven and a new earth wherein will dwell righteousness, where no sin will ever darken the place, where the glory of that celestial place will be wonderful.

I John saw the holy city, new Jerusalem, coming down from God out of heaven, prepared as a bride adorned for her husband. (Revelation 21:2)

A city, figurative—not exactly figurative; luminous, in fact—will be, sure to be, cannot miss. A city greater than any city ever known. Millions, billions, trillions, all ready for the marriage, making a great city—architecture, domes, pinnacles, cornishes, foundations—the whole city made up of saints coming to a marriage.

The glory of it! I'll be there. I shall be one of it. I do not know what part, but it will be glorious to be in it anyhow. All these billions of people will have come through tribulation, washed their robes, come through distress, brokenness of spirit, hard times, strange perplexities, weariness, and all kinds of conditions in the earth, will be quickened and made like Him, to reign with Him for ever and ever.

What a thought God had when He was forming creation and making it so that we could bring forth through our loins sons and daughters in the natural, quickened by the Spirit in the supernatural, and received up to glory, and then to be made ready for a marriage! May God reveal to us our position in this Holy Ghost order that we may see how wonderful that the Lord has His mind upon us. I want you to see security—absolute security, where there will be no shaking, no trembling, no fear, absolute soundness in every way, knowing that, as sure as the city is formed, you are going out to the city.

> *Eternal life came to us when we believed, but the process of eternal life can begin today, making us know that now we are sons of God.*

Salvation is glory, new life is resurrection, new life is ascension, and this new life in God has no place for its feet anywhere between here and the glory.

The Spirit of the Lord is with us, revealing the Word, bringing to us not eternal life, for we have that—we believe and are in this place because of that eternal life—but bringing to us a process of this eternal life, showing to us that it puts to death everything else. Eternal life came to us when we believed, but the process of eternal life can begin today, making us know that now we are sons of God.

Interpretation of Tongues:

Let thy whole heart be in a responsive place. Yield absolutely to the Spirit cry within thee. Do not be afraid of being so harmonized by the power of the Spirit that the Spirit in thee becomes so one that thou art altogether as He desires thee to be.

Do not let fear in any way come in. Let the harmonizing, spiritual life of God breathe through you that oneness. And when we get into oneness today—oh, the lift; oh, the difference—when our hearts are all blended in one thought, how the Spirit lifts us, how revelation can come! God is ready to take us far beyond anything we have had before.

Notice some more verses in the sixth chapter of John:

The Jews therefore strove among themselves, saying, How can this man give us his flesh to eat? Then Jesus said unto them, Verily, verily, I say unto you, Except ye eat the flesh of the Son of man, and drink his blood, ye have no life in you. Whoso eateth my flesh, and drinketh my blood, hath eternal life; and I will raise him up at the last day. For my flesh is meat indeed, and my blood is drink indeed. He that eateth my flesh, and drinketh my blood, dwelleth in me, and I in him. (John 6:52–56)

There is another word which is very lovely in the fourth chapter of the first epistle of John: "*He that dwelleth in love dwelleth in God, and God in him*" (1 John 4:16). You cannot separate these divine personalities. If you begin to separate the life from the nature, you will not know where you are. You will have to see that, right in you, the new nature is formed.

You got a glimpse of it in a very clear way in the fourth chapter of Hebrews:

> *For the word of God is quick, and powerful, and sharper than any twoedged sword, piercing even to the dividing asunder of soul and spirit, and of the joints and marrow, and is a discerner of the thoughts and intents of the heart.*
> (Hebrews 4:12)

The Word of God—the Word, the Life, the Son, the Bread, the Spirit, in you, separating you from soulishness. The same power, the same Spirit, separating soul and spirit, joint and marrow, right in you. The Life, the Word, the power by the Spirit, quickening the mortal body. It is resurrection force. It is divine order. The stiff knee, the inactive limb, the strained position of the back, the muscle—everything in your nature—resurrection power by the Word, the living Word in the body, discerning, opening, revealing hidden thoughts of the heart till the heart cannot have one thing that is absolutely contrary to God. The heart separated in thought, in life, till the whole man is brought into life divine, living in this life, moving by this power, quickened by this principle.

Oh! This is resurrection! This is resurrection! Is it anything else? Yes. This is that which will leave.

I do not know how far this goes, but I am told that when the spiritual life of a man is very wonderfully active, the white corpuscles in his blood are very mightily quickened, going through the body, and after the spirit goes, they cannot find them in any way. I do not know how far that goes, but to me, it is a reality. The Spirit of the living God flows through every vein of my body, through every tissue of my blood, and I find this life will have to go. It will have to go!

Interpretation of Tongues:

It is not by might or power, it is by My Spirit, saith the Lord. It is not the letter, it is the Spirit that quickeneth; it is the resurrection which He brought into us. "I am the resurrection and the life. He that believeth in Me hath resurrection life in him, resurrection power through him, and he will decrease and the resurrection will increase."

God, manifest that through us. Give us that. Oh, for this spiritual, divine appointment for us today, to see this deep, holy, inward reviving in our hearts!

I must press on—I am pressing on. The only difficulty is, He is pressing in and keeps us in, holding on but laying hold. Not until in these last days have I been able to understand Paul's words to Timothy when he tells him he is to lay hold of eternal life. We cannot imagine any human man in the world laying hold of eternal life; it never could be. But a supernatural human man has power to lay hold, take hold. So it is the supernatural divine which lays hold, laying hold of eternal life.

Eternal life, which was with the Father, was brought to us by the Son and is of Him.

As the living Father hath sent me, and I live by the Father: so he that eateth me, even he shall live by me.
(John 6:57)

Here is a divine principle: He had His life from the Father. "As I live by the Father and have life in Myself by the Father, so ye shall live by Me and have life from Me as I take it from the Father."

Oh, that the Lord would inspire thought and revelation in our hearts to claim this today!

> *This is that bread which came down from heaven: not as*
> *your fathers did eat manna, and are dead: he that eateth of*
> *this bread shall live forever.* (John 6:58)

It was wonderful bread that they had, it was a wonderful provision—but they ate it and they died. But God's Son became the Bread of Life, and as we eat of this bread, we live forever, forever, *forever!*

Interpretation of Tongues:

> *It is the Spirit that giveth life, for He giveth His life for us*
> *that we, being dead, should have eternal life. For He came*
> *to give us His own life that we henceforth should not die but*
> *live forever.*

> > *Breathe upon us, breathe upon us,*
> > *With Thy love our hearts inspire.*
> > *Breathe upon us, breathe upon us,*
> > *Lord, baptize us now with fire.*

Thank God for the breath of the Spirit, the new creation dawning. Thank God for the spiritual revelation. Fire, holy fire, burning fire, purging fire, taking the dross, everything out, making us pure gold. Fire! "He shall baptize you with the Holy Ghost, and with fire." (See Matthew 3:11; Luke 3:16.) It is a different burning to anything else; it is a burning without consuming. It is illumining. It is a different illumination to anything else; it so illumines the very nature of the man till within the inner recesses of his human nature there is a burning, holy, divine purging through till every part of dross is consumed. Carnality in all its darkness, human mind with all its blotches, inadequate to reach out, are destroyed by the fire. We shall be burned by fire till the very purity of the Christ of God shall be through and through and through, till the body shall be, as it were, consumed.

It seems to me the whole of the flesh of Jesus was finished up, was consumed in the Garden, on the cross, in His tragic moments, in the twelfth chapter of John's gospel as He speaks about seed falling, and as He says in the great agony, with sweat upon His brow, *"If it be possible…"* (Matthew 26:39).

There is a consuming of the flesh till the invisible shall become so mighty that that which is visible shall only hold its own for the invisible to come forth into the glorious blessed position of God's sonship.

These things said he in the synagogue, as he taught in Capernaum. Many therefore of his disciples, when they had heard this, said, This is an hard saying; who can hear it?
(John 6:59–60)

It may be difficult for some of you clearly to understand this ministry we are giving you. Now, I tell you what to do: if you are not sitting in judgment but allowing the Spirit to come forth to you, you will find out that even that which is a mystery will be unfolded to you and that which is a difficulty will be cleared up. These people sat in judgment without being willing to enter into the spiritual revelation of it. As I read on, I want you to see how it divided the situation.

When Jesus knew in himself that his disciples murmured at it, he said unto them, Doth this offend you?
(John 6:61)

Jesus was a perceptive person. We, too, may get to the place where we rightly understand these things and can perceive the difference in the meeting. Whether the people are receptive or not, I am sensitive to the fact immediately when there is anybody in the meeting who is sitting in the judgment of the meeting. Jesus felt this and said unto them:

> *Doth this offend you? What and if ye shall see the Son of man ascend up where he was before? It is the spirit that quickeneth; the flesh profiteth nothing: the words that I speak unto you, they are spirit, and they are life.*
>
> (John 6:61–63)

We have been having the Word, which is life and spirit. *There is not a particle of your flesh which will ever be of any advantage to you as long as you live. It has pleased God to give you a body, but only that it may be able to contain the fullness of the Godhead principles and life, and it has only been given to you that it might be so quickened with a new generation of the Spirit that you can pass through this world with salt in your life, with seasoning qualities, with light divine, with a perfect position.*

He wants you walking up and down the breadth of the land, overcoming the powers of Satan, living this spiritual touch with God till your body is only used to cause you to take the spirit and the life from one quarter of the globe to the other. Quickened by the Spirit. The flesh never had anything for you. The Spirit is the only property that shall help you anytime. In my flesh, there never has, there never will be any good thing. Only the body can be the temple of the Holy One.

Oh, to live! "If I live, I live unto Christ. If I die, I die unto Christ. Living or dying, I am the Lord's." (See Philippians 1:20.) What a wonderful word comes to us by this saintly, holy, divine person, full of holy richness! I want to say a word more about this holy man, Paul, so filled with the power of the Holy Ghost till, when his flesh was torn to pieces with the rocks, the Spirit moved in his mortal life, and though his fleshly body was all the time under great privation, the Spirit moved in the life. In death oft—quickened in the Spirit. Laid out for dead—again quickened and brought to life. What a wonderful position!

"I am now ready to be offered" (2 Timothy 4:6)—offered on the altar of sacrifice. By the mercy of God, he lived, he moved, energized and filled with a power a million times larger than himself. In death oft, in prisons, in infirmities, in weaknesses, in all kinds of trials—but the Spirit filled his human body, and he comes to us in a climax, as it were, of soul and body mingled, with the words, "I am ready to be offered. There is the guillotine; I am ready to be offered." Already he has been on the altar of living sacrifice, and taught us how to be, but here he comes to another sacrifice: "I am ready to be offered."

It is said Paul was sawn asunder. I do not know how it was, but I thank God he was ready to be offered. What a life. What a consummation. Human life consummate, eaten up by the life of another. Mortality eaten up till it has not a vestige of the human nature to say, "You shan't do that, Paul." What a consummation! What a holy invocation! What an entire separation! What a prospect of glorification!

Can it be? Yes, as surely as you are in the flesh, the same power of the quickening of the Spirit can come to you till, whether in your body or out of your body, you can only say, "I am not particular, just so I know."

> *Christ liveth in me!*
> *Christ liveth in me!*
> *Oh! What a salvation this,*
> *That Christ liveth in me.*

But there are some of you that believe not. For Jesus knew from the beginning who they were that believed not, and who should betray him. And he said, Therefore said I unto you, that no man can come unto me, except it were given unto him of my Father.   (John 6:64–65)

It is so precisely divine in its origin that God will give this life only to those which attain unto eternal life. Do not get away from this. Every person that has eternal life, it is the purpose of the Father, it is the loyalty of God's Son, it is the assembly of the firstborn, it is the new begotten of God, it is the new creation, it is a heaven-designed race that is going to equip and get you through everything.

As sure as you are seeking now, you are in the glory. There is a bridge of eternal security for you if you dare believe in the Word of God. There is not a drop between you and the glory; it is divine, it is eternal, it is holy, it is the life of God, and He gives it, and no man can take the life that God gives to you from you. Wonderful! It is almightiness. Its production is absolutely unique. It is so essential, in the first place; it is so to be productive, in the next place; it is so to be changed, in the third place; it is so to be seated, in the fourth place. It is God's nature which cannot rest in the earth. It is His nature from heaven; it is a divine nature. It is an eternal power. It is an eternal life; it belongs to heaven. It must go back from whence it came.

I hope no person will say, "Wigglesworth is preaching eternal security." I am not. I have a thousand times better things in my mind than that. My preaching is this: I know I have that which shall not be taken away from me. *"Mary hath chosen that good part, which shall not be taken away from her"* (Luke 10:42).

I am dwelling upon the sovereignty, the mercy, and the boundless love of God. I am dwelling upon the wonderful power of God's order. The heavens, the earth, and under the earth is submissive to the Most High God. All demon power has to give place to the royal kinship of God's eternal throne. Every knee shall bow, every devil shall be submitted, and God will bring us, someday, right in the fullness of the blaze of eternal bliss, and the brightness of His presence will cast every unclean spirit and every power of devils into the pit for ever and ever and ever.

Interpretation of Tongues:

> Why faint, then, at tribulation when these light afflictions, which are only for a moment, are working out for us an eternal, glorious weight of glory? For we see this: that God, in His great plan of preparing, has delivered us from the corruption of the world and transformed us and made us able to come into the image of the Most Holy One. We are made free from the law of sin and death because the life of Christ has been manifest in our mortal body. Therefore, we live—and yet we live not, but another life, another power, and eternal force, a resurrection glory.

O Jesus! If our fellowship here be so sweet, if the touches of the eternal glory move out inspiration, what must it be to be there!

> From that time many of his disciples went back, and walked no more with him. Then said Jesus unto the twelve, Will ye also go away? Then Simon Peter answered him, Lord, to whom shall we go? thou hast the words of eternal life.
> (John 6:66–68)

Where will you go? If you leave the Master, where will you go? Where can we go? If we need a touch in our bodies, where can we go? If we want life, where can we go? Is there anywhere? This world is a big world, but tell me if you can get it.

Could you get it if you soared the heights of the Alps of Switzerland and looked over those glassy mountains where the sun is shining? As I peeped over one of those mountains one morning, I saw eleven glaciers and three lakes like diamonds before me in the glittering sun. I wept and I wept, but

I did not get consolation. Then I dropped on my knees and looked to God—then I got consolation.

Where shall we go? There are all the grandeurs and the glories of earth to be seen, but they do not satisfy me. They all belong to time. They will all fold up like a garment that is laid aside. (See Hebrews 1:11–12.) They will all melt with fervent heat. (See 2 Peter 3:10.)

Where shall we go? *"Thou hast the words of eternal life"* (John 6:68). Jesus, You fed us with bread from heaven. Jesus, give us Your life. Oh, breathe it into us! Then we will eat and drink and breathe and think in God's Son till our own nature is eaten up with the life divine, where we are perpetually in the sweetness of His divine will, in the glory—already in! Praise Him!

You can always be holy. You can always be pure. It is the mind of the Spirit that is making you know holiness, righteousness, rapture.

QUESTIONS AND ANSWERS

Q: Is any part of the mission of the Holy Ghost to purify and cleanse from sin?

A: We have nowhere specified in the Scriptures that the Holy Ghost is a cleanser, but there is a great power in the Spirit. Rudiments of evil, sins, covetousness, adultery, fornication, and a thousand other things that may have been in the body, when the Spirit got revelation through that body, He would bring Christ in evidence so that the Word of God would come true, as in Romans 8:10: *"And if Christ be in you, the body is dead because of sin; but the Spirit is life because of righteousness."*

Wherever Jesus is manifested in the body, sin is dethroned in that body. Jesus is the dethroner of sin and the cleanser by His blood and the purifier of the mind, and sets the whole body in perfect contract with heaven, as He is made manifest in the mortal body.

The moment sin is dethroned, the moment every carnal power is removed, the next thing that happens in the body: he wants to do justly, he wants to live righteously. And the moment righteousness takes place in the body, then the Holy Spirit has greater illumination to that soul, and he leaps and leaps and goes on and sees new things in Christ than he saw before.

The sanctification of the Spirit, as referred to in 1 Peter 1:2, keeps the baptized believer humble, keeps him broken, keeps him separate, keeps him realizing the spirit of revelation of the powers of demon power. When the evil power, as an angel of light, comes and says, "You are wonderful! You are mighty! There is no one like you!" then the Holy Spirit can so lay hold of you and make you broken, empty, helpless, weakened before God—and that is the sanctification of the Spirit. God help us to see that we need the sanctification of the Spirit in the day of triumph.

Q: There is a teaching that the emblems we partake of at the Communion time are the actual flesh and blood of Jesus, our Lord. Is that right?

A: Jesus said it was His blood, He said it was His body and that they had to eat of it. If they had actually eaten Him around that table, He would have been incomplete as a sacrifice. But He was as whole after they had that meal as He was before.

The people who teach this are deluded, and it is the delusion of the devil. The Romans have been deluded all through the years.

It never is, and never will be, the body and the blood of Jesus. It is an emblem and leads you to the real presence of the Lord.

Q: Is the husband that is not saved a hindrance to the wife receiving her healing?

A: Corinthians has a big place for the husband and wife. Every unsaved husband can be sanctified by the sanctification of the wife, and vice versa. If the husband or the wife is not saved, or if they are both not saved and are seeking healing, if any ministering saint of God would go, God would minister life and healing for revelation to those people and bring them to a knowledge of the truth by a manifestation. God worked in Australia and in New Zealand, bringing family after family into the knowledge of the truth because one person was healed in the family—a manifestation of the power of God. I believe that nothing in the home will interfere with divine healing except unbelief.

Q: Please explain the Scripture that says, "Believe on the Lord Jesus Christ, and thou shalt be saved, and thy house" (Acts 16:31).

A: A lot of people are terribly troubled about their families. I wish you would get to the place of faith—God's Word says it, you believe it, and they will be saved. Why should you take anything else? My wife and I agreed together to believe this Scripture, and He was faithful who promised and saved our children.

Q: Will you explain what place testimony should have in the service and what place the Word should have? Is it in the proper order that testimony should crowd out the preaching of the Word?

A: If you do not allow testimony in your meetings, you will impoverish the church. The more you testify, the more sure you are in your salvation. Every time you testify, the spring of prophecy will come forth and make you know your glorious originality is perfect in God. It would help any meeting to have half an hour's testimony at the commencement, if you felt the spirit of testimony coming. Then you have a right to let the Word follow that, because it ought to follow that. There must be order on the line of the prophecy. If there is a great unction on the people to testify, and you see there is prophecy coming through them, patiently say, "Now beloved, it is time for the ministry of the Word. Let us see how many testimonies we can have in the next five minutes."

People want love. They want grace, and they want it administered in love.

Q: Are the results mentioned in Mark 16:16–18 to be only to those who are baptized with the Holy Spirit?

A: Thousands of people who have never received the baptism of the Holy Ghost are very specially led and blessed in healing the sick. The finest people that ever I did know have never come into the same experience as I am in today regarding the baptism of the Holy Spirit, are mightily used with all kinds of sicknesses wonderfully. But they did not have that which is in the sixteenth chapter of Mark. Only baptized believers speak in tongues. "If you believe, you shall lay hands on the sick, and if you believe, you shall speak in new tongues"—meaning to say, after the Holy Ghost is come, you are in the place of command. You can command. How do I know it? Because Paul, in 2 Timothy, is very clear when he says, *"Stir up the gift"* (2 Timothy 1:6). What was the trouble with Timothy? He was downcast. He was a young man, called out by Paul, had been amongst the presbytery, and because of his youth, he had been somewhat put to one side; and he was grieved. Paul found him in a distressed place, so Paul stirred him up.

Every one of you, if you have faith, can stir up the gift within you. The Holy Ghost can be so manifest in you that you can speak. It may not be in gift, but speak in utterances by tongues. And I believe everybody baptized in the Holy Ghost has a right to allow the Spirit to have perfect control and speak every day—morning, noon, and night—in this order.

Do not put out your hand to stop anybody that is doing good, but encourage them to do good. Then, bring them in the baptism of much good.

I want to repeat the words which are ringing through my heart as the real knowledge of truth: when we are filled with the joy of the Lord, then there comes forth a glad "praise the Lord!" David knew that, and he wished all the powers that had breath to praise the Lord. It is a tragedy if there is not a divine spring within you pressing forth praise. God wants you so in the Spirit that your whole life is a praise.

How my soul longs for you to catch fire!

Four things which are emblematic, divinely ascertained, or revealed by the Lord are fire, love, zeal, and faith.

- Fire, burning up intensely, making us full of activity on a new line with God.

- Love, where there is nothing but pure, undefiled willingness, yieldedness, knows no sacrifice.

- Zeal, so in the will and the mighty power of God until we press beyond measure into that which pleases God.

- Faith that laughs at impossibilities and cries, "It shall be done!"

May God make these things immediately real before our eyes and give us these emblematic displays of inward flame!

Our message on the fifth chapter of Romans is to take us further on into God. These messages have been dealing with the reception of the life, of the nature of the Son of God, and we have been seeing that the nature of the Son of God could be transmitted unto us by the Word, and the Spirit could fill the vessel till the Word could be made life, as the Spirit went through the vessel and took the Word and poured it into the body till the body became quickened by the same nature of Jesus, with the same power over all weaknesses. An incorruptible force, pressing through human order, changing human order, bringing it to the place where it was resurrection life, eternal life, quickened by the Spirit, and changed from one state of grace to another, even from glory to glory.

Many people in these days are receiving a clear knowledge of an inward working of the power of the Spirit, which is not only quickening their mortal bodies, but also pressing into that same natural body an incorruptible power that is manifesting itself, getting ready for the rapture. The divine teaching of the Lord has revealed unto us that it is the inward life, the new man in the old man, the new nature in the old nature, the resurrection power in the dead form, the quickening of all, the divine order of God manifested in the human body. In us, the life, the nature of the living Christ; in us, power over all death. Do not be afraid to claim it: power over all sin, power over all disease. In the body, the Christ life forming, quickening, till every vestige of natural order is eaten up by the life divine.

The former law was of the natural man. Now the new law is of the life of the Spirit, or the manifestation of the new creation, which was Christ in us, the manifested power of the glory. Glory is a manifestation of the nature divine in the human body.

Now I want to go on from that, reading the fifth chapter of Romans. *"Therefore being justified by faith, we have peace with God through our Lord Jesus Christ"* (Romans 5:1).

You are justified, you are being made at peace. And remember, the peace of God is different from any other peace—it passeth all understanding; it takes you away from being disturbed. You are not moved by earthly things. It is a deep peace, created by the knowledge of a living faith which is the living principle of the foundation of all truth. Christ in us, a manifestation of God in us, which is the glory, or which is the nature of the glory, or which is the transportation of the glory, or the power to transport the glory. Christ in us, the hope, the evidence of the glory.

I want you to see how rich you are. *"By whom also* [that is, by the Lord Jesus Christ, the nature] *we have access by faith into this grace wherein we stand, and rejoice in hope of the glory of God"* (Romans 5:2).

This is perhaps the greatest of all thoughts we have reached: faith having access through Jesus Christ into all the fullness of God. It was by grace first. You were saved through grace, but now another grace, a grace of access, a grace of entering in, a grace of understanding the unfolding of the mystery, a grace which shall bring us into a place of knowledge of God.

In 2 Peter, we have a very special word that will help us here. There is one special thought we should dwell on: *"like precious faith"* (2 Peter 1:1). We have received like precious faith of all that have passed through Abraham, I say it with grace. Jesus, I say it with grace. The Father, I say it with grace. The Holy Ghost. All that the Father has, all that Jesus has, all the Holy Ghost has, we have access into, we have right into, we have an open door into. There is nothing can keep us out of it. Jesus Christ is the Alpha and the Omega for us, that we may know grace, favor, mercy, to lift us into and take us through.

Into what? Into grace and peace multiplied. *"Grace and peace be multiplied unto you through the knowledge of God, and of Jesus our Lord"* (2 Peter 1:2).

You want grace multiplied this morning? You want peace multiplied? You have it here, if you dare to believe. We have access; we have a right to it.

> *According as his divine power hath given unto us all things that pertain unto life and godliness, through the knowledge of him that hath called us to glory and virtue: whereby are given unto us exceeding great and precious promises: that by these ye might be partakers of the divine nature.*
>
> (2 Peter 1:3–4)

Access into the right to the promises; yea and amen, the right to all the heirship which He has made us heirs of.

It is true that He came to us in grace, He met us in need, and transformed us by His power. It is right to say that now we have within us an inheritance, right to say it is incorruptible and undefiled. We have a right to say it is filled with glory and virtue. We have a right to say we have the same nature as the Lord Jesus Christ.

The nature of His flesh? No—and yes. It is true He was made in likeness of our single flesh, and for sin, condemned sin in the flesh. But a higher order now, a spiritual order, a divine order, a divine nature, a super-nature, a holy nature, a nature of love, a nature of faith.

The nature of faith, divine nature, the same nature as He was spiritually. His faith He has committed to us. What by? All human weaknesses in believers are spoiled when it is a mixture. If your faith is not perfect, your victories are uncertain, your prayers have lost the anointing, your pressing into the kingdom of God is somewhat veiled, and your personality of divine power to lay hold is hindered. Why? God comes to us, breathes into us a new life, shows us we have access into this grace where we stand, that we may have a new nature that has no variableness, neither shadow of turning, but believes all things, hopeth all things, endureth all things, and is all the time being changed.

Interpretation of Tongues:

> *It is the law of the Spirit of Christ, which is the hope, which is the glory in the hope, which is the revelation in the glory of the hope, which is filled with opening of keen perception of things above, where Christ is sitting at the right hand of God, and we see jointly the Father and the Son. And so filled with purity of unmixed reality, faith rises, changes its order, lays hold and believes, dethrones, and stands fast to see the kingdom of God manifested.*

Faith, the power of access. Unfeigned faith. Faith which never has a mixture. Faith which never wavers. Faith which has audacity. Faith which is purified. Faith which is sensitive to the breath of God. Faith which is the very nature of the Son of God. Faith which came from the Author of faith, the very same as He, holy in act, daring to believe, testing assured, and seeing the mighty power of God made manifest through this living faith.

This is that which takes us into claim all He has. Faith is sight. The crooked are to be made straight, the lame are to leap with joy, the blind have to be made free. God has creation finished, forever completed, by the perfect work of our Lord. We are complete in Him, belonging to the Living Head. We are His righteousness, born into, created for, His purpose, that we might be in the world over all the powers of the world.

This eighth chapter of Romans is one of those marvelous masterpiece chapters. Yet all of God's Word lifts. You can feel yourself lifted. Gravitation is the only thing that causes you to remain. The Spirit lifts, the Word of Incarnation moves, the life divine operates, the Spirit quickeneth. You are being changed, made right, made ready, changed by regenerating. The power of the Word is quickening into, out of, unto. Whatever you were this morning, you are never to be as you were again, but as you were not, you have to be now. Nothing will move you as much as knowing what you were, so that you may be what you were not. Believe it: God's plan, purpose, revelation is for us today that we may leap gloriously.

Interpretation of Tongues:

> *The Lord's life is moving. The Lord's life is flowing. Put thy spirit into the joy of the Breath and let yourself go on the bosom of His love, to be transformed by all the Spirit life from above.*

"And rejoice in hope of the glory of God" (Romans 5:2). The hope of the glory of all saints is what we are laying foundations for in these studies. The hope of the glory is *you must know that you are going*. The great, mighty masterpiece of all is the great plan of rapture. It is the hope of the glory. It is the life divine. It is the peace of God. It is the enrichment of the soul. It is shed abroad in our hearts by the Holy Ghost.

The Holy Ghost is the manifestation of God's Son. The manifestation of the revelation of God's Son by the Holy Ghost, the Holy Ghost, always revealing Him to us as divine, as so uniquely divine that He is in power of overcoming, He is in power of purity, He is in power of rising all the time. And the Holy Ghost is shed abroad in our hearts for the very purpose that we may know that that which is in us has to go on to development. It must not cease development. The Holy Ghost is there for creating development and for moving us out as the Lord would have us to be.

> *For when we were yet without strength, in due time Christ died for the ungodly. For scarcely for a righteous man will*

one die: yet peradventure for a good man some would even
dare to die. But God commendeth his love toward us, in
that, while we were yet sinners, Christ died for us. Much
more then, being now justified by his blood, we shall be
saved from wrath through him. For if, when we were en-
emies, we were reconciled to God by the death of his Son,
much more, being reconciled, we shall be saved by his life.

(Romans 5:6–10)

Saved by His life. Now we have received salvation, He wants to open our eyes to understand what Christ really did for us. In due time, at the end of the weeks of the law, when there was no aim to save, when there was no hope, when law had failed, Christ took our place, delivered us from all the powers of human weaknesses and failure, and so came to us in our sins. When we were in sin, Christ died for us in due time; at the end of failure, at the right moment, He died for us and delivered us from the power of the devil—delivered us from death, delivered us from sin, delivered us from the grave—and gave us a hope of immortality through His life. We are saved by His life.

Jesus had eternal properties. Jesus had power to impart eternal gifts. He is here now. He has delivered us from the curse of the law and set us free. Who loves the gospel as do those who have been delivered by the gospel? What is the gospel? It is the power of God unto salvation. It has power to bring immortality and life immortality, and life is the nature of the Lord Jesus, and through this life in us, we are delivered from all things and being prepared for the glorious hope of the coming of the Lord.

Christ arose, a victor over death's domain.
He arose, forever with His saints to reign.
He arose! He arose!
Hallelujah, Christ arose!

What was it that rose? Christ's life. How did He rise? Out of death, over death victorious. Were we not planted with Him?

Were we not risen with Him? Then the only thing that can happen is to be seated with Him. The past is under the blood; the whole thing is finished.

Now entering into another step of this divine order, the Lord will speak to us.

> *And not only so, but we also joy in God through our Lord Jesus Christ, by whom we have now received the atonement.*
> (Romans 5:11)

Atonement—at-one-ment. One-ment, perfect association. Whatever His appointment in the earth, whatever He was, we have been joined to Him in "one-ment." The atonement is one-ment, meaning that He has absolutely taken every vestige of human deformity, depravity, lack of comprehension, and inactivity of faith, and has nailed it to the cross. Forever on the cross. You died with Him on the cross, and—if you will only believe you are dead with Him—you are dead indeed to sin and alive to righteousness.

The atonement, the one-ment, the principle, the working out of this wonderful regenerative power of God, is, "I am complete in His oneness." There is not a vestige of human weakness if I dare believe; I am so in order with God's Son that He makes me perfect—at one with Him, no sin, no blemish, no failure, absolutely a perfect. Atonement—till there isn't a vestige of weakness left.

Dare you believe it? It may not be easy for you, but I want to make it easy. Faith is the substance of things hoped for. Everything the Word of God speaks to you, faith lends its help. Faith stirs you; faith says to you, "If you believe, it is now. If you dare believe now, oneness, purity, power, eternal fact is working through you." Oneness—all one in Christ, perfectly covered, hidden, lost in God's Son. He has made us whole through the blood. Oneness, purity, divine association.

> *Wherefore, as by one man sin entered into the world, and death by sin; and so death passed upon all men, for that all have sinned: (For until the law sin was in the world: but sin is not imputed when there is no law. Nevertheless death reigned from Adam to Moses, even over them that had not sinned after the similitude of Adam's transgression, who is the figure of him that was to come. But not as the offence, so also is the free gift. For if through the offence of one many be dead, much more the grace of God, and the gift by grace, which is by one man, Jesus Christ, hath abounded unto many.*
>
> (Romans 5:12–15)

Through one man's disobedience, through one man's sin, death came and reigned. Now, here is another. Here is a new man, Adam, the first; Christ, the second. One earthly, the other heavenly. As sin reigned, as death reigned by one, so now the new man, the Christ man, shall make us so awake to righteousness, to peace, to abounding in God till, just as death had its power, through a new man, life has to have its power and victory. Through a new man, we have to come into a new divine order, abounding.

It is difficult probably for you to claim it. Abounding!

"I cannot understand it, Wigglesworth."

No, brother, you never will; it is a thousand times bigger than your mind. But Christ's mind replanted in your natural order will give you vision that you may see what you cannot understand. What you never will understand, God thoroughly understands and abounds to you in blessing, and says, "Only believe, brother, and it shall be abounding to you." God will make it rich to you.

You know how sin was abounding, how we were held, how we were defeated, how we groaned and travailed. Has sin abounded? Now grace, now the life, now the ministry abounding unto us.

Take a leap that you may never know what defeat is anymore. This is a real divine healing chapter. This is a real ascension chapter. This is a real ascending chapter. This is a real power of resurrection chapter. It looses you from your limitations and brings an unlimitation. It takes away all your former place and brings you into a place of covered grace; it takes your weaknesses and sins and abounds to you with atonement. It covers you with atonement. And now it reveals to you all that Adam ever had that bound you. All that Christ ever had, or will have, abounds toward you to liberate you from all human and bring you into all divine, separating you forever. This is the glorious liberty of the gospel of Christ. This is abounding measure.

> *And not as it was by one that sinned, so is the gift: for the judgment was by one to condemnation, but the free gift is of many offences unto justification.* (Romans 5:16)

We have been condemned and lost. How human nature destroys! We all know sin had its reign, but there is a justification, a mighty power of justifying, God working in the lower order with His mighty, higher order. He touches human weaknesses with His touch of finite, infinite, glorious resurrection power. He transforms you.

> *For if by one man's offence death reigned by one; much more they which receive abundance of grace and of the gift of righteousness shall reign in life by one, Jesus Christ.*
> (Romans 5:17)

Oh, how rich we are! There was a death life, but it has been supplanted. Now there is a righteous life. You were in death, and it was the death life, but now you have got the righteous life over death, over all weaknesses.

How much have you gotten it? *"Much more they which receive abundance of grace"* (Romans 5:17). Abundance of grace. What does it mean? Your grace has run out years ago. My grace has been spun out years ago, but I realized and got to know, by the revelation of the Spirit, that His grace should take the place of my grace. His power in the grace should cover me where I could not cover myself. He would stand beside me when I was sure to go down. Where sin abounded, grace abounded. His love abounded. He stretched out His hand; He was in mercy. He never failed. He was there every time when I was sure to go down. Grace abounded.

Oh, the mercy, the boundless mercy of the love of God to us! I hope you are getting—and I hope you are thriving in it and triumphing in it. God must give you these divine attributes of the Spirit that you may come into likemindedness with Him in this wonderful provision.

Any number of people fail to come into access to the divine personality of God's gift because they are always fearful because of their knowledge of their own imperfection. The devil has a tremendous trap all the time trying to catch poor people who have made a little slip or not just said the right thing. There has been nothing special, but the devil tries to make it like a mountain when it is not more than a molehill. I like the thought that God's Son is so gracious toward us. Beloved, where you fail in your righteousness, Jesus Christ has a gift of righteousness, a supplanting of your righteousness, a taking away of your filthy garment and clothing you with a new garment. He has power to take away even thy tongue and thy thoughts of evil. If you believe, it is abounding towards us much more. God wants to supply you with His righteousness.

It is the righteousness of the Son of God; it has no adulteration in it. It has no judgment in it. It is full of mercy and en-
treaty. It is the righteousness of the law of God's Spirit. Dare
you come into it? It is a reigning in it.

I go into this slowly lest you miss it. There is line upon line
and precept upon precept. There is a lot of truth about being
saved. It is a reality. There is a great deal of truth about having
the peace of God. There is a great deal of knowledge in the fact
that you know you are free, and there is wonderful manifestation of power to keep you free. But I find Satan dethrones
some of the most lovely people because he catches them at a
time when they are unaware. I find them all the time—poor
souls!—deceived by the power of Satan.

Hear this word: *when Satan is the nearest, God is nearer with
abounding measure of His grace.* When you feel almost as although you would be defeated, He has a banner waving over
you to cover you at that moment. He is abounding to you. He
covers you with His grace. He covers you with His righteousness. It is the very nature of the Son of God. It is the very life
of God.

This life is impossible to remain in the body. When you
are intoxicated with the Spirit, the Spirit life flows through
the avenues of your mind and the keen perception of the
heart with deep throbbings, and you are filled with the passion of the grace of God till you may be so filled with illumination by the power of the new wine—the wine of the
kingdom, the Holy Ghost—till your whole body is intoxicated. This is rapture. This will have to leave the body. There
is no natural body will be able to stand the process of this
going forth. It will have to leave the body. But the body will
be a preserver to it until the sons of God are made marvelously manifested.

Sonship is a position of rightful heirship. Sons have a right to the first claiming of the will—sons of God not only in that, but sons in heirship, and then sons in joint heirship.

I would like you to realize that redemption is so perfect to get you rid of all your judging yourself, believing God has a righteous judgment for you. Get away from all the powers of the devil. Liberality of grace is much more abounding toward you. Grace abounding, righteousness abounding, liberty for the soul, transformation of the mind, lifting you out of all your earthly place into God's power and authority.

This holy new life, this preservative of the Son of God in your human body, this life in you is so after the order of God that it is not ashamed in any way to say you are coming into coequality with the Father, with the Son, and with the Holy Ghost.

God has been showing to me that Jesus meant us when He said, "I will give you power to remit sin. Whosoever sin you remit, it will be remitted. And I will also give you power to do the opposite":

Whose soever sins ye remit, they are remitted unto them; and whose soever sins ye retain, they are retained.

(John 20:23)

It was manifested in the days of our first apostles. When was it? When Simon stood in the way of the power of the Holy Ghost. The apostle said to him, "*Thou shalt be blind, not seeing the sun for a season*" (Acts 13:11). "*For I perceive that thou art in the gall of bitterness*" (Acts 8:23). And immediately his eyes were closed.

When there was a man in the church who was living in fornication, the apostle cast him over to Satan for the destruction of the flesh. And then, a few months after, when they saw that Satan had done such havoc with his body, they saw that this power of evil would take him to the grave, so they took him out of the power of Satan and placed him back in the church.

So we have to see that God, in the Holy Ghost order, is bringing us into likemindedness of faith. I speak this to you because I know the Holy Ghost is bringing this church through. She has passed through many dark days of misunderstanding, but God is showing us that we have power to defeat the powers of the enemy. We have power to reign in this life by another. God has mightily justified us with grace abounding, filled us with the Holy Ghost, and given us the hope of the glory. When we were helpless, Jesus Christ came and took our place. And seeing through Adam we all received these evil things, Jesus gave a new impetus, so grace could be where sin was, righteousness could be where there was no righteousness, till we move from grace to grace, travailing in the Spirit till the whole man is longing for redemption. Bless God! It is not far off; it is very near, at the door. Ah, there will be a shout someday; it will not be long before He shall be here!

> *Therefore as by the offence of one judgment came upon all men to condemnation; even so by the righteousness of one the free gift came upon all men unto justification of life. For as by one man's disobedience many were made sinners, so by the obedience of one shall many be made righteous. Moreover the law entered, that the offence might abound. But where sin abounded, grace did much more abound: that as sin hath reigned unto death, even so might grace reign through righteousness unto eternal life by Jesus Christ our Lord.*
> (Romans 5:18–21)

Eternal life is resurrection. Eternal life is with the Father and with the Son. Eternal life has come into us, and as the Father is, so are we. As the Son is, so are we, and the glory itself will not be able to contain His position without the glory of the earth comes to the glory which is in heaven. This life eternal is manifested in mortal bodies that the life of Christ shall be so manifested in our mortal bodies that everything shall be dead indeed unto sin and alive unto God by the Spirit.

We are ready, we are gloriously ready. Oh, hallelujah! The life, the redemption, the glorious life in the Spirit! Have you got it? Have you entered into it? Is it reality to you? Do you know that it would not be possible for Him to move at all in the glory without your moving that way? It would be impossible for the Lord, in His life, to come without taking you.

I saw one day a great big magnet let down amongst iron, and it picked up loads of iron and carried them away. That is a natural older, but ours is a spiritual order of a holy magnet. That which is in thee is holy. That which is in thee is pure. And when the Lord of righteousness shall appear, who is our life, then that which is holy, which is His nature, which is His life, shall go, and we shall be forever with the Lord.

You have not gone yet—but you are sure to go. Seeing we are here, comforting one another, building up one another in the most holy faith, we would say, "No, Lord; let it please Thee that we remain. But please, Father, let us be more holy, let us be more pure. Please, Father, let this life of Thy Son eat up all mortality till there is nothing left but that which is to be changed in a moment, in the twinkling of an eye."

Do not let one thought, one act, one thing in any way interfere with more rapture. Ask God that every moment shall be a moment of purifying, a moment of rapture seeking, a moment in your body of a new order of the Spirit. Let God take you into the fullness of redemption in a wonderful way. Covet to be more holy. Covet to be more separate. Covet God. Covet gifts. Covet the graces. Covet the beatitudes. Covet earnestly.

May God show us that divine order that love shall eat us up no sacrifice, love eating our very nature till we love and love, till the whole church is love. "A new commandment I give you, that you should love." (See John 13:34.) Oh, breathe this holy, intense love in our bosom this morning—love! Love! Love! Let it please Thee, Lord, that this bond of union, this holy covenant with Thee, shall be so strong that no man shall be able to separate us from this love of God in Christ Jesus. And whom the Lord hath joined together, let no power in the world put asunder. May love, *love*, **love** take us on to the summit of the perfection of *"God so loved"* (John 3:16).

About the Author
Smith Wigglesworth (1859–1947)

An encounter with Smith Wigglesworth was an unforgettable experience. This seems to be the universal reaction of all who knew him or heard him speak. Smith Wigglesworth was a simple yet remarkable man who was used in an extraordinary way by our extraordinary God. He had a contagious and inspiring faith. Under his ministry, thousands of people came to salvation, committed themselves to a deeper faith in Christ, received the baptism in the Holy Spirit, and were miraculously healed. The power that brought these kinds of results was the presence of the Holy Spirit, who filled Smith Wigglesworth and used him in bringing the good news of the Gospel to people all over the world. Wigglesworth gave glory to God for everything that was accomplished through his ministry, and he wanted people to understand his work only in this context, because his sole desire was that people would see Jesus and not himself.

Smith Wigglesworth was born in England in 1859. Immediately after his conversion as a boy, he had a concern for the salvation of others and won people to Christ, including his mother. Even so, as a young man, he could not express himself well enough to give a testimony in church, much less preach a sermon. Wigglesworth said that his mother had the same difficulty in expressing herself that he did. This family trait, coupled with the fact that he had no formal education because he began working twelve hours a day at the age of seven to help support the family, contributed to Wigglesworth's awkward speaking style. He became a plumber by trade, yet he continued to devote himself to winning many people to Christ on an individual basis.

In 1882, he married Polly Featherstone, a vivacious young woman who loved God and had a gift of preaching and evangelism. It was she who taught him to read and who became his closest confidant and strongest supporter. They both had compassion for the poor and needy in their community, and they opened a mission, at which Polly preached. Significantly, people were miraculously healed when Wigglesworth prayed for them.

In 1907, Wigglesworth's circumstances changed dramatically when, at the age of forty-eight, he was baptized in the Holy Spirit. Suddenly, he had a new power that enabled him to preach, and even his wife was amazed at the transformation. This was the beginning of what became a worldwide evangelistic and healing ministry that reached thousands. He eventually ministered in the United States, Australia, South Africa, and all over Europe. His ministry extended up to the time of his death in 1947.

Several emphases in Smith Wigglesworth's life and ministry characterize him: a genuine, deep compassion for the unsaved and sick; an unflinching belief in the Word of God; a desire that Christ should increase and he should decrease (John 3:30); a belief that he was called to exhort people to enlarge their faith and trust in God; an emphasis on the baptism in the Holy Spirit with the manifestation of the gifts of the Spirit as in the early church; and a belief in complete healing for everyone of all sickness.

Smith Wigglesworth was called "The Apostle of Faith" because absolute trust in God was a constant theme of both his life and his messages. In his meetings, he would quote passages from the Word of God and lead lively singing to help build people's faith and encourage them to act on it. He emphasized belief in the fact that God could do the impossible. He had great faith in what God could do, and God did great things through him.

Wigglesworth's unorthodox methods were often questioned. As a person, Wigglesworth was reportedly courteous, kind, and gentle. However, he became forceful when dealing with the Devil, whom he believed caused all sickness. Wigglesworth said the reason he spoke bluntly and acted forcefully with people was that he knew he needed to get their attention so they could focus on God. He also had such anger toward the Devil and sickness that he acted in a seemingly rough way. When he prayed for people to be healed, he would often hit or punch them at the place of their problem or illness. Yet, no one was hurt by this startling treatment. Instead, they were remarkably healed. When he was asked why he treated people in this manner, he said that he was not hitting the people but that he was hitting the Devil. He believed that Satan should never be treated gently or allowed to get away with anything. About twenty people were reportedly raised from the dead after he prayed for them. Wigglesworth himself was healed of appendicitis and kidney stones, after which his personality softened and he was more gentle with those who came to him for prayer for healing. His abrupt manner in ministering may be attributed to the fact that he was very serious about his calling and got down to business quickly.

Although Wigglesworth believed in complete healing, he encountered illnesses and deaths that were difficult to understand. These included the deaths of his wife and son, his daughter's lifelong deafness, and his own battles with kidney stones and sciatica.

He often seemed paradoxical: compassionate but forceful, blunt but gentle, a well-dressed gentleman whose speech was often ungrammatical or confusing. However, he loved God with everything he had, he was steadfastly committed to God and to His Word, and he didn't rest until he saw God move in the lives of those who needed Him.

In 1936, Smith Wigglesworth prophesied about what we now know as the charismatic movement. He accurately predicted that the established mainline denominations would experience revival and the gifts of the Spirit in a way that would surpass even the Pentecostal movement. Wigglesworth did not live to see the renewal, but as an evangelist and prophet with a remarkable healing ministry, he had a tremendous influence on both the Pentecostal and charismatic movements, and his example and influence on believers are felt to this day.

Without the power of God that was so obviously present in his life and ministry, we might not be reading transcripts of his sermons, for his spoken messages were often disjointed and ungrammatical. However, true gems of spiritual insight shine through them because of the revelation he received through the Holy Spirit. It was his life of complete devotion and belief in God and his reliance on the Holy Spirit that brought the life-changing power of God into his messages. Today, the words of Smith Wigglesworth continue to convey to readers everywhere his complete trust and unwavering faith in God and impact their lives with one of his favorite sayings: "Only believe!"

ABOUT THE COMPILER
Roberts Liardon

R oberts Liardon, author, public speaker, spiritual leader, church historian, and humanitarian, was born in Tulsa, Oklahoma, the first male child born at Oral Roberts University. For this distinction, he was named in honor of the university founder. Thus, from the start of his life, Roberts was destined to be one of the most well-known Christian authors and speakers of the twentieth century. To date, he has sold over six million books worldwide in over fifty languages and is internationally renowned.

An author of over forty-eight Christian and self-help books, Roberts's career in ministry began when he gave his first public address at the age of thirteen. At seventeen, he published his first book, *I Saw Heaven*, which catapulted him into the public eye. By the time he was eighteen years old, he was one of the leading public speakers in the world. Later, he would write and produce a book and video series entitled *God's Generals*. This became one of the best-selling Christian series in history and established Roberts as a leading Protestant church historian.

Roberts's notoriety increased outside Christendom as well. Twice he was voted as Outstanding Young Man in America, and his career has taken him to over one hundred nations around the world, having been hosted by presidents, kings, leading political and religious leaders, and other world dignitaries. Roberts had an introduction with former President Ronald Reagan, Billy Graham, and with Former Prime Minister Lady Margaret Thatcher. Roberts received a letter from President George Bush honoring him for his commitment and contribution to improve the quality of life in his community.

In 1990, at the age of twenty-five, Roberts moved to Southern California and established his worldwide headquarters in Orange County. There, he founded Embassy Christian Center, which would become a base for his humanitarian work that would include assistance to the poor and needy, not only in Southern California, but throughout the world. He also built one of the largest Christian churches and Bible colleges in Orange County. He has established, financed, and sent forth more than 250 men and women to various nations. These humanitarian missionary teams took food, clothing, medical supplies, and spiritual teachings, and they are providing expertise and assistance to those who receive their help.

Overall, Roberts Liardon, humanitarian, pastor, teacher, and philanthropist, has paid the price for his accomplishments in prayer to God and service to mankind. He has dedicated his entire life and finances to the work of God's kingdom and the welfare of his fellow man, keeping a watchful eye on those less fortunate and doing all he can to ease their pain and help their dreams come to pass.

ABOUT ROBERTS LIARDON
MINISTRIES
Church History Is Valuable to Us

*I*f you have any materials pertaining to church history, we would like to know about them. Roberts Liardon Ministries is committed to preserving Christian archives in our Reformers and Revivalists Historical Museum. Memorabilia from our past is very valuable and vital to future church growth.

We are looking for magazines, letters, books, manuscripts, photographs, audio and video tapes, movies, diaries, scrapbooks, and any other personal items that would portray our church history. If you have anything you would like to donate to Christian history, no matter how large or how small, or if you know of someone who would like to contribute, please contact our research department in California. (See the next page for the contact information.)

Thank you for sharing your portion of history with the world and with generations to come. Only heaven can reveal the lives you will have touched by your thoughtful generosity.

Roberts Liardon Ministries International Offices:

USA

Roberts Liardon Ministries
P.O. Box 2989
Sarasota, FL 34230
Phone: 941-373-3883 • Fax: 941-373-3884
www.robertsliardon.org • www.godsgenerals.org

United Kingdom/Europe

Roberts Liardon Ministries
P.O. Box 5318
London, England
WC1N3XX

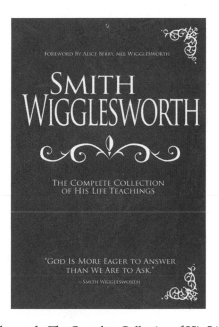

Smith Wigglesworth: The Complete Collection of His Life Teachings
Smith Wigglesworth
Compiled by Roberts Liardon

God confirmed Smith Wigglesworth's ministry through powerful signs and wonders. A few of these included the restoration of hearing and sight, the creative formation of missing limbs, the disappearance of cancerous growths, the recovery of mental wholeness by the violently insane, and the raising of several people from the dead. His words continue to provide spiritual, financial, emotional, and physical healing as they inspire and build faith.

ISBN: 978-1-60374-083-8 • Hardcover • 864 pages

WHITAKER
HOUSE

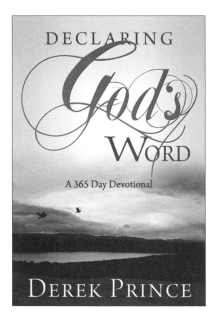

Declaring God's Word
Derek Prince

According to Scripture, Satan can be defeated if believers will stand on God's Word and testify to what it says about the mighty and powerful blood of Jesus—blood that cleanses us from sin and makes us righteous. For the first time, acclaimed Bible teacher Derek Prince will lead you to power and victory in this yearlong daily devotional. By *Declaring God's Word*, you will become steeped in the Scriptures and overcome satanic oppression and attacks. Begin each new day by confessing the truth of God's Word, and you will experience the love, power, and wisdom of God all year long.

ISBN: 978-1-60374-067-8 ♦ Trade ♦ 432 pages

WHITAKER
HOUSE

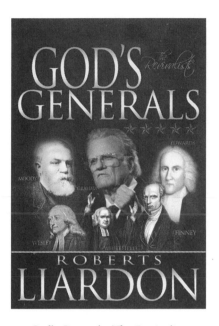

God's Generals: The Revivalists
Roberts Liardon

Roberts Liardon chronicles compelling spiritual biographies of some of the most powerful preachers ever to ignite the fires of revival. Follow the faith journeys and lives of the great generals of God, including John and Charles Wesley, George Whitefield, Jonathan Edwards, William and Catherine Booth, Billy Graham, and more. Liardon goes beyond history, drawing crucial life application and inspiration from the lives of these mighty warriors. You will learn how to fulfill God's call on your life, experience the joy of winning souls, and be led by the Spirit of God. Let these revivalists inspire your life and revitalize your ministry!

ISBN: 978-1-60374-025-8 • Hardcover • 496 pages

WHITAKER
HOUSE

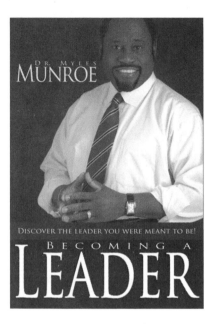

Becoming a Leader
Myles Munroe

Best-selling author Dr. Myles Munroe dispels the myth that only some are destined to be leaders while everyone else is destined to be a follower. You can become the leader God intended you to be. Learn how to activate your leadership potential, develop a positive legacy, find resources to fulfill your vision, empower others for leadership, and discover your unique role in life. Recognize your inborn leadership abilities and become the leader you were meant to be!

ISBN: 978-1-60374-027-2 ◆ Hardcover ◆ 224 pages

WHITAKER
HOUSE